A VICTORIAN HOUSEHOLD

BY

SHIRLEY NICHOLSON

BASED ON THE DIARIES OF

MARION SAMBOURNE

COLOUR PHOTOGRAPHS BY

SNOWDON

BARRIE & JENKINS

LONDON

First published in Great Britain in 1988 by
Barrie & Jenkins Ltd
289 Westbourne Grove, London W11 2QA

British Library Cataloguing in Publication Data

Nicholson, Shirley
    A Victorian household : based on the
    diaries of Marion Sambourne.
    1. London. Kensington and Chelsea (London
    Borough). Kensington. Household management.
    Sambourne, Marion, 1851–1914. Biographies
    I. Title   II. Sambourne, Marion, *1851–1914*
    640′.92′4

    ISBN 0-7126-2055-9

Typeset by Florencetype Ltd, Kewstoke, Avon
Printed in Italy by Graphicom SRL, Vicenza

*The photograph on p. 2 shows the fireplace in the
morning-room, with its handpainted Dutch tiles.
Above the mantelboard (covered in green velvet and
studded with brass-headed nailes) are shelves holding
terra-cotta figurines, Chinese jars and family portraits.*

CONTENTS

FAMILY TREE

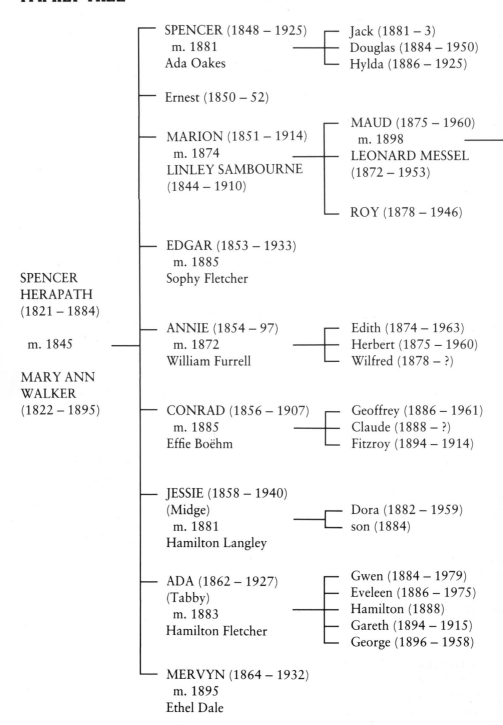

SPENCER (1848 – 1925)
  m. 1881
Ada Oakes

— Jack (1881 – 3)
— Douglas (1884 – 1950)
— Hylda (1886 – 1925)

Ernest (1850 – 52)

MARION (1851 – 1914)
  m. 1874
LINLEY SAMBOURNE
(1844 – 1910)

— MAUD (1875 – 1960)
   m. 1898
  LEONARD MESSEL
  (1872 – 1953)

— ROY (1878 – 1946)

EDGAR (1853 – 1933)
  m. 1885
Sophy Fletcher

SPENCER
HERAPATH
(1821 – 1884)

m. 1845

MARY ANN
WALKER
(1822 – 1895)

ANNIE (1854 – 97)
  m. 1872
William Furrell

— Edith (1874 – 1963)
— Herbert (1875 – 1960)
— Wilfred (1878 – ?)

CONRAD (1856 – 1907)
  m. 1885
Effie Boëhm

— Geoffrey (1886 – 1961)
— Claude (1888 – ?)
— Fitzroy (1894 – 1914)

JESSIE (1858 – 1940)
(Midge)
  m. 1881
Hamilton Langley

— Dora (1882 – 1959)
— son (1884)

ADA (1862 – 1927)
(Tabby)
  m. 1883
Hamilton Fletcher

— Gwen (1884 – 1979)
— Eveleen (1886 – 1975)
— Hamilton (1888)
— Gareth (1894 – 1915)
— George (1896 – 1958)

MERVYN (1864 – 1932)
  m. 1895
Ethel Dale

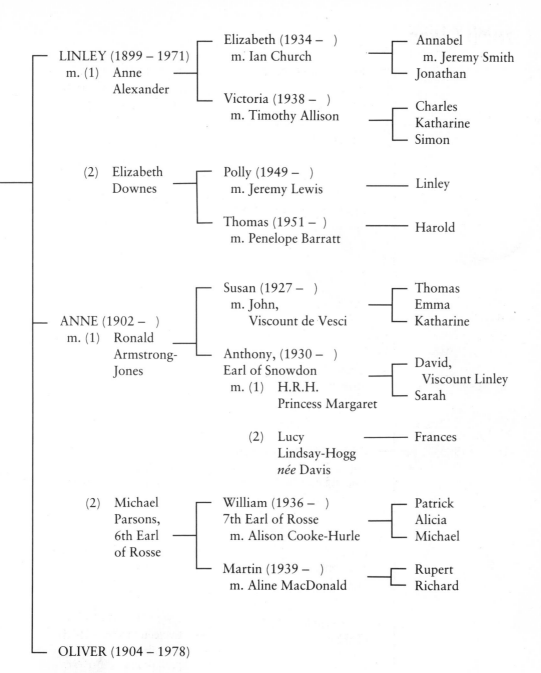

LINLEY (1899 – 1971)
m. (1) Anne Alexander

- Elizabeth (1934 –   )
  m. Ian Church
  - Annabel
    m. Jeremy Smith
  - Jonathan

- Victoria (1938 –   )
  m. Timothy Allison
  - Charles
  - Katharine
  - Simon

(2) Elizabeth Downes

- Polly (1949 –   )
  m. Jeremy Lewis
  - Linley

- Thomas (1951 –   )
  m. Penelope Barratt
  - Harold

ANNE (1902 –   )
m. (1) Ronald Armstrong-Jones

- Susan (1927 –   )
  m. John, Viscount de Vesci
  - Thomas
  - Emma
  - Katharine

- Anthony, (1930 –   )
  Earl of Snowdon
  m. (1) H.R.H. Princess Margaret
  - David, Viscount Linley
  - Sarah

  (2) Lucy Lindsay-Hogg née Davis
  - Frances

(2) Michael Parsons, 6th Earl of Rosse

- William (1936 –   )
  7th Earl of Rosse
  m. Alison Cooke-Hurle
  - Patrick
  - Alicia
  - Michael

- Martin (1939 –   )
  m. Aline MacDonald
  - Rupert
  - Richard

OLIVER (1904 – 1978)

NOTE: *Most of Marion's nieces and nephews married and had children, but for the sake of clarity their names have been omitted from this family tree. Only the direct descendants of Marion and Linley Sambourne are shown here.*

INTRODUCTION

 INLEY SAMBOURNE HOUSE, in the London Borough of Kensington, was opened as a museum in 1980. It is entirely due to the generosity and foresight of Sambourne's granddaughter, Anne, Countess of Rosse, that the public is now able to see inside a genuine Victorian home where the original decorative scheme, devised in the 1870s, is almost unaltered. Fifty years ago an interior such as this was commonplace, the background for comfortable middle-class living all over England, but the accelerating pace of change has swept so much away that it has become a rare and precious survivor.

Edward Linley Sambourne was born in 1844. He was a black-and-white artist who worked as a cartoonist for *Punch*, one of the most successful of nineteenth century periodicals. For over forty years at least one drawing signed by him appeared in its pages every week and his talents were much admired by his contemporaries. Because of his energetic and gregarious nature he was on friendly terms with a wide circle of well known artists, sportsmen and literary men, many of whom were entertained at his home. After his death in 1910 his reputation suffered an eclipse, so that it is only now, with the revival of interest in late Victorian art and the opening of his house at 18 Stafford Terrace, that his talents are being reappraised.

Visitors today are fascinated by the atmosphere of this house, whose rooms in all their dark and crowded richness seem so far removed from our own age. Of the family who lived here a century ago the most important figure is that of the artist himself: his ebullient nature is perfectly caught in the caricature by "Spy" which hangs in the drawing-room. Here he stands, short and plump in his favourite riding clothes, waving his cigar, and no doubt regaling the assembled company with one of his celebrated funny stories. His presence can still be felt throughout the house: the

Left: Linley and Marion Sambourne. Photographed in Rome when they were on their wedding tour, 1874.

easel and camera which he used daily stand ready for work, while his heterogeneous collection of paintings, prints and photographs, together with his own framed drawings, hang edge to edge on all the walls. The furniture, the books, and the dozens of *objets d'art* are hardly changed since he moved in after his marriage in 1874, when as an ambitious young man he was striving to create an aesthetically pleasing background against which to display his talent.

Though Sambourne's aura is so strong, there was another person responsible for the arrangement of the rooms at Stafford Terrace. This was his wife, Marion, whose contribution has had little recognition and to whom we owe the preservation of many other treasures which are not on view. Marion Sambourne did not expect to be remembered. It was her husband's achievement which mattered, so to preserve his memory and enhance his reputation she carefully stored away anything which related to his life and work: not only his drawings and his huge collection of photographs, but also the newspaper articles written about him, his diaries, and most of the hundreds of letters which he wrote to her during the thirty-six years that they were married. Public tastes and interests change, and today it is her unobtrusive way of life and her ordering of the household which are as much a matter of interest and curiosity to visitors as her husband's work.

Marion could not claim to be an artist, or a writer, or a social reformer, or even a famous beauty. She was just a typical middle-class Victorian wife, wrapped up in her husband and children in the security of a happy home, and having no desire to break away from the conventions of her upbringing. Sambourne's artistic gifts were to be inherited by his daughter, Maud, a talented artist and needlewoman, by his grandson, Oliver Messel, the successful stage designer, and by his great-grandson, Lord Snowdon, the photographer. But many strands make up an inheritance, and Marion's contribution to her descendants was as important as that of her husband. Her loving spirit and her delight in people and parties are traits which have passed down the female line, as has her romantic attachment to the past with its attendant urge to preserve every relic of happy days gone by. As well as the letters from her husband, she also kept those written by her children, her son's school reports, her daughter's wedding invitation, and much other memorabilia which form the basis of a wonderful archive about an interesting artistic family; yet there is not a single reference to Marion Sambourne—other than her name—in any of the recollections of the time, or in later articles written about Linley Sambourne and his descendants. She would have joined those many millions who have no memorial had it not been for the fact that she kept a diary. In this, for thirty-three consecutive years, she set down not only what she did each day, but what she bought, how much she paid the servants, whom she entertained, what the family ate, and a thousand other mundane details. It is these diaries which have provided the inspiration for a book about her life, her family and her home.

PART ONE
1881-1887

18 Stafford Terrace, Kensington.

Russell & Sons

17. BAKER STREET. W. &
49. BRECKNOCK ROAD. N.

PHOTOGRAPHERS TO H.M. THE QUEEN.

CHAPTER ONE
HUSBAND & FAMILY:
HOME & FURNISHINGS

ARION SAMBOURNE began to keep a diary on 1 January 1881. She was twenty-nine years old; her husband, Linley, had his thirty-sixth birthday on 4 January. The couple had lived at 18 Stafford Terrace, Kensington, since their marriage in October 1874 and now had two young children, Maud and Roy. From the beginning of her married life Marion had written dinner-party menus and recipes in a little notebook which was divided into alphabetical sections: this was full up by the end of 1880, so she began afresh in 1881 with a larger, diary-type book. It was probably her intention to use this just to record the meals which were set before the family each day (as at first these are the only regular entries) but they only filled a quarter of the page so she began to list her engagements as well. From there it was easy to slip into the habit of noting what the weather was like and what the rest of the family were doing, and by the end of the year she was writing a few sentences every day. It may have been his wife's enthusiasm for this new venture which inspired Linley to follow her example, as in January 1882 they embarked on proper diary-writing together. Marion's entries gradually became more informative (though they were hardly ever more than statements of fact) until her bold sprawling hand filled every page. Linley's was a neater script, but he wrote in the same terse and impersonal way. With both of them, diary-writing became an essential part of their daily routine, and they continued to fill volume after volume until their lives were nearly ended. Though the information is sparse at first, over a long period such a multitude of tiny clues is presented that a picture gradually emerges of two interesting people, both busy and preoccupied in their individual spheres but happily united in their appreciation of each other, their family, and their home.

Marion recorded her husband's activities as well as her own. She referred to him as "Lin" in her diary (usually "dear Lin") and he called her "M" in his, in spite of

---

Left: Linley working at his easel in the drawing-room. Behind him is an engraver's globe and a 100 candle-power gas lamp, made to his own design.

the fact that his letters to her always began "My dearest Polly" and were signed "Your affectionate husband, Dickie". It is quite clear that he was the most important person in the household and she mentioned him with affection, or sometimes with a natural wifely exasperation, almost every day. Though Linley did some book illustrations and the occasional drawing for other periodicals, *Punch* was his chief source of income. He was one of the team of artists and writers employed on that paper, whose custom it was to meet for dinner every Wednesday night when the captions for the cartoons and the subjects of the articles which would go into the next issue were thrashed out. The drawings were done on wood blocks, and had to be delivered to the engravers by Saturday morning where they were prepared for publication a week later. This meant that Thursday and Friday were high-pressure days for the contributors, while the rest of their time could be passed in a more leisurely fashion. In Linley's case sport and a full social life were given high priority.

Linley worked at home, with his easel set up by the big south-facing window in the upstairs drawing-room. (The house was not large enough, nor was he rich

One of Linley's cartoons. This shows Mr Punch in his favourite role as "Detector of Nuisances" castigating the Duke of Bedford (owner of Covent Garden market) for being a bad landlord.

MUD-SALAD MARKET AGAIN, AND WORSE THAN EVER!

Mr. Punch (Sanitary Officer and General Inspector and Detector of Nuisances everywhere). "Now then, your Grace, cart off this muck!"

Duke of Mudford. "But it's not my place—it's——"

Mr. Punch. "Isn't it? Then whose is it? Anyhow, it's *a matter that wants clearing up immediately.*"

Duke of Mudford. "I offered the Corporation——"

Mr. Punch. "You did. If it's yours to sell, isn't it yours to deal with? Come!"

[*Vide Letter in* "*Times*," *Thursday, June 26. Under Our Eyes, and under Our very Nose! An Offal Nuisance!*]

enough, to have a separate studio.) Though Victorian artists often complained of the difficulties of working in dark and foggy London—so different from the clear air and sunshine of Italy—Linley was not so hampered as the colourists, and he often worked far into the night. Beside his chair he had a portable gas lamp and an engraver's globe, which could be used to focus a beam of bright light on to his drawing board. A typical entry in his diary is "Up at 7:45 worked hard and fast on drawing much pushed finished 11:00 pm. Exhausted. Bed 12:00." Marion corroborates this, often writing "Lin hard at work all day", while "Lin worked till 3 o'clock in the morning" was not unusual. She was his most ardent admirer, mentioning his drawing repeatedly in her diary: "Lin doing awfully good block" or "Lin's work beautiful" and she glowed with pride whenever she heard him praised: "Sir F. Goldsmith took me in to tea, like him, admires Lin's work." She did everything she could to help and encourage her husband; sitting beside him for many hours while he drew, chatting, or reading aloud, to ease the tedium of endless meticulous shading. "Lin very hard at work, sat with him all day till 2 am" she wrote, and it is not surprising that she sometimes added, "Wish he did not have to slave so."

Though Linley did not have to supply the caption for his cartoon, he had to decide how the idea could be best presented. If he did not like the subject he could be very dilatory, and his Editor was not pleased. He found it very hard to work without a deadline (some projects were started and never finished) so that "Wish Lin would get more forward with work" alternated with Marion's fears that her husband was over-doing it. Linley was a superb draughtsman, but it was his obsessive passion for accurate detail—coupled with an inability to draw without a model—which often made work a struggle. By the middle of the 1880s he had discovered that photography was the perfect tool for an artist in a hurry and from then on he devoted many hours to his camera. He would decide on the design for his cartoon on Thursday morning and then get his family or the servants to model for a photograph; often he himself posed while someone else took the picture. He then developed the plates and was ready to start his drawing in the afternoon. The chests of drawers at Stafford Terrace contain quantities of photographs showing people wearing fancy costume and striking attitudes. (The self-portraits are the most amusing of all, as Linley was quite uninhibited in his contortions.) All the photography was done in the garden at the back of the house where the light was good, and no attempt was made to flatter the models or create artistic effects: these pictures were for work purposes only, and they were added to the archive of purchased photographs, newspaper cuttings and postcards which Linley steadily amassed over the years.

It has been estimated that there are over 10,000 pictures in Linley's collection. It is difficult to believe that so many were essential; much more likely that he used work as an excuse for indulging in what became an all-absorbing hobby. Marion certainly did not think that so much photography was either desirable or necessary, and it became quite a bone of contention between them. She frequently vented her irritation in the diary, "Lin at those everlasting photos" she wrote. "More of those

Linley in the back garden at Stafford Terrace, posing for his cartoon drawings.

hateful photos, Lin wastes time, late with work", or "Bitterly cold in morning room. Lin busy with photos, in & out, curtains taken down for it." From Linley's diary it can be seen that he spent many hours developing and enlarging his photographs, to say nothing of the time taken sorting and filing them, and then hunting for those which he had mislaid. "Put things in order" was an almost daily entry, and any task which involved photography was undertaken with as much care and concentration as work done at the drawing board.

Apart from the nights when he had to work late, Linley led a very full social life. He and Marion went out to dinner parties and theatres together, as well as entertaining their friends at home, but the number of his acquaintances was very large and included many people that she never met. Gentlemen belonged to clubs, where they could gather to talk politics and sport, or smoke and read the papers in peace. Linley was a member of the Garrick Club, and he lunched or dined there at least once a week. No lady was ever admitted to these establishments, nor to the many Gentlemen Only functions which were so popular. Thus Linley was out in the evenings quite often and he sometimes came back "not all he should be". Marion disliked having her nights disturbed by his late homecomings, and even when he came to bed early wrote "Slept badly, Lin snores so." She also disapproved when he over-indulged himself at table: "Lin looks seedy—must have eaten too much last night."

On balance, though, Marion's criticisms were few and the marriage would seem to have been extremely happy. The mere fact that she mentioned her husband so many times in her diary and clearly enjoyed everything they did together shows that she was certainly not unhappy. Nor was she ever bored, but filled the time to her own satisfaction, frequently recording her appreciation of the good things which came her way. Many Victorian women found the conventions of middle-class life restrictive, if not stifling, and used their surplus energies in good works, art or

16

literature. Today more is known about those who rebelled against the system than about the vast majority who were happy and fulfilled in the role of wife and mother. To keep a man contented, bear his children, look after his home and entertain his friends was the main object in life for most young women, and there is nothing to show that Marion ever considered the possibilities of a wider sphere of activity outside her own close-knit domestic circle. Only once or twice does her diary indicate any resentment about the unfairness of a social system which gave so much freedom and intellectual scope to men and so few opportunities to women.

As well as adhering closely to the model of an ideal Victorian wife, Marion was a devoted daughter. She seems almost too devoted, as her diary gives the impression that she clung to her parents longer than was necessary, and that Linley and the children sometimes had to take second place in her affections. From Stafford Terrace to her old home at 18 Upper Phillimore Gardens was a distance of only a few hundred yards, so Marion walked round there nearly every day to see her mother and father: "Lunch at Mother's", Tea at Mother's", she wrote over and over again. Mr and Mrs Herapath were always ready with help and advice and were most generous towards their eldest (and perhaps best-loved) daughter. "Mother sent pineapple", "Cheque from Mother for dress", "Papa gave me bottle of port", "Mother brought Maud shoes", record some of the presents which Marion received. The Sambourne children were much petted whenever they went to visit their grandparents; one affectionate note from Mr Herapath survives: "Put the enclosed in dear little baby's money box with grandpapa's best love and wishing her many many happy returns of her birthday."

Marion's grandfather, John Herapath, had come from a West Country family. He was the author of the first book ever written on mathematical physics, a successful designer of early locomotives, and the founder of an important periodical, *Herapath's Railway Journal*. His second son, Spencer (Marion's father) married Mary Ann Walker in 1845, and the couple decided to move to London, then as now the recognised goal for those aspiring to make their way in the world. They settled in Kensington, a rapidly expanding village on the western outskirts of town, and their first child, Spencer John, was born in 1848 at 18a Holland Street. Soon afterwards they moved to 2 Notting Hill Grove—now called 4 Aubrey Walk—where a second son, Ernest (who did not survive infancy) was born. On 29 September 1851, the Herapaths had a daughter. Though this child was christened Mary Ann after her mother, from an early age she preferred the more romantic and fashionable spelling of her name. She appears as "Marion" in the census of 1871 and also in the newspaper report of her wedding in 1874, even though on the marriage certificate she was still plain Mary Ann. In a family where all the girls had pet-names she was called "Polly", and it is this name which her husband was to use throughout their married life.

Spencer Herapath worked his way up to become a wealthy and respected stockbroker with his own firm in the City. He was closely involved with railway construction, especially in the expanding market of South America, and became a director of the Buenos Aires and Great Southern Railway, the City of Buenos Aires Tramways, the Great Western Brazil Railway and the Central Argentine Railway. In addition he had a great interest in all scientific subjects, being a Fellow of the Royal Society and the Statistical Society, as well as a founder member of the Institute of Civil Engineers. Success on the Stock Market and an increasing family caused him to move house several times, though he always favoured the same part of Kensington. Another son, Edgar, was born at Notting Hill Grove in 1853, but the next three children, Annie (1854), Conrad (1856) and Jessie (1858) were born at 19 Sheffield Terrace. A move to 46 Argyll Road followed, where Ada (1862) and Mervyn (1864) were born. Finally the family settled at 18 Upper Phillimore Gardens and the 1871 records a household of two adults, eight children and five indoor servants.

Little is known about Marion's life before her marriage. From her father's few surviving letters to her it would seem that she spent two years in Brussels, learning French, German and music. French was her favourite language in later life, and her diaries are scattered with little French phrases. Unlike Charlotte Brontë, twenty-five years earlier, she had no need to use her languages as a career, and the visit to Brussels was primarily to put a polish on her education. It must also have relieved her of the burden of helping to look after so many little brothers and sisters, who

Marion, aged eighteen, ready to be launched on a London season.

The four younger Herapath children: Conrad, Jessie, Ada and Mervyn. Taken soon after Marion's marriage.

when she left home were aged between fourteen and six years old. When Marion returned to England in November 1869 she was aged eighteen, and ready to be launched on a London season. It is likely that her parents arranged for her to have a delightful round of parties and visits (similar to the well documented experiences of her daughter, Maud, in the 1890s), but there is nothing to show how she met her future husband, Linley Sambourne, how long their courtship lasted, or whether her parents were pleased with what, in worldly terms, could hardly be called a brilliant match. As Spencer Herapath's eldest daughter she could have been expected to do better for herself than to marry an artist of little fortune and no great prospects.

Linley's father had been in trade, a partner in a firm importing furs from America. Both his mother and his paternal grandmother were related to an eighteenth-century family of musicians, known as the Linleys of Bath, whose portraits by Gainsborough hang in Dulwich Picture Gallery. He was christened Edward Linley, but when he grew up he chose to be known by his more prestigious middle name. As a child he had been for ever drawing, so to turn this talent to good account his father had apprenticed him to an engineering firm when he was sixteen. Young Linley quite enjoyed the work there, but all his spare time was spent sketching and making caricatures. A friend showed some of his work to Mark Lemon, the Editor of *Punch*, and his first drawing was published in that paper in

19

1867. Over the next four years Linley submitted more work, but it was not until he was offered the post of "Cartoon Junior" in 1871 that he was properly launched on what was to be a very successful career, though it always rated higher in satisfaction and esteem than in monetary reward.

Linley's father had died in 1866, without leaving a will, so that his widow and son may have found themselves rather hard up. It seems likely that they went to live with his father's sister, Mrs Barr, as they were at her house in Uxbridge (a village a few miles west of London) when the 1871 census was taken. Jane Barr, then a widow in comfortable circumstances, was a talented amateur water-colourist who had given her nephew his early lessons in drawing. She died in March 1874, leaving her personal possessions to her sister-in-law, Frances Sambourne; more importantly her death released other family property (always referred to as "the Barr Estate") which was to bring Linley a steady income of £650 a year for the next twenty years. This inheritance must have greatly improved the young man's prospects of marriage, and enabled him to be bold enough to apply for Marion Herapath's hand. His obvious talent, energy and charm were also important assets in persuading her parents to agree to a betrothal. The absence of a great fortune makes it clear that Marion married for love; it does not seem as if she ever regretted it.

The only surviving letters from Linley to Marion which pre-date their wedding were written from Uxbridge:

> 20 June 1874. My darling Marion. I got your letter dearest this morning and have read it so many times. I gather from it that your Papa has not refused to let us be married in October. It has made me so happy. I only trust that we may be able to get things sufficently ready by that time. You don't tell me what he said and I have not heard from him yet. . . . I can't bear to be here alone so far from you besides my mother is very unwell, she goes back to Yorkshire next week I hope. I won't forget the dinner if you care to have me with you. It's been raining all day and if it was not for the hope of seeing you tomorrow I should be awfully in the blues. I wonder if I could get rooms reasonably anywhere in Kensington and then I could pop in and see you after work. Give my best love to your mamma, Jessie and all of them and with thousands of kisses believe me my sweet darling pet yours for ever Linley Sambourne.

Marion and Linley were married on 20 October 1874; the bride was just twenty-three, the bridegroom thirty. They went abroad for their wedding tour, and had their photograph taken in Rome. Linley looks rather stolid, with no hint of the sense of humour for which he was famed; Marion, posed with her hand on his shoulder to display her wedding ring, is wearing a saucy hat and a simple elegant dress which shows off her trim figure. Photographs taken later in life are less flattering, but in this one she appears a lively pretty girl with more sparkle than her husband.

Spencer Herapath advanced his daughter the sum of £1,000 on her marriage to help set her up in the manner to which she was accustomed. He may have stipulated

that Marion and Linley should settle near the parental home, so it was a piece of luck when a house only three streets away from Upper Phillimore Gardens and with the same number—18—came on the market. The fields which sloped southwards from the crown of Campden Hill to Kensington High Street belonged to the Phillimore family and had been leased for building development in 1855. Progress had been very slow at first and the layout was not complete until nearly twenty years later. The Herapaths lived in one of the large houses on the northern side of the estate; Stafford Terrace, on the southern boundary, was made up of much smaller houses and was only finished a year or two before Marion was married. The same rather old-fashioned Italianate style (light-coloured brick, stucco trim and classical details) was used throughout the development. Had Linley been richer he might have preferred something more exciting—like the detached red brick villas which had just been put up for Leighton and Prinsep in nearby Holland Park Road—but once settled at Stafford Terrace he showed no desire to move.

The Phillimore Estate was built to house the newly affluent and rapidly expanding professional classes, and was never to decline (as so many similar Victorian developments did) into slum property. Today it is considered to be part of inner London and houses here are highly desirable and very expensive, but all through the 1860s and 1870s the area was not much more than a vast building site on the very edge of the metropolis. Throughout her childhood Marion must have been familiar with timber scaffolding, muddy pot-holed roads, and cartloads of builders' rubbish. The shouts of the workmen and the clink of the bricklayers' trowels would have filled the air, and over everything hung the smell of the brick-kilns—what a contemporary described as the "curious stuffy oven odour" so typical of London during this period of rapid expansion. By 1874 the population of Kensington was five times larger than it had been when the Herapaths first arrived, and the developers were moving to fresh fields. Thus Marion began her married life in a smart new suburb within easy reach of the West End and the City. Houses here were to remain fashionable for the middle classes until the end of the century, only gradually being overtaken in popularity by the much larger terraces of Bayswater and the big red brick blocks of flats in Knightsbridge and Chelsea. Between the two World Wars Kensington had an aging population and a rather dowdy image: young professional couples were taking advantage of easy commuting and making their homes further out in leafier suburbs. During the last thirty years this trend has been reversed and the area is thriving once again.

For some unexplained reason, a full inventory of everything in the Sambournes' new home was taken by a qualified valuer soon after the furnishing was completed. This document, dated December 1877, adds enormously to the interest of the house and its contents, as most of the things listed are still in the places they were bought to fill. The title page reads: "The Inventory of the Household furniture, Pictures, Plate,

An Inventory of—

The Household Furniture, Pictures, Plate, Articles of Vertu, Ornaments, China, Glass, Linen Fixtures, Fittings Utensils and Effects in and upon the Premises No 18 Stafford Terrace, Kensington Middlesex W which are the property of E. Linley Sambourne Esquire——

Taken this 1st day of December 1877.

by

Jas. Willis & Son
Auctioneers & Valuers
90 Saint Andrews
Uxbridge

The first page of the 1877 Inventory.

articles of Vertu, Ornaments, China, Glass, Linen, Fixtures, Utensils and Effects in and upon the premises No 18 Stafford Terrace Kensington Middlesex which are the property of E. Linley Sambourne Esquire." Every object was priced, right down to the hearth-brush, and details were also included of the alterations which the young couple had thought necessary for a comfortable standard of living. The Inventory gives an astonishing picture of the amount of furniture and the number of decorative objects considered essential at the time. To modern eyes the house seems impossibly full; naturally some articles have been added and others lost or broken over the years, but taken overall there were probably even more things here in 1877 than there are today. There were, for instance, sixty-six upright chairs; ten of these were in the dining-room and twelve in the drawing-room (which is perhaps not excessive), but there were ten in the best bedroom and another ten in the day-nursery, leaving twenty-four distributed among the other rooms. There were also more framed photographs (as opposed to drawings) on the walls than there are now: sixty-two in the front hall, thirty-five in the rear hall, and ninety-four on the staircase. Even during the Sambournes' lifetime people commented on the quantity of pictures at Stafford Terrace, though contemporary drawings and photographs of other interiors show that most homes were just as crowded with furniture and miscellaneous *objets d'art*.

The Inventory tells us that the "Lease of eighty nine years unexpired" was purchased from the estate of the late Mrs Bentley for the sum of £2,000. (She had not lived there long, as the house was not finished until after the 1871 census was taken and she died in February 1874.) The Sambournes paid £150 for the fixtures (the venetian blinds, the gas brackets and pendants, the pegs on the doors, gilt cornices, brass curtain rods and so on) which were already there, but they did not care for Mrs Bentley's taste in decoration, as "Wallpapers throughout the house" were ordered from Messrs Morris and Company at a cost of £35.5s. Mr Smith of Baker Street was paid £17.10s. for painting, Messrs Jackson and Graham and Messrs Christies were paid £1.5s. and £5 respectively for unspecified work, but the biggest sum of all went to Mr Walter Nash, Builder. "Making alterations and extension of Morning Room, paper hanging, painting, laying on water, fixing picture rods, dado rails, and general reparations", cost £240. It was also necessary to pay ten guineas to "Mr J.G. Davies the Ground Landlord, being his commission on the alteration of the morning-room". The stained glass in the windows is listed separately: that in the garden door was valued at 15 guineas, the dining-room window at 12 guineas and the morning-room at 18 guineas, which shows that it was considered an extravagant extra embellishment to the house, not something provided by the developer.

The houses in Stafford Terrace were built to a formula which had already been standard in London for over a hundred years, and which can still provide attractive and flexible accommodation for a modern family. Behind a narrow frontage the typical town house has two rooms on each floor; the staircase rises from the back of the hall with bathrooms and lavatories off the half-landings. The size of the ground-plan and the number of floors built on it was all that distinguished an artisan's house from a rich man's; the treatment of the façade differed hardly at all. The uses to which the various rooms were put were the same for everyone except the very poor: the kitchen and servants' rooms were in the basement, the dining-room and morning-room (or study) on the ground floor, and the main entertaining rooms on the first floor. On the second floor were the principal bedrooms, with small rooms for the children and servants above that. Though 18 Stafford Terrace seems large and extravagantly decorated by present day standards, it perfectly suited the young Sambournes' position in life, standing as they did on the lower ranks of the professional ladder with a joint income which probably amounted to a little over £2,000 a year.

It is fairly safe to assume that it was Linley rather than Marion who decided on the style of decoration for their new house. At thirty years old he knew what he liked, and his young wife would have been full of admiration for his knowledge and taste. The Aesthetic Movement had come into being in the late 1860s, and *Hints on Household Taste* by C.L. Eastlake (published in 1867) was the Bible which preached

this new fashion to all who wanted their homes to be *avant-garde* and "artistic". We have no proof that Marion and Linley ever read this book, but they adopted many of its precepts and the house survives today as an excellent example of the style. Of all the rooms, the dining-room is the one which remains closest to the original decorative scheme. The olive-green paint and the division of the walls into three bands of colour with a William Morris wallpaper on the central portion are typically "Aesthetic" devices. The design called "Fruit" (or "Pomegranate") was very popular among those with a Pre-Raphaelite tendency, and was used in Burne-Jones's house in nearby Fulham, as well as in many other homes where the owners had advanced artistic ideas. This may not be the original paper, but that on the frieze, embossed and gilded to represent Spanish leather, probably is. This was of a type made by an English firm in Japan for export to European markets, a nice example of Victorian eclecticism. The pictures are all listed in the Inventory: "Right of fireplace 1 drawing in oak frame, 3 engravings in ditto, 7 photographs in ditto, 1 photograph in gilt ditto. Left of fireplace 13 photographs in oak frames, 2 engravings in ditto", and so on around the room. Above this arrangement—which is exactly the same now as it was in 1877—is a shelf on brackets, especially designed for the display of blue and white china. This fashion had been initiated by Whistler and Rossetti and taken up enthusiastically by the Aesthetes. There is more china in the "Delft case" above the fireplace, and here too is a fine example of the popular "upholstered mantleboard" in olive-green velvet ornamented with brass-headed nails and tasselled fringe. The original oak suite of octagonal dining table and eight chairs, together with sideboard, cabinet and two easy chairs, is complete. The Inventory states that the chairs were upholstered in green morocco leather, while the handsome sideboard with its inset panels of mirror, tiles, carvings and paintings of fruit (valued at £62.10s), was the most expensive single item in the house. The "bay for ferns" built out from the window of the dining-room is also mentioned in the Inventory, but the "shells and geological specimens" in it were later moved to the Water Garden on the landing. The Victorians had a passion for ferns and indoor plants, and caring for these was thought to be a very suitable occupation for the ladies. A rubber plant was much prized, and one in a brass pot in the morning-room was successfully tended for thirty years. Marion noted in her diary whenever she bought new plants, and often wrote "did fern cases" or "watered plants".

The morning-room was generally considered to be the sanctum of the lady of the house. At Stafford Terrace it faced south and would certainly have been easier to heat and keep cosy than the vast drawing-room upstairs, especially when one considers that all the fires had to be freshly lit each morning. Here Marion would have done her sewing, interviewed Cook, and received her callers. Though she occasionally recorded using it after dinner, most evening entertaining would have taken place in the drawing-room, in spite of the fact that this room had to double as Linley's studio. It seems likely that the decoration of the morning-room would have been to Marion's choice rather than her husband's, and it does have a different character from the rest of the house. Though the wallpaper is again the Morris "Fruit" pattern, this time the background colour is blue for the walls and cream for

the ceiling. None of the other rooms in the house has a brightly coloured paper on the ceiling, and the morning-room is also unique in that it is not hung with photographs and drawings. We can assume that Marion insisted on something approximating to Old Masters, which we know she admired. The "magnificent copy of a Van Dyck" and the four rather undistinguished classical canvases were here in 1877: the Anton Mauve and Luke Fildes oil paintings both came later as gifts.

On the first floor the Sambournes chose to throw the usual two rooms into one large L-shaped drawing-room. It was at first papered in a William Morris yellow and white "Larkspur" design, which made a light and pretty, though still typically Aesthetic background for more pictures (only fifty-two then instead of the present ninety) and more blue and white china. Some of this paper can still be seen behind the pictures, although exposed areas were later covered with more of the sumptuous-looking imitation Spanish leather. There were no comfortable upholstered chairs here or anywhere else in the house in 1877: deep buttoned upholstery was popular in most homes at this time, but the Sambournes must have considered it incompatible with the Aesthetic mood. The other pieces of furniture—the tables, writing desks and commodes —are mostly late eighteenth-century French (Louis-seize) or good quality Victorian copies in the same style. The parquet in this room was not put down until much later, so a felt drugget covered the floor. On it lay "three oriental rugs, a sheepskin dried and a tiger-skin mounted"—sadly the last two have disappeared. The Inventory lists a multitude of little objects on all the surfaces, but in 1877 there were not any of the bronzes and other statuettes which are such a feature of the room today, though they appear in the photographs which Linley took of the drawing-room in the early 1890s. Among the pictures on the walls are several watercolours by Linley's aunt, Mrs Barr, which he thought worthy of hanging beside drawings by his successful contemporaries and photographs of famous paintings by Old Masters.

On the second floor the principal bedroom no longer retains much of the original decoration, which is a pity as here we might have been able to feel Marion's presence most clearly. Replacement wallpaper, modern curtains and carpet, and white paint make it difficult to visualize the way it looked at first, even though the matching set of wardrobe, dressing table, bedside cupboard, towel rail and eight chairs is all just as it was in 1877. Ebonised furniture such as this had first been seen at the International Exhibition in London in 1871, and had immediately become a craze. The washstand, which was originally listed as part of the set, was replaced— perhaps ten years later—by basin and taps. Although the furniture is dark, the white stencilling gives it a certain lightness and charm. With the "cane blinds and scarlet window curtains" the "brass half tester bedstead with the lined chintz furniture to the same" and "a sofa and a box covered in cretonne" the room must have looked very bright and cheerful. The numerous smaller pieces of furniture mentioned in the Inventory have all gone. There were "two occasional chairs mounted in needle-work" (making ten chairs in all), "an octagonal table with lace", another table, a black and gilt bookcase, a linen basket, a mahogany bidet, a small portmanteau, a toilet vase, a waterproof mat and a pair of blue and white jardinières. Moving about and getting dressed amongst all these items must have been quite difficult.

Marion's love of pretty little bits and pieces was apparent from her dressing table: the Inventory lists five jewel caskets, an ivory brush set, a card case, two sachets, six needlework doileys, three ring trays, a pin cushion and "a velvet mouchoir case". On the bedside table were "two splendid Prayer Books"; beside the bed were two hassocks and on the wall hung a crucifix (Marion had High Church leanings). She was also well endowed with jewellery; it was worth £300 and was kept in the "iron-plate safe" which was probably built into the wall near the door. Her clothes were valued at £100, Linley's at £80.

The second bedroom on this floor was designated the spare-room. The two gentleman's wardrobes and the brass bedstead are listed in the Inventory, but the basin was most likely installed at the same time as the one in the front bedroom. Roy moved into this room in the early nineties, and he continued to sleep here during the thirty-two years that he lived alone after his mother's death. A few relics of his occupation have been gathered together, but Roy has left curiously little imprint on the house: the photographs of his pretty cousins and actress girl friends on the walls are the only things which distinguish this room from the others. Upstairs on the third floor the Inventory gives details of the contents of day-nursery, night-nursery and servant's bedroom, but these are now quite altered, with not a trace of the furniture or decorations of 1877 remaining.

By 1880 *Punch* had taken to mocking the Aesthetic Movement and Linley's drawings of that time show that he was quite capable of laughing at the extremes of a fashion which he had happily adopted in his own home a few years earlier. Modifications to the arrangements at Stafford Terrace over the years show a gradual move away from Aestheticism; the surprising thing is that so much of it was kept. It was a long time before any new fashion arrived which was strong enough to dictate a complete change in the way the English middle-class home was furnished. Things did alter slowly between the wars, but when Roy died in 1946 the decoration of 18 Stafford Terrace, though very old-fashioned, was by no means unique. It was only the urge to be "modern" during the 1950s which finally swept away all but a tiny handful of Victorian interiors.

CHAPTER TWO
WESTWOOD:
BROTHERS & SISTERS

HE SAMBOURNES' FIRST CHILD, Maud, was born on 5 August 1875, not at 18 Stafford Terrace, but at her grand-parents' house in Upper Phillimore Gardens. It was natural for a daughter to return to the parental home for her first confinement; twenty-three years later Maud herself was to do just the same. Marion's father was away in the country at the time, and his letter of congratulations is the only one remaining to mark this important event:

> My very dear Marion. Ma has arrived all safely. The account she gives of your dear little newcomer is quite glowing. She says it is a *perfect little model*. Ma is an authority on matters relating to babies so I am sure your baby is all that you and Linley could wish. May God spare her to be as great a source of pleasure to you and Linley as you have ever been to Ma and me. . . . With earnest wishes for your speedy recovery and a fond father's love to you and your dear little babe and Lin, believe me your affectionate father, Spencer Herapath.

The habit of keeping every scrap of paper—which became so marked in Marion's later life—was not fully developed in the early years of her marriage. No letters from her husband survive for the period between 1874 and 1879, nor is there anything from her parents about the birth of Roy at Stafford Terrace on 19 August 1878. Linley's letters begin again in 1880 with a packet sent from a yachting holiday, containing glowing accounts of the thrills of taking part in a Regatta:

> . . . Yachting life gives one an utter distaste for the shore—fancy no dust smuts or flies, everything clean as a new pin. I wish I could afford to keep a yacht such as this. . . . I hope you and dear babes are happy and comfortable—although this life is tremendously jolly I am longing to be back with you all again. Goodbye darling and with many kisses believe me your ever loving husband, Dickie.

Linley never lost his boyish enthusiasm for all kinds of sport. In London he kept his own horse, and felt that he could not do without an hour's ride every morning; usually he went to Hyde Park, but if there was time to spare he would go to Richmond Park, sometimes even further afield. He also liked to walk from Stafford Terrace to the *Punch* office in Bouverie Street, a distance of nearly four miles. Any new sport was always taken up with the greatest enthusiasm; a craze in the eighties was roller-skating, and another was lawn tennis. This game was invented in the mid-1870s and at first was played on any large piece of grass. Linley's friend, Mr Tuer, had a tennis court and so did Mr Lewis; on summer afternoons Marion would walk up Campden Hill to Moray Lodge to have tea with Mrs Lewis and watch her husband enjoying four or five sets of tennis. (In latter years Linley used Sir Alfred Hickman's court in Kensington Palace Gardens, and went on playing vigorously right up until the last year of his life.) When the Serpentine in Hyde Park was frozen during hard winters he went skating every day, and in the country he liked to go hunting, or take long walks, no matter how bad the weather. Marion never rebuked him for spending so much time in these pursuits, but was proud that he excelled in everything he tried. Besides, gentlemen were expected to be keen sportsmen, and she knew that exercise was essential to her husband's well-being.

There was hardly a year when Linley did not accept an invitation from friends to go up to Scotland in September for the shooting. Marion went with him in 1882 and 1883, but for the next few years she stayed behind with the children at her parents' country house. This was Westwood Lodge near Ramsgate in Kent, which her father had built in 1865 to give his family much needed space and fresh air. The young Herapaths had probably spent a large part of their childhood there; most of them returned regularly to Westwood long after they were grown up, and it was clearly a much loved second home, one of Mr Herapath's happiest investments. Marion and Linley had been married from there, with the wedding ceremony taking place at St Peter's Church, Thanet, only a few minutes drive from the house.

Westwood Lodge was situated in the centre of that part of Kent known as the Isle of Thanet, so called because it had once been separated from the mainland by a narrow channel. The little towns around the coast—Ramsgate, Margate, Westgate and Broadstairs—had originated as hamlets for fishermen wherever there was a gap in the cliffs. Their expansion to accommodate the visitors who came for the newly discovered benefits of sea bathing began before the end of the eighteenth century, and fifty years later the area had become a highly fashionable playground. *A Guide to Thanet*, dated 1736, describes it. "Anciently a good Part of the Island was Woodland, which is now almost all grub'd up and converted into sowing land. Several of the little Vills hereabouts still preserve the Memory of these Woods, viz West-wood, North-wood, South-wood . . ." Mr Herapath must have decided to restore the timber on his newly acquired estate; today his house lies at the centre of a green and secret oasis, surrounded no longer by open fields but by an unlovely twentieth-century clutter of roads, petrol stations and little factories. The imposing entrance gates open on to a drive which winds through dense woodland, past stable block, gardener's cottage and walled garden, before reaching the house. This still looks as

Westwood Lodge, 1882. Maud is on the donkey, riding side-saddle, with Roy watching her. The Herapath's coachman, Tassel, holds the horses' heads.

bright and new as it did in 1882 (when the photographs hanging on the stairs at Stafford Terrace were taken) but Westwood Lodge can no longer be called an elegant model villa, typical home of a successful stockbroker. Gone are the crisp lawn edges; the glossy horses and the liveried coachman on the immaculate gravel sweep seem more than a century away. The ornamental trees are huge and past their prime, while the gabled roof with its coloured tiles and fancy cresting, the bell turret and the oriel window, the curly bargeboards and the gothic trimmings, and especially the Kentish ragstone with its resemblance to a box of sweets, conspire to give the house the air of a Hansel and Gretel cottage in a clearing, faintly comic but still endearing.

By the 1840s the London Chatham and Dover Railway had begun to bring crowds of day-trippers down to Margate, and the English seaside holiday was entering its period of greatest popularity. In 1863 a station was built right on the sea-front at Ramsgate, and a big hotel, *The Granville*, was erected on the cliff top for the ever increasing number of visitors. The Herapaths' house was only twenty minutes drive from either Margate on the north coast or Ramsgate on the south, but it remained sufficiently isolated to feel genuinely rural up until the turn of the century.

Marion went down to Thanet to see her parents for visits of varying length throughout the year. Sometimes she only spent a few days with them, but more often she stayed for several weeks at a stretch. She was deeply attached to Westwood; to her it always seemed a sort of paradise, a panacea for all ills, from which she drew strength and comfort. She wrote "To Westwood, D.V." before each visit and was full of praise for its beauty when she arrived. "To Westwood, all looking so lovely", "Walked in grounds, picked violets *any amount*", "Heavenly day, sat in sun", and "Lovely day, lay in hammock all morning." The late-Victorian summers were nearly all long and hot, and though there might be wet or windy days, or times when Marion did not feel well, the general impression given in the diary is of one golden day after another. Whenever she was there Linley would come down from London every two or three days, sleep a night or two, and then return for various engagements in town. He always wrote her a letter as soon as he got back to Stafford Terrace, and one—often two or even three—on every day that they were parted. The communications system was excellent: a letter posted in the morning would reach its destination by the afternoon, and one which caught the last post at ten o'clock would be on the breakfast table the following morning. In addition a telegram sent just before leaving London would ensure that the traveller was met on arrival at the station. Linley's letters were brief, but they brought him almost as close to his wife as a telephone call does today. This one was written in 1880:

> My dearest Polly. Glad to get your letter. Wretched day here today, pouring. I shall try to come down tomorrow Friday by evening train if I do I'll wire if not I shall come 1st train Saturday. I have caught a slight cold I fear in the wind yesterday. Bradbury has engaged us all the 21st inst, a garden party. Same day as Mrs Messel's. Take care of yourself. Must get on with work if I am to come down so goodbye, ever your affectionate husband, Dickie.

Linley's style did not change, nor did the content of his letters vary very much, over the next thirty years, but Marion seldom failed to note in her diary "Letter from dearest Lin" each time she received one.

A combination of London and country living was the ideal arrangement for those who could afford it; Marion persisted in the habit all her life and as much as a quarter or even a third of her time was spent away from Stafford Terrace. Her diary for 1882 gives the outline of a typical year. A week in the early spring was spent with her parents at Westwood, followed by a fortnight in May, during which she looked around for a house to rent later so that the children and Nurse could have a separate establishment for the summer months—an excellent idea which allowed the grown-ups pleasant freedom from childish demands. She returned to London to be with her husband for June and July (the party season) and by 1 August the children were installed in their seaside lodgings, with Marion staying at Westwood and going over every day to see how they were getting on. At the end of August she went to Scotland with Linley for three weeks, and then came back to keep her parents company until the end of November when the whole family returned to London for the winter.

30

This pattern was repeated for several years with only minor variations. The availability of Westwood must have been a great blessing when Maud and Roy were little and they would have had a wonderful time playing in the extensive grounds, or going for rambles round the country lanes. There were breezy walks along the cliff tops for those in need of strenuous exercise, as well as miles of perfect sands around the coast for days with bucket and spade. People were always coming to stay: jolly uncles ready to play games of cricket or tennis, and aunts to take them shopping in Ramsgate. Mrs Herapath kept a watchful eye on them when their mother was away:

> My own dear Polly. Just a few lines to tell you your darlings are here and look so sweet and are so good. They are spending the day with us and I am going to take them back this evening. With dearest love from Pa and self, always your devoted and loving mother, M.A. Herapath.

Besides staying at Westwood with her parents, Marion sometimes accompanied them to other places. In 1883 she went with them to Bournemouth for three weeks, where it was hoped that the change of air would help her father's cough. Linley was a good son-in-law too; when Marion was about to return from Bournemouth with her ailing father he wrote to her with great concern:

Mrs Herapath and her eldest son, Spencer. Taken about 1872.

Dearest Polly. Very cold again. I think it would be madness for the Guv to come up in this east wind. He ought not to run the risk. When you do come the carriage ought to meet Pa at Vauxhall and then he should get in and drive straight away leaving the luggage etc to wait after. The pottering about at the station would be the worst of the journey. Above all see that you don't change trains, go up to the station-master and see the carriage reserved and footwarmers put in.

Mrs Herapath was three years younger than Queen Victoria and, just like the Queen, had borne a family of nine sons and daughters over a span of sixteen years. These children, with their marriage partners and their offspring, created the extended family so typical of the Victorian age. Marion, being the eldest girl, took it upon herself to keep in touch with all her brothers and sisters. Their affection and comradeship formed a most important part of her life and she saw most of them regularly, or wrote to them with news and gossip whenever they were far away. Though very different from each other in character and achievements, taken together they form a perfect cross-section of English middle-class life.

Marion's eldest brother, Spencer John, was often mentioned during the early years of her diary. He was something of a ne'er-do-well, never demonstrating the intelligence and capacity for hard work that had made his father and grandfather so successful. On 12 January 1881 he married Ada Oakes, so that this wedding was the first big family event for Marion to record: "Spencer's wedding day. Glorious day, drove to church with Papa, Mother & Auntie. Bride looked charming, lovely dress." Ada's father had been a wealthy East India merchant and had left a substantial fortune to his widow, who lived in a large detached house (called Derwent Lodge) in Addison Road, not far from Stafford Terrace. Ada was considered a very good match, and Spencer a lucky man. At first Marion got on well enough with her new sister-in-law, whom she always referred to as "Ada Sp" to distinguish her from her own youngest sister Ada. Spencer and Ada often came to dinner and the Sambournes went out with them to the theatre several times a year. In October 1881 their first child was born. "Took Maud with me to call on Ada Sp & baby" wrote Marion. Sadly this baby did not live long: "Poor little Jack died after three months suffering" was the diary entry in March 1883. Another son, Douglas, was born to Spencer and Ada in 1884 and a daughter, Hylda, followed two years later.

Marion admired Ada's clothes very much, and often described her outfits in the diary. A touch of envy is discernible in her comments: "Ada gorgeousely attired in fawn coloured ensemble", or "Mrs Boëhm's at home, Sp & Ada there, A. covered up with diamonds and taken for Indian princess!!!" As time went on she began to find her less congenial. In March 1886 she wrote "Spencer & Ada to dinner, utterly spoilt our evening, will *not* have Ada again, most trying person, always looking out for defects." This disagreement seemed soon forgotten: "Lin, Spencer, Ada & self

The hall and staircase. The walls are hung with photographs of statuary, inscribed Museo Vaticano; these were probably bought by the Sambournes when they were in Rome on their wedding tour. On the half-landing is the Water Garden: here ivy, ferns and Solomon's seal surround a glass tank in which a miniature fountain plays on a collection of semi-precious stones. The stained glass window contains the monogram LMS, Linley and Marion Sambourne's initials.

Above: A corner of the
dining-room. The
doors of all the main
rooms have painted
panels by Linley
Sambourne. The
bronze lamp has a
green glass shade and a
beaded fringe.

Left: Stained glass in
the dining-room:
Titania and Ariel in the
centre, surrounded by
birds and flowers.

(ii)

dined at Café Royal, excellent dinner", but Marion continued to find the difference in temperament a barrier: "Ada called, unapproachable as ever, shall never understand her."

Though the young Spencer Herapaths had a fine house in Scotland, much of their time was spent in London staying with Ada's mother at Derwent Lodge. This cannot have been a very satisfactory arrangement and it probably accounts for Spencer being so often at Stafford Terrace. He liked to call round for a chat nearly every day, and sometimes he helped Linley with his photography. He was very generous, often bringing Marion and the children presents; he also took his sister out to meals or to the theatre when her husband was busy. He was always asking Linley to go on jaunts with him—to Henley, to the Boat Race, to the Derby, as well as the occasional trip to Paris. It seems as if he had more money than was good for him and not enough to do; perhaps he too found Ada rather difficult to live with.

A large Victorian family usually contained one black sheep, and the child who fits this description is the Herapath's second daughter, Annie. Family tradition has been hard on her: she was said to have always been wayward, and her father was thankful to get her married off (at the early age of seventeen) without a scandal. Annie's husband was a solicitor much older than herself, called William Furrell. The marriage had taken place in March 1872 and a daughter, Edith, was born in 1873, followed by two sons. But domesticity did not alter Annie's character; her activities continued to shock her relations and in 1881 her husband divorced her, naming two co-respondents on the petition. In the moral climate of the time this meant complete social disgrace, so Annie and her two little boys were dispatched to Australia to start a new life as far away from home as possible. Edith was left behind, to spend her childhood at a school in the Isle of Wight. Some time later the boys were abandoned in Adelaide, where they remained in an orphanage until they were old enough to make their own way in the world. The scandal and the shame of Annie's behaviour must have been deeply painful for the whole family, and it seems that most of them responded by cutting her out of their lives completely.

The date of Annie's return to England is not known, but her name appears in Marion's diary for the first time on 26 March 1885, "Dear Mother called, had letter from Annie." Five days later Marion wrote, "Went with Mother to see poor Annie, very ill." Two years then elapsed before the next mention of this errant sister. In February 1887 Maud was taken ill and Linley summoned Marion back from Westwood, "Mother & self to London, v.anxious about dear Maud. Shocked to see her, struck with her likeness to Annie." Marion obviously felt a pang—was it sorrow for the past or fear of what the future might hold? There is another long gap before the next reference, "Mother worried about Annie", but we do not know if Marion worried too. What her sister was doing all those years, and what had become of her unfortunate children, were problems which were firmly set aside, although it is the very lack of references to Annie in the diary that stirs the interest of the modern reader. Her name does not occur again until early in 1890: Marion had caught a train up to London from Kent, "Saw Annie get in at Westgate. Did not see her at Victoria" was her entry that day and it seems a sad cold comment from one whose

own life was so much blessed. But this bleak encounter between two sisters perfectly illustrates those great divisions, so marked in Victorian society, between moral and immoral, lucky and unlucky, rich and poor. Very few people were prepared to defy convention to reach across the gap.

Jessie, the third Herapath daughter, was married in September 1881 to Hamilton Langley, a businessman with large estates in Argentina. Apparently he and Mr Herapath had negotiated the construction of a railway line to their mutual benefit: Langley had sold the land on condition that he would have a station on his ranch. The wedding took place at St Peter's Church, Thanet, seven years after Marion and Linley had been married there. The new bride and groom probably left for Buenos Aires directly after the wedding, as they were not mentioned again until 1882, "May 1st, Jessie & Ham arrive home." Their daughter, Dora, was born that July; like her cousin Maud before her, she first saw the light at 18 Upper Phillimore Gardens under Mrs Herapath's care. The Langleys soon returned to South America but all Jessie's letters to Marion from Argentina (and there are frequent entries "Long letter from Jess") have disappeared—a sad loss.

The youngest girl in the family, Ada, was married in London in April 1883 to George Hamilton Fletcher, the son of the founder of the White Star shipping line.

On the lawn at Westwood, 1883. Seated: Mr Herapath, Jessie, baby Dora. Standing: Spencer, a friend, Mrs Herapath and Nurse Waddie.

Ada (Tabby) and Hamilton Fletcher. They were married in 1883.

ELLIOTT & FRY.   55&56, BAKER S.T LONDON. W

The names of Marion's relatives are most confusing: not only were her father and brother both called Spencer, but she had a sister and a sister-in-law called Ada and now two brothers-in-law called Hamilton, both always referred to as Ham. Fortunately her sister Ada was called "Tabby" after her marriage, presumably a nickname invented by her husband. The Fletchers' first child, a girl, was born in September 1884.

Information about the early lives of the three younger Herapath boys is scanty. Edgar became a Regular Army officer (probably at an early age), while Marion's diary tells us that Conrad and Mervyn went out to Argentina in 1882. Journeys across the Atlantic, though still uncomfortable and time consuming, were no longer considered very hazardous and seem to have been undertaken quite lightly by various members of the family. Whether the two young men were engaged in their father's railway enterprises or merely travelling to broaden their horizons is not clear, but while he was in South America Conrad invested a small sum of money so successfully that he seems never to have been obliged to work for his living. He returned to England after a few months, but Mervyn stayed abroad for two years.

One aspect of Marion's diary that particularly strikes the modern reader is its pre-occupation with ill-health. An obsessive, almost morbid, interest in every kind of sickness was a very Victorian characteristic and the letters which Marion received from her father when she was at Brussels all had this subject as their main theme. "I am sorry to say that Mama continues in a very indifferent state of health—so much so that I am seriously concerned about her. She is getting so thin and looks so pale I only hope under God's goodness she will shortly be better but I am very sad and miserable about her. What should we do if anything happened to her," wrote Mr Herapath. Another letter, about Marion's younger sister, followed soon afterwards: "Poor Jessie is decidedly worse that is the fever has more hold on her. I have from the beginning had great fears and now I am very very anxious. I dread the effect upon poor Ma. I don't know what I should do if she were laid up which I fear will be the case unless she takes rest and gets a little relief from her constant watching. . . ." With her large family Mrs Herapath must have passed many weary hours watching and waiting. Prayers, will-power and devoted nursing were the only weapons which a loving heart could employ against the Angel of Death, but Marion's father did not think it unkind to transmit his anxiety to a sensitive sixteen-year-old girl, far away from home for the first time.

Marion shared her father's concern about health: a large part of her life was spent worrying about her loved ones. It was impossible for her to meet anyone without remarking on how well or ill they looked (usually the latter) and how concerned she felt about them. In addition hardly a day passed without a mention in her diary about how unwell she felt herself. The Victorians believed that men were by nature strong and active, women weak and passive, and they lost no opportunity of underlining that stereotype. Ladies were expected to show refinement in both mind and body; this they often demonstrated by adopting a pose of frailty and ill-health. To be "delicate" was to be interesting, and to lie on a sofa was a mark of status. Country girls were different: they were assumed to lack sensibility and it was this coarseness of fibre which made them so suitable as domestic servants, able to work long hours without complaint. Curiously enough it was not only those with too little to do who were constantly pandering to imaginary weaknesses. The diaries and letters of many forceful and pioneering women of the period show a similar absorption with ill-health, and it would seem that some kind of psychosomatic disorder affected most middle and upper-class females.

Marion probably never saw her own ill-health as a form of protest or a way of escape. Both her father and her husband were intelligent men of broad liberal views who treated their wives and daughters with affection and respect, and she did not have a restless or dissatisfied nature struggling to break out of the mould. The general low status of women was thus not something which she regarded as a problem, and in later years she found the antics of the Suffragettes very shocking. Her ill-health was—in part at least—genuine, and she probably suffered from some kind of chronic anaemia. Innumerable troublesome symptoms afflicted her—a pain in the side, neuralgia in the face, sore throat, sleeplessness,—but all were incidental to the main complaint, which she called "the old weakness". Nearly every day she

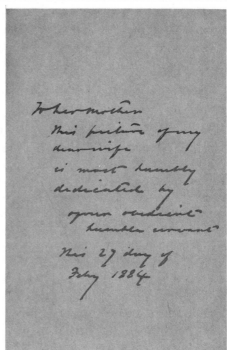
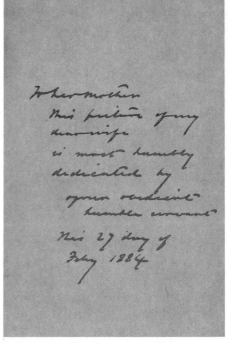

Marion in 1884. Poor health has spoiled her looks; she is hardly recognisable as the girl photographed in Rome ten years earlier. Linley inscribed the back of this to Mrs Herapath.

was "tired" or "very tired", and her diary was filled with pathetic little notes, "Feel so seedy & weak, can't think why", "Very poorly", or "Wretched & seedy, still feel so sick." A typical start to the day was "In bed as usual till 12 o'clock—feel a wreck generally." Though she took advice from several doctors no improvement seemed to last for long. A popular treatment was a change of diet: at one time a quart of milk a day was recommended, but then "Dr L came, altered diet, no more milk, no potatoes; pint of claret, turkish bath once a week." The turkish bath was only attempted once ("very droll") and the claret did not do much good either.

One cannot help wondering whether modern medicine would have provided a simple cure, or whether anything could have eased another (probably related) trial, her monthly periods. Nowadays women are not allowed to consider themselves "unwell" at these times, and those who suffer usually do so in silence, but among Victorian ladies this type of ill-health was all part of the inherent weakness and inferiority of their sex. Marion probably made more fuss than she need, but what was known as "the spinster's curse and married woman's friend" certainly made her feel wretched. She called it her *petit ami* or "little friend", and never failed to mark the days with an inky cross. It meant the morning spent in bed, sometimes the whole day, and cancelled engagements if she had not planned ahead properly. "Could not go on account of little F" was quite a usual entry. One wonders how

much she complained aloud, or if only her diary knew how ill she felt. Her husband seems to have been sympathetic, "To Crystal Palace, had Bath chair and quite enjoyed day, dear Lin helped wheel me about, did not feel a bit tired." But there must surely have been times when Linley felt impatient—perhaps his enthusiasm for early morning rides in the park was an excuse to escape from Marion's seediness.

This constant harping on the theme of ill-health generates a certain amount of irritation in the reader, until the other side of the coin becomes apparent—the number of times that Marion rose from her sick-bed to go to a party. A morning filled with sighs of self-pity was frequently followed by "To theatre & dinner, very jolly evening, enjoyed it", or "Delightful dinner, most amusing", or (her favourite expression) "Enjoyed it *immensely*." Clearly she was one of those people who needed the stimulus of company to make her sparkle: parties and outings, laughing and talking, seeing old friends and meeting new ones, were all activities essential to her well-being. Time after time she wrote "All in good spirits", or "Laughed immoderately". One of the reasons for marrying Linley must have been that he made her laugh so much, "Lin told joke at dinner, very amusing", and "Lin awfully funny, made Mother & self laugh immensely." One feels that the days when she wrote in her diary "Very quiet, nobody called" were dull indeed, not a blessed respite from the social round.

CHAPTER THREE
MAUD & ROY:
MRS S:
COUNTRY HOLIDAYS

 T IS CLEAR from reading the Sambournes' letters and diaries that Maud and Roy were the much cherished centre of a very loving family. Both the children had their birthdays in August, so that Maud was five and a half and Roy two and a half when Marion began writing. Admittedly during the early years of marriage she was so busy fulfilling the roles of dutiful daughter and loving wife that there was not a great deal of time left for her children. Victorian babies were very much the property of Nurse and parents were not expected to interfere: thus Maud and Roy are mentioned very little at first, and there were long periods when Marion was away from home and quite happy to leave them in Nurse's care. But gradually, as they grew older, the children absorbed more and more of her attention, and in later years their doings occupied a large part of her diary space.

Maud seems always to have been a good little girl, with a very affectionate and sensitive nature. In early photographs she looks rather frail and small for her age, which probably accounts for the nickname "Mite", which her father always used. Roy was a complete contrast. From the very start he was much more trouble: "Baby v.fretful" is his first appearance in the diary, followed by "Took baby out, rather naughty." His parents called him "Bar", and in May 1882 Linley wrote in a letter to Marion: "Bar is very well but oh so rough we shall be like the Frankensteins soon I fear", and drew a little sketch of themselves terrorized by a giant baby. By December that year babyhood had ended: "Darling Bar in long suit for first time, looks a duck." Soon after that he began to be referred to as "Roy". Though he had been baptised "Mawdley" (after some shadowy seventeenth-century ancestor), this name was never used, and in later life he always signed himself "Roy Sambourne".

No harsh separation between the generations existed in this family, as sometimes happened higher up the social scale. Maud and Roy (always called "the chicks") were made much of by their parents and were often taken out for treats, though of course there was always Nurse in the background to take over when they

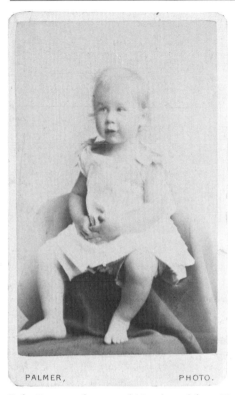

PALMER, PHOTO. PALMER, PHOTO.

Baby Roy, aged one, and Maud aged four. Taken in Ramsgate in the summer of 1879.

became troublesome. "Took Nurse Maud & Baby to zoo. Enjoyed it, chicks very happy" wrote Marion, and any special occasion was fun: "Xmas dinner, very jolly with chicks." Several of Linley's friends have left on record his skill with little children—how he had an inexhaustible store of jokes and games for their amusement, and a natural sympathy with their joys and sorrows. Maud's adult letters show that she thought her parents the best in the world; she loved them and her home and everything in it with an unusual intensity. Roy had more of a struggle to conform, and never seemed to find the key to a successful life.

The children were mentioned very often in Linley's letters. In April 1883 Marion had taken Maud to the country for a week, and Linley sent her daily reports on Roy (then aged four) left in London with himself and Nurse:

> Pleased to hear you got down safely and dear little Maud enjoying herself picking flowers. Roy well good and happy, not heard to cry since you went. He had twice of everything at dinner—two muttons, two potatoes, two oranges, and two goes of water and washed after and is now heavily sleeping it off. Shall be thankful to have you home again, and dear little Maud too. . . .

During their early years Nurse (or Nana as the children called her) was an important figure at Stafford Terrace. The Victorian nanny was the prop and stay of every middle-class household, and was very often passed round the family when new babies came. From her age (given in the 1881 census as thirty-two) the Sambournes' nurse was not old enough to have been a family retainer of very long standing. Later, when Roy began school, she went for a time to Marion's youngest sister's children, but returned occasionally to have tea with her former charges. Nurse slept with the children in the night-nursery, and supervised their every waking moment. Meals would have been brought up to the day-nursery until the children were considered old enough to eat with their parents downstairs. Once when Linley was away Marion wrote, "Maud sat down to dinner with me alone", which must have been a very special treat for a six-year-old. Although Marion occasionally recorded buying clothes and shoes for the children, Nurse really had charge of what they wore, and made sure that they were always clean and tidy. Nurse controlled their regular exercise, and it was nearly always she who took them to church; she also had entire responsibility for their welfare when their parents were away.

However Nurse did have her disadvantages. Mindful of her superior position in the household she quarrelled with the other servants, "Mary wants to leave at once, dislikes Nurse", "Jane cross with children just to spite Nurse", and she lacked subservience, "Nurse will argue about every blessed thing, so annoying." One wonders why Marion put up with her for so long, when she was always writing "Trouble with Nurse," or "*Bruit avec la bonne*" (strong feelings that were better suppressed were nearly always couched in French). On one occasion she was really put out: "*Tapage terrible avec la bonne, et grande pleurage de ma fille malheureuse à cause d'elle.*" Again, in English this time, "Had awful rumpus with Nurse about Roy, feel sorry I was so angry, always suffer keen regret after." In spite of all this, the children were devoted to Nurse, and she to them. One of the only faults Marion could find with Maud was that whenever there was any difficulty with Nurse, "Maud wept as usual."

Nurse supplied the children's early instructions in manners, and probably their first lessons in reading and writing too, but for further education a governess was necessary. When Maud was little Marion sent her to play with other children whose mothers she knew. In April 1883 she wrote "Maud's first day with Mrs Coward's governess". When Roy was old enough to need lessons it was time for the Sambournes to employ their own governess, so in November 1884 it was "Miss Penn's term begins £12 the quarter." Nothing is said about what Miss Penn did for the children; they were so often away for long holidays or out on various treats that the governess's work cannot have been very arduous. A picture-book of animals is the only thing which survives from these schoolroom days, inscribed "To Roy from Miss Penn", but she probably taught a smattering of all subjects, except the extra French conversation which was arranged for Maud. The children learnt to read and write quite early, but (for girls at any rate) a high level of intellectual accomplishment was not expected. Marion herself must have had a very similar upbringing; her writing may be hard to read but it is seldom misspelt, and her French was fluent.

Maud's artistic bent was encouraged from the very first. The 1877 Inventory records 240 prints pasted on to the nursery walls—it is sad indeed that later decoration has obliterated this attempt to foster her infant perception. She was taken to the Royal Academy Private View in 1882 (when she was six years old) and went every year thereafter, as well as going with her parents to numerous other exhibitions and important artistic events. She drew well from an early age. "Letter from Lin, drawings from Maud", wrote Marion in 1883, and, "Mr Fildes thinks Maud's drawing very clever." In 1887 she recorded with pride, "Dinner with Mrs Stone & Mrs Perugini, they are delighted with Maud's painting, Mrs P anxious to paint M and teach her, quite enthusiastic."

Though Maud had inherited Linley's talent, it was Roy who had his father's energy and bounce. He was full of noisy high spirits so that "Roy v.tiresome" was his mother's constant refrain. "Roy rampageous as usual" she wrote in 1885, and

Maud, aged five and a half.
Dated March 1881.

PALMER,   PHOTO.

"Roy fell out of cart", "Roy v. naughty", "Roy broke flower pot, thankful he was not hurt." The older he got the more troublesome he became: "Conservatory window put in, Roy pulled out putty after", "Roy nearly set house on fire playing with matches", and "Roy v. good, perhaps to make up for yesterday cutting Jane's dress." In spite of his naughtiness, he must have had plenty of charm: "Roy sweet & good", or "Roy very funny", was compensation for much bad behaviour.

Tucked into Miss Penn's *Book of Animals* is a list, drawn up by Roy, of all the toys in the nursery at Stafford Terrace:

> Roy has a bank of England pencil and so has Maud both of them has got a little Indian rubber. Roy has got a lot of pens Maud has only a few. Maud has got from twenty five to thirty five dolls and Roy has got nearly twenty boxes of soldiers with three hundred and thirty soldiers. Maud has a lovely theatre Roy has a fly that flys along Maud has a large dolls house Roy has a pair of horses you can drive. Maud and Roy have a nice pair of reins . . .

The list goes on to cover both sides of the paper, ending up:

> Maud has nine or ten doll sets of chairs and tables and Roy has nine or ten boxes of bricks. Roy is fonder of soldiers little fish to swim precious stones coins and puppys that go along. Maud is fonder of dolls and little chiner tea sets. Roy has three pounds seven shillings Maud has twelve shillings Roy and Maud have threepence a week.

The sheer quantity of toys possessed by this little pair is quite startling—one of the advantages of having parents with a wide circle of rich friends and numerous aunts and uncles. Love and pampering the children certainly had in plenty, and discipline seems to have been lax. The only instance recorded of either child being punished was when Roy played with matches after having been expressly forbidden to do so: "Sent him to bed at once" wrote his mother with unaccustomed firmness.

Though Roy did not draw, when he grew up he quite enjoyed writing. A notebook survives containing an essay of his, which gives a delightful glimpse of life at Stafford Terrace. It begins:

> Never shall I forget our first Christmas at home. We had always had our Christmas dinner at grandpapa's house, Nana Maud and I in the dear old schoolroom and plenty of interruptions we had with so many uncles and aunties coming in to see how we were getting on with the plum pudding and mince-pies. But this particular Christmas as Maud was eleven and I was eight we were to dine late at home. . . .

Roy was writing about Christmas 1886, but he must have been looking back quite a few years as the style is too mature for an eight-year-old. On Christmas morning the children opened their presents in bed:

There was a pack of cards, some crackers, a box of chocolates and a pen-wiper in the shape of an elephant's head. . . . Granny H gave us each a box of sweets with a sovereign inside, Papa and Mama a large magic lantern with 120 slides and a musical box which nearly drove Granny mad, for we kept it going all day. Directly we were dressed we rushed down to mother's room with our own little present for each. . . . After breakfast we all went to church and very pretty it looked with its lovely white flowers and wreaths. Then came luncheon after which Papa took Maud and me to St Paul's Cathedral, which I like even better than Westminster Abbey where I had been the Sunday before.

We reached home just in time for tea and very hard work it was cutting the cake with its casing of sugar. What a romp we had after tea, whilst the musical box played thro' its little tunes, until it was time to dress for dinner. Oh! how lovely the table looked, such flowers, such fruit, such crackers, and all the candles on a dish with the sweetest little shades. . . . With dinner over we rushed up to the drawing room. Here we found the sheet all ready for the Magic Lantern display. So we took our places whilst Papa had the lights all lowered or put out. There were all the different cathedrals which Papa had brought for myself especially, knowing I had a weakness for churches, then some comic pictures, a man in bed swallowing rats at a great rate, and a woman whose nose grew an inordinate length, besides many more I have almost forgotten. . . . Then came a dance of Sir Roger and how stiff Granny's back was after for days. Then Blind Man's Buff and several uncomfortable encounters had I against odd corners of furniture, our rooms are a little too crowded for these romps.

The Magic Lantern which their parents gave the children that Christmas is still in the drawing-room, although the slides which went with it are not. Neither is the musical box—perhaps Maud took it away with her when she married.

The children led a very full social life, as the Sambournes had many friends with young families. Among the engagements listed in the early part of 1881 were "Mrs Bradbury's juvenile party" and "Mrs Arthur Lewis' juvenile party". Only Maud was old enough to go that year, but in every succeeding year both children were asked out often: "Chicks to two parties, came home laden with toys." Sometimes fancy dress was required, and these parties could be very grand affairs. After one of them Marion wrote, "Maud's dress v. successful", and another time she cut out a short article from *The World* dated 14 January 1885, which began, "The juvenile fancy-dress ball given by the Lord and Lady Mayoress at the Mansion House was a particularly brilliant one . . ." and went on to mention "Master Sambourne as an executioner" among the twelve hundred guests. Linley made a drawing of his son wearing this costume which he titled *Heads I Win*. Roy kept it as a memento for the rest of his life and it still hangs on his bedroom wall.

Going to the theatre was a favourite treat for the whole family. Maud was taken

Roy in the executioner's costume which he wore to the Lord Mayor's children's fancy dress party in January 1885.

twice to the Pantomime in the early months of 1882, and Roy soon began to go too. There are a great many references to plays and pantomimes in Marion's diary; like Queen Victoria before her, she liked nothing better than to take her children to a matinée. Sometimes Linley took them; in June 1884 his friend Edwin Abbey had laid on a party and he wrote to Marion at Westwood, "I went this afternoon [to the Pantomime] and was with dear little Roy the whole time and held his hand. He was very excited especially with the wolf and the grandmother! I think it very kind of Abbey to give such a treat, there were 5 little Messels 1 Fildes & 2 Sambournes. Roy amused Miss Parsons very much by saying that a Pantomime was better than the Circus, but *Church* was better than all!"

In Roy's case this early initiation into the joys of theatre-going resulted in an enthusiasm which lasted all his life. Another thing to which he became passionately addicted was sport; as soon as he was old enough his father took him to cricket matches and to watch the Boat Race. Something all the family enjoyed was a visit to the Natural History Museum, a vast impressive building which had been opened in 1881. A visit to the Zoological Gardens in Regent's Park was another treat. Any new acquisition there was always considered worth a special visit; on 12 March 1882 Marion wrote, "To Zoo to see Jumbo, great crowds." Linley often went there to take photographs of the animals for his cartoon work.

45

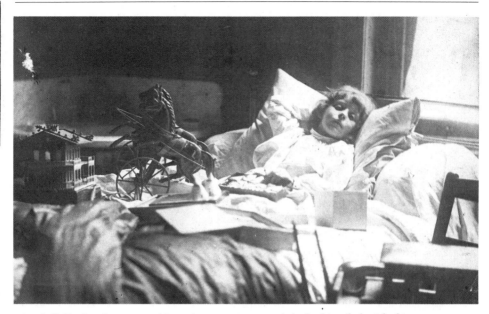

Maud ill. She has been moved into the spare room and the bed is piled with things to amuse a sick child. There was no shortage of toys in the Sambourne nursery.

The only thing to spoil Maud and Roy's happiness was the usual succession of childhood illnesses. These were mostly of a minor nature, but in 1887 Maud was taken seriously ill. On 2 February she had a bad throat, and on 10 February Marion wrote, "Maudie no better, v.feverish & in pain, Dr O came four times." A second opinion was called in, "Dr West came at 3, confirmed all my dreadful fears of yesterday." The diary does not record what the diagnosis was— diphtheria and scarlet fever were potent killers in the days before antibiotics—but the progress of Maud's illness seems too erratic for either of these. "Darling Maud a little better" alternated with "Dear Maudie looks awfully bad, Lin so anxious." A month after the onset of the illness Marion wrote, "Dear Maud improving, sitting up enjoying an egg for her breakfast", but the child continued poorly and had an alarming relapse on 8 April. "Dear little Maud very ill all night, sent for Dr O, ordered ice & champagne." Another ten days of anxiety followed before Marion could write: "Maudie much better, drove with her to Barnes, walked a little way." Maud had been ill for nearly three months, so it was no wonder that her mother considered her "delicate" for a long time afterwards.

As Maud had been the centre of everyone's attention for so long it was hardly surprising that Roy felt neglected. "Roy very noisy and rough, dear Maudie must be kept v.quiet" wrote Marion. Quiet was what Roy could never be, and the next day his exasperated mother added "Roy getting *quite* beyond control." Stafford Terrace was too cramped for an active little boy; Nurse could not manage him any longer, nor did Miss Penn attempt to discipline him. His parents began to make plans for

sending him to school, but in the meantime they could gain a little peace at home by arranging for both children to go to the country with Nurse for a period of recuperation.

All through the 1880s there was another person who occupied a central position in the pattern of life at Stafford Terrace: Linley's mother, old Mrs Sambourne. As an elderly widow of restricted means, with no home of her own, Mrs Sambourne must have thought it quite right and natural that a large part of her time should be spent with her only son and his family. Although she was with them for several months of the year, she was not a permanent fixture, but seems to have been perpetually on the move from one sister or niece to another. It was her custom to arrive at Stafford Terrace shortly before Christmas and to remain there for about three months, and she often stayed with the family for a month or two during the summer as well. As so often happens, she did not see eye to eye with her daughter-in-law. Marion tried very hard to be welcoming and kind, but it was a real effort, and it is soon obvious that the relationship with her mother-in-law (always called simply "Mrs S") was fraught with difficulties.

Frances Sambourne had been widowed when she was fifty-five. She was seventy years old when first encountered in the diary and still full of vigour. She needed constant amusing and Marion had to work hard arranging something different for her to do each day: "With Mrs S to shops", "With Mrs S & Maud to theatre", Mrs S & self dine at Mother's", and so on. Mrs Sambourne made a great fuss over her health, but here her daughter-in-law was less sympathetic than usual: "Mrs S seedy & depressed" was followed by "Mrs S not so ill as she thinks she is", and differences of opinion often rankled: "Tiff at dinner, annoyed, Mrs S will interfere" wrote Marion, "*Fracas avec la belle-mère*" and "*La belle-mère très désagreable.*" Not even Mrs Sambourne's usefulness as a child minder ("Mrs S up with baby all night" or "Mrs S all day with chicks on sands") could outweigh her disadvantages. By the end of each long visit Marion's nerves were at breaking point: "Mrs S left. *Je me suis un peu contente d'être seul encore*" was written with real thankfulness. At a Christmas party in 1886 there was an open rift: "Mrs S said my health very trying for Linley, feel extremely annoyed." It was, alas, a home truth, and one which Marion was never able to forget or forgive.

Mr Herapath died on 13 March 1884. He had not been well for some years, but his death (after only three days illness) came as a great grief and shock to his family. "Darling Father taken from us. He fell asleep at 7 o'clock in the morning and was taken without pain at 3.20' wrote Marion. All her relations wrote kind and sympathetic letters. From one of her aunts: "Your dear father was the dearest of all my brothers and you darling Polly were his most loving child . . . It will be a comfort to you darling to know that you have never caused him trouble or hastened his untimely end." (This was a pointed reference to the misdemeanours of Annie and

young Spencer), and from a cousin, "I know your sad loss is equally great to you all but you have always been dear Uncle Spencer's especial daughter and the blank seems almost saddest for you." Marion did indeed grieve for her father and his death marked the end of her childhood in a way that her marriage ten years earlier had not done. In the days that followed she was her mother's best comforter, "Spent all day with dear mother, who keeps up wonderfully well, thank God." But without her father's beloved presence everything was changed and during the next few weeks the words "very miserable" and "dreadfully depressed" appeared repeatedly in the pages of her diary.

All Mr Herapath's property and effects were left in trust to his wife, together with the income from his investments after certain annuities had been deducted; she was to chose which of their two houses she would live in, and sell the other. There was an annuity of £250 each for the three younger sons, Edgar, Conrad and Mervyn, but the eldest son got nothing. This may have been because young Spencer was a partner in his father's firm, and thus amply provided for, but it might be interpreted as a rebuke, for he had long been a drain on his father's purse. Each Herapath daughter was to receive £100 a year from the trust until her marriage when the allowance was to be increased to £150. Under the terms of their marriage settlements Marion and Annie were already receiving their annuities, but the will explains why Marion was allotted less than her sisters: To my daughter Mary Ann Sambourne to whom I have already advanced the sum of £1,000, an annuity of £100." The two younger girls, Jessie and Ada, later married very well and hardly needed their allowances: Marion must often have thought what good use she could have made of that extra £50 a year.

Spencer Herapath put another clause into his will, typical of the careful self-made man that he was: "I direct that my executors shall conduct my funeral in the quietest and most inexpensive manner possible." Arrangements were made for him to be buried in the country, and on 18 March Marion wrote, "Darling Father taken to Westwood and St Peter's. I spent day with dear Mother." As was customary in those days, the ladies stayed at home and only the men of the family accompanied the coffin and attended the funeral service, returning to London by train late that same evening.

Mrs Herapath chose to sell the house in Upper Phillimore Gardens and to reside at Westwood. The long business of settling her father's affairs depressed Marion more than ever. In May she wrote "Dined at Mother's. Felt v.sad, it no longer seems the same home to me", and on 2 July, "Feel wretched about house sold for £4000, Mr Nash bought it." Mrs Herapath's move was completed by the end of July, and it was decided that Jessie (who was in England, expecting her second baby) would, with little Dora, keep her mother company during the first months of her widowhood. In August the Sambournes went down to Kent for their usual holiday, but this time they all stayed together in a rented house near to Westwood for three months, going over daily to see Mrs Herapath. Hamilton Langley went back to Buenos Aires and thus was not present on 22 October when Marion wrote, "Jessie's little son born, very wee, cannot live. In Dora's doll's cot—Mother in her element."

Above: The dining-room. The octagonal table and eight chairs, the pictures, the china and the brass chimney furniture are all listed in the 1877 Inventory.

Left: The morning-room ceiling, papered with a William Morris design, "Fruit" or "Pomegranate".

The drawing-room. The magnificent
stained glass window, designed by
Linley Sambourne, was installed in
1887. In front of it a bronze statuette of
Cupid and Psyche embracing stands on
a marquetrie chest. On the right is a
camera on an adjustable tripod base.

The baby died next day, "Mother nearly broken-hearted about the poor little thing." It had been a sad year for all the family, but for Mrs Herapath the baby's death would have brought back poignant memories of the loss of her little boy, Ernest.

Even though Marion missed her father, Westwood meant as much to her as ever, and she re-lived her happy childhood days each time she went there. Most of her nervous anxiety was now centred on her mother, and during the next few years she visited Westwood as often as possible, leaving Linley and the children behind in London. The two women clung together in their bereavement, and seemed to vie with each other as to who could suffer most. "Feel very seedy indeed, worried to see Mother looking so poorly" wrote Marion repeatedly. Sometimes it was Mrs Herapath who had to do the most comforting: she cosseted her daughter and encouraged her to indulge her hypochondria to the full. "Bad night, went in to Mother's bed at 5 o'clock" was the type of entry which appeared in Marion's diary during these visits. It was only when she was at Westwood with her beloved mother that she felt her troublesome health received all the attention and sympathy it deserved. Another conviction was that country air did her more good than any medicine, and she would write "Feel Londony already, tired and back-achey" on her return to Stafford Terrace.

Maud and Roy with their grandmothers in the conservatory at Westwood. Mrs Herapath on the left, Mrs Sambourne on the right, Marion behind.

Marion's two middle brothers, Edgar and Conrad, did not marry until all four of their sisters had found husbands. Naturally enough she did her best to find them suitable wives, and one of the girls whom she introduced to Conrad was Effie Boëhm. Effie's parents, though older than the Sambournes, were very dear friends of long standing. Joseph Edgar Boëhm was a successful sculptor, much liked by Queen Victoria, and teacher of her talented daughter, Princess Louise. Marion entertained Conrad and Effie together several times at Stafford Terrace, but she had some doubts about the suitability of the match. On Christmas Eve 1884 she wrote, "Letter from Con actually proposed to Effie, hope no harm will come of it." Conrad was not considered nearly good enough by Effie's parents: "Mrs Boëhm called about Effie. Long talk all to no point. Sorry we ever introduced them." However four months later everything was satisfactorily resolved. "Lin dined with Con, bachelor dinner. Mother & self at Mrs Boëhm's" wrote Marion, and next day, "April 29th 1885: Con and Effie's wedding day—all went off splendidly."

Meanwhile Marion's other brother, Edgar, had been busy courting Sophy Fletcher, sister of Tabby's husband, Hamilton. Sophy was an intelligent girl, one of the first graduates of Girton College, Cambridge. She and Edgar were married on 9 June 1885, and their marriage, though childless, was to last longer and be happier than Conrad and Effie's. During the summer both newly married couples went to stay at Westwood with Mrs Herapath for a few weeks. Marion and Linley were there too, and all joined together in the perennial country pleasures—walks and rides, jaunts in the pony cart, picnics on the sands and photographs on the lawn.

The youngest of Marion's four brothers, Mervyn, was seventeen when she began her diary. He was only eleven years older than Maud, so it is hardly surprising that he makes his first appearance having tea in the nursery with the little Sambournes. He returned to England from his visit to South America in March 1884, a week before his father died, and went down to Westwood with his brothers for the funeral. He was best man at Conrad's wedding, but during the next few years was so restless and unsettled. For a time he was very keen on acting: "Mervyn has interview about going on stage" wrote Marion in February 1887, and the next day, "Wire from Mervyn, interview satisfactory, great excitement." Though he did secure a few small parts, fame eluded him, and he decided to travel abroad.

Mrs Herapath was by no means totally retired at Westwood after her husband's death, but made regular forays up to London to stay for several weeks at a time at her favourite Bath Hotel. Her children (with the exception of Annie and Spencer) were devoted to her, taking it in turns to stay at Westwood as well as visiting her regularly when she was in London. As the family grew larger and more scattered, Westwood gradually became less of a meeting place. The centre of entertainment shifted to the youngest daughter, Tabby, and her husband, Hamilton Fletcher. Tabby loved to gather people round her; she and Hamilton moved about the country renting various large and comfortable houses where there was always plenty of room for visitors. Thus Marion had a different place to admire every time she visited her

Left: Conrad and Effie taken in Paris on their wedding tour. Right: Edgar and Sophy.

sister. In August 1885 the Sambournes went to the south coast, near Christchurch: "We all go to Tabby's, lovely place, 'Sandhills'. Dear little baby, pink-cheeked thing exactly like Ham." Conrad and Effie were invited at the same time, as well as Mervyn, so there was a cheerful family party with something for everyone to enjoy: "Chicks delighted to be on sands all day" wrote Marion, "Con Mervyn & self rowed up river, lovely, & sailed back", "Ham & Mervyn painted boat", "Tabs Effie & self shopping in Christchurch", "Went sand-eeling, great fun, Roy got wet", and so on, for three happy weeks. Linley came down at intervals, and of course "Lin took all our photos on verandah."

At Christmas Tabby invited the Sambournes again, this time to a house near Evesham. "Xmas tree, village children, great success" wrote Marion, and later, "Deep snow, Lin could not go to town. Went tobogganing, great fun." In the evenings they made themselves cosy, "Tabs & self had baby down, sat over fire and talked." The following September Tabby had a second daughter, "Telegram from Ham. So sorry another girl." The two little girls were called Gwen and Eveleen and Conrad's son (born in July 1886) was called Geoffrey, but Marion referred to all her nieces and nephews as "baby" until they reached the age of reason.

Marion spent most of the summer of 1886 at Westwood, but the following year the Sambournes again holidayed with Tabby at the seaside while other members of

the family came and went. This August holiday with the Fletchers became an established feature of Herapath family life, and if Jessie and Hamilton Langley were on one of their periodic visits to England, they too joined the party. The Langleys would arrive from Buenos Aires laden with exotic presents: Bahia oranges, pineapples, South American partridge, and once a pair of love-birds for Maud. Hamilton also imported horses; one year he lost fifty on the voyage due to violent storms in the Atlantic. After the first few years of their marriage Jessie was able to spend much more time in England. Her nickname, "Midge", soon began to be used in all Marion's diary entries. "Lin & Ham to horse show, Midge & self to shops" she wrote when the Langleys were staying in London, and "Midge Ham & Dora called, Ham bought three polo ponies to play at Hambledon."

The Langleys, like Tabby and Hamilton Fletcher, rented a series of houses in various parts of the country from which they dispensed generous hospitality. Conrad and Effie had houses in both London and Sussex; when Marion went to stay with them in the country she wrote, "Very jolly day, to Arundel, went up river in 3 boats, picnic on brow of hill. V.delicious lunch, played cricket after, made one run, v.proud!" But it was the regular August seaside visit to Tabby that Marion looked forward to most, a wonderful opportunity to relax in the lap of luxury with all her loved ones round her. Year after year the pattern was the same: "On sands with Tabs & Midge, children all so happy together, delightful to see them" she wrote, "Bathed with children, enjoyed it", "Heavenly day, sat on sands while all the little ones paddled." As the children grew up, there was plenty to keep the more energetic members of the family happy: "Roy & Lin played tennis, Roy improving", or "Lin long walk with dogs & swim", and "Ham off to Cowes for regatta." Marion was always sorry when the time came to an end: "Envy Tabby and Ham their opportunity of giving so much pleasure to others."

One combination of relatives which rather surprisingly did not occur was Tabby and Hamilton with Edgar and Sophy. In spite of the double relationship, it seems that these two couples had little in common. Naturally Edgar and Sophy had their own group of Army friends, very different from the artistic circle in which the Sambournes moved or the wealthy set around the Fletchers, but Edgar and Tabby had never got on well. "Had long talk with Tabs about her row with Edgar" wrote Marion, and she made a point of not entertaining them together. Edgar may have been rather a pompous bore, and here Roy's Christmas essay is revealing: "After dinner Uncle Edgar made a speech. I never heard one before and I do not think I would care to hear another. I noticed Mother looked very uncomfortable and I could see tears in Granny H's eyes. I am determined when I am a man not to make a speech unless I can make people laugh and not cry." Marion was sometimes rather impatient with Edgar; at this stage of their lives she saw less of him than of Conrad, Tabby, or Midge, but in later years she grew very fond of him.

CHAPTER FOUR
FRIENDS & ARTISTS: MUSIC & THEATRE

LARGE PART of Marion's diary was taken up with her social engagements. By far the most important activity of the middle-class Victorian lady was "calling". Although calls could be made on any day, many people established an at home day once a week when they held open house for any of their friends who might care to drop in for conversation and a little light refreshment. Marion made a list of these days in the front pages of her diary and this is a most useful guide for determining the composition of her social circle. Most of the names on the list mean nothing to us now, but many are of well known artists and writers—for instance Mrs Alma-Tadema had her at home day on Monday, Mrs Rider Haggard on Wednesday, Mrs du Maurier on Thursday and Mrs Marcus Stone on Sunday. Marion's own at home was on Tuesday, and she could generally expect four or five people on that day: "Mrs Boëhm & Flossie, Mrs Rainbow & Mrs Ross, Mrs Wilson & friend called." These friends would all be offered tea and cakes and a pleasant gossip, though they were not expected to stay too long. Sometimes gentlemen called too, and then the conversation took a more lofty tone. Occasionally the visitors were very boring, "Mr Emery & sister called, both densely slow", and sometimes no one called at all. It was not necessary always to receive callers, as if the lady of the house was too busy, or indisposed, she would instruct her maid to say that she was "not at home". The caller would then leave her visiting card, and convention would be satisfied. Not to call "to enquire" if there was serious illness in the house would be considered very remiss. When Maud was very ill Marion wrote "Great many callers", but she probably would not have seen them, nor would they have expected it. There were other rules designed to avoid embarrassment: for instance it was considered rude and "forward" to call uninvited on a lady above one in the social scale. Thus when Marion wrote "Mrs X asked me to call", she was recording a compliment. Conversely, one did not call on those who were lower in the hierarchy, although charitable ladies would "visit" the poor and sick.

Much time was spent returning calls, as it was impolite to ignore even a visiting

53

card. Sometimes Marion only did one or two calls in an afternoon, but more often she fitted in a great number, taking tea two or three times on her round. "Called on Mrs Kemp, Mrs Christopher, Mrs Humphreys, all out. Had tea at Mrs Holmes, stayed some time. Called & had tea at Mrs Tuer's and at Miss Hogarth's, saw Mrs Andrews and girls there, sent carriage home & walked back," was one busy afternoon, and another: "After lunch called at Mrs Baines (lots of people there) Mrs Smiles (too ill to see anyone) Mrs Sington (little girl v.ill) Marion Pollock (out) Mrs Kemp (had tea there) Mrs Eykyn (out) and round park to Mrs V.Cole. Sent carriage home, tea there. Walked back, left card at Miss Winthorp's and enquired after Dr Harcourt, little better." When Maud was old enough it was considered part of her education to accompany her mother on these visits.

Marion thoroughly enjoyed the social round. Some women found the ritual of polite visiting and idle chatter infinitely boring, but this was never her attitude. She loved people: the exchange of conversation and the general airing of views on all topics was a very important part of her life. "Amusing" was one of her favourite words, and her best friends were always those who made her laugh. She was full of curiosity about other people's affairs, their health, their children, and their clothes. She liked seeing their new furnishing schemes, "To Friths' at home, sweetly pretty

Marcus Stone's house in Melbury Road. Luke Fildes, G.F. Watts, Frederic Leighton, Val Princep and Colin Hunter all lived within a few hundred yards of each other.

drawing room, yellow blue & white", and "To Oscar Wilde's weird house, dullish." No doubt she hoped that people who came to call on her would be suitably impressed by the artistic interior of 18 Stafford Terrace. Marion had a keen eye for beauty in any form and she often recorded her admiration for other women: "Mrs G, lovelier than ever all in white", "Admire Mrs A. v.much, exceedingly handsome", or "Mrs D looking v.nice in pretty plush tea-grown." Even people that she did not know drew a comment; more than once she wrote "Saw v. pretty woman in train." Her diary is remarkable for its lack of carping or criticism of her fellow mortals; only very occasionally did she say something derogatory, "Mme de Sembrich sang, pity she squints so!"

Apart from the casual afternoon calling, there were written invitations to at home parties in the evening, intended for both husbands and wives. These sometimes took place before dinner, or often quite late in the evening as an after-dinner or after-theatre entertainment. Dinner parties were usually grand and very formal. Marion always noted who escorted her in to the meal, and who sat next to her at table. Social rank was most significant, so the table seating was carefully worked out and it was a great compliment to be given a place next to the host or the guest of honour. "Sir R. Webster's dinner. Very delightful, Sir Arthur Blyth took me in & sat on left of Sir R. Mr & Mrs Stafford Northcote there, & Sir C. Owen. Music after, v.charming evening." Or "Very jolly dinner at Mrs C's. Mr Twiss took me in, Sir W. Hardman on other side." Sometimes she was not best pleased: "Rather slow dinner. O. Wilde sat next me & spilt all his claret all over my dress." Again, "Awfully slow dinner at Hunters'—frightful glare in studio & dining room. Smelly old gentleman on my right & Mr Black on left. Lin & self v.bored." But usually Marion thoroughly enjoyed herself: "Exquisite dinner at Mrs de la Rue's. Pleasant company & left late", "To Messels', v. jolly party, good fun at supper", "Charming evening at German Reed's, singing dancing etc, home at 3 o'clock", and "Mrs Burnand's dinner. Stayed until 3:30 am, came home in broad daylight."

Marion found entertaining in her own home great fun too. "Delightful dinner here, room looked v.pretty with new lamp-shades", or "Table looked lovely, yellow green and orange. Arranged flowers & fruits", and "Enjoyed having Mr Tenniel to dinner, as charming as ever, stayed till ¼ to twelve." Although she took great care over her arrangements, things did not always go right: "Sat in morning room after dinner, pretty but uncomfortable", or "Dinner not quite a success—Burnands & Haggards *not* sympathetic." Being a busy hostess had its hazards, and it was not unknown for her to make a mistake. Once Linley had to write her a scolding letter, "You must *not* ask people to dinner and then go away. We shall make serious enemies if you do. The Grossmiths were within an ace of coming on Sunday, only Mrs G being ill prevented it. Write at once to Mrs Grossmith and say how sorry you are that she is ill and that they could not come. The rest you must get out of as best you can. . . ."

Punch was of course the mainstay of Linley's life. Not only did he have to draw for his living, but he had to work very closely with the other members of the staff. Marion's first duty as a wife was to keep on friendly terms with all his colleagues; fortunately for her, Frank Burnand (the Editor of *Punch* since 1880) and his wife, Rosie, were among her favourite friends, and they dined together often. John Tenniel held the position of "First Cartoon" for many years and, although much older than Linley, was another valued friend. (He is better known to posterity as the illustrator of *Alice in Wonderland*.) Other connections with *Punch* were more tenuous: Agnew and Bradbury (the proprietors of the paper), Lehmann, a'Beckett, Keene, May, du Maurier and all the other writers and illustrators appeared frequently in Linley's diary but Marion hardly mentioned them and they were seldom, if ever, invited to Stafford Terrace.

During the eighties it was the artistic world which supplied the Sambournes with most of their friends. Scattered through Marion's diary are the names of a host of minor Victorian painters—among them Frank Holl, William Orchardson, Walter Crane, Felix Moscheles, and the Americans Edwin Abbey and George Boughton. The Sambournes knew everybody who lived in nearby Melbury Road and Holland Park Road, where there was a flourishing colony of artists. Its most illustrious inhabitant was Frederic Leighton, who had begun building his remarkable house there in 1866. He had become President of the Royal Academy in 1878, was made a baronet in 1886, and just before his death in 1896 was raised to the peerage; thus he was always rather an Olympian figure to the Sambournes. As he was a bachelor it was difficult for Marion to get to know him, and she does not record going to any of his famous parties and musical soirées. Val Prinsep, G.F.Watts, Colin Hunter and the sculptor Thorneycroft also lived in the same area, but (except for Hunter) the Sambournes did not mix much with this group. Their really close friends in Melbury Road were Mr and Mrs Marcus Stone and Mr and Mrs Luke Fildes. Both these couples lived in large detached red-brick houses designed for them (in 1875 and 1876 respectively) by the architect Richard Norman Shaw. Luke Fildes was Roy's godfather, and Marion often walked round to call on Fanny Fildes or Laura Stone. In July 1884 she wrote, "Went to Mrs Fildes, Luke showed us the lovely picture he has done for us." This picture, *Head of a Girl*, hangs in the morning-room at Stafford Terrace. Such a painting was very welcome as a gift; the Sambournes did not spend money on collecting contemporary art.

Fanny Fildes was an artist in her own right, as were several other of Marion's female acquaintances—Mrs Alma-Tadema, Mrs Perugini (Charles Dickens' daughter, Kate), Mrs Jopling, Mrs Stokes and Mrs Allingham. They had all exhibited before marriage, and their talents were respected by their male colleagues. Nor were these ladies exceptional; well-educated girls were expected to be able to sketch and paint a little, and a surprising number of them took up art seriously, had their own studios, and exhibited at the Royal Academy. Some of them were daughters of artists, like Blanche Vicat Cole (whose mother was an old friend of Marion's) or of sculptors, like the Thorneycroft sisters. Art, music and literature were the only acceptable modes of expression for a Victorian lady. Acting was still

frowned upon (though not so much by the Sambournes who had many theatrical friends), while teaching was considered a very lowly occupation.

Linley was familiar with many more artists than Marion, for the ones who adopted a Bohemian life style would not have been introduced to his wife; all her friends combined artistic talent with the utmost respectability. Marion seldom ventured down to Chelsea, the haunt of raffish characters such as Whistler; of the artists who clustered in St John's Wood only Mrs Alma Tadema was on her calling list. Nor did she know any of the Pre-Raphaelites, who in their youth had set out to shock the establishment. Rossetti died in 1882, and Holman Hunt did not come to live in Melbury Road until 1903. Burne-Jones had a house in Fulham, and William Morris one in Hammersmith, both very close to Kensington, but Marion never mentioned either of them. Millais was still a very important figure in the art world, (he was said to earn £30,000 a year), but like Leighton was rather too grand to be a friend of the Sambournes. Although Linley admired him, Marion did not mention his wife; perhaps she felt, as Queen Victoria did, that Mrs Millais (who had divorced John Ruskin, her first husband) was not respectable. The Queen made Millais a baronet in 1885, and after that dispensed honours freely amongst those connected with the arts. Of the Sambournes' close friends, Boëhm was made a baronet in 1890, and several others were later knighted: Tenniel in 1893, Irving in 1895, Alma Tadema in 1899, Burnand in 1902, and Fildes in 1906. When Marion began her diary these friends were already successful, but had not yet become part of the Establishment. If Linley had lived longer it is quite possible that he, too, would have received a knighthood.

As he was only a black-and-white artist Linley was debarred from being elected a member of the Royal Academy, but he did exhibit there from 1885 onwards, and always took a keen interest in the work of other artists. A successful oil painter could sell a single picture for a price well above Linley's annual salary, but he himself never appears to have tried his hand at any medium other than pen or pencil. In January 1884 he finished his drawing for the Diploma of the International Exhibition of Fisheries, which he had been working on for over six months. This design is generally held to be his masterpiece, and it hangs today in a prominent position on the stairs at Stafford Terrace. It was the fashion for artists to hold an open day on the completion of an important work, and Marion wrote proudly in her diary "Thirty five people called to see Diploma." However this achievement pales beside that of a popular oil painter: the previous year Mrs Fildes had recorded over seven hundred people calling at the house in Melbury Road to see her husband's latest big picture.

On "Picture Sunday" (just before the sending-in date for the Royal Academy annual exhibition) the Sambournes would do a tour of the artists' studios, where the pictures destined for submission to this most important event were on display. In April 1883 Marion was away and Linley wrote to her: "Went round the Studios yesterday. . . . Orchardson's *the* picture I think. Mrs O sorry you were away seedy. Mrs Stone, Mrs Fildes etc etc asked after you. Obliged to miss some of them, did not go to Wells, Calderon, Yeames or Hodgson." In another year Marion recorded calling at the studios of Prinsep, Hunter, Fildes, Leighton, Millais and Alma-

Tadema, as well as several lesser artists. A month later she and Linley would go to see the same pictures on Private View Day at the Royal Academy. It is difficult now to realise the immense power and prestige of the Academy during the nineteenth century, and how necessary it was for an artist to have its seal of approval. The interest taken by both press and public in each year's crop of pictures was astonishing. All the papers carried long critical reviews, and people crowded into the Academy to see the "Picture of the Year". An artist was assured of success if a barrier had to be erected in front of his work to protect it from the milling throng. Private View Day was the greatest social occasion in the artists' calendar, just the sort of party Marion loved best. She seldom missed a year: "To Academy, met heaps of friends", she wrote, or "Private View Academy, enjoyed it, v.crowded."

The Grosvenor Gallery was also very important. It had been opened in 1877 as a rival showplace for anyone who either disapproved of the Academy's monopoly, or who had been unfairly (as they thought) excluded. It was the focus of the Aesthetic Movement, and thus a favourite subject for caricature in *Punch*. "Private View Grosvenor Gallery, met shoals of people, v.amusing" wrote Marion, but she never mentioned the pictures on the walls at these affairs, nor made any critical appraisal of work done by her friends. Her preference was for Old Masters: "Lovely pictures" was her comment after seeing a collection of Rembrandts and Titians.

Many of Marion's close friends were not connected with the art world at all. Scattered through the diary are the names of her unmarried friends and cousins, who came to tea, helped to entertain the children, or sat for a morning sewing and gossiping. Judy, Alice, Geraldine, Nelly, Tilda, and so on, appear and disappear over the years. Other friendships which lasted a long time were with those matrons who had little girls the same age as Maud—Mrs Coward, Mrs Orchardson, Mrs Paxton, and Mrs Burnand. Then there was a quite different set of acquaintances, probably made through her father's interests in stockbroking and banking. Of these the most important were the Messels, and through them it is likely that she and Linley met several rich couples of European origin—the Joachims, Seligmans, Ionides, and Joshuas. These people all liked to entertain on a lavish scale and the Sambournes thoroughly enjoyed going to their parties, but return invitations to dine at Stafford Terrace were never proffered, nor did their names appear on Marion's calling list. It is impossible to study the Sambournes' circle of friends, or the families into which Marion's brothers and sisters married, without noticing one salient characteristic: they were nearly all much more affluent than she was. We know where most of them lived and there is no doubt that Stafford Terrace was, in comparison, a fairly humble home. Coming as she did from a wealthy background, Marion had no inhibitions about mingling with the rich and famous, but it is to her credit that not once in her diary does she show any envy of those in easier financial circumstances than herself, or more than a normal anxiety about the difficulty of keeping pace with high society. On the other hand *Punch* was increasingly popular and prestigious, and Linley's connection with it gave her a certain position in the world which she obviously relished. From this vantage point she had ample opportunity to practise that most Victorian of pastimes, social climbing.

The Sambournes did not have what we like to call a typical Victorian attitude to religion. Sunday for them was not a special day set apart from the rest of the week, hedged about with restrictions. Although Marion went to church, Linley did not. He would attend a funeral as a mark of respect, or go to admire the architecture of a famous cathedral, but he never went to Sunday service. If he had a lot of work to do, he would sit over it for as long on a Sunday as any other day, but his favourite way of passing the time was to go riding with friends. Entertainment went on as usual: though Marion never approved of playing cards of any kind or gambling on a Sunday, it was considered a good day for holding a dinner party. The women of the family were all regular church-goers, but never at any time in her diary did Marion mention her husband's lack of religious observance: they must have agreed to differ early in their married life. The children were usually taken to morning service by Nurse, or by their grandmother, Mrs S, but seldom went with their mother. Marion did not feel it necessary to go to church every single Sunday—sometimes she was too seedy, or thought it too cold or too wet to go out—but she did seem to be looking for salvation, albeit in a rather half-hearted way. Kensington's period of greatest expansion had taken place during a time when church-going was at a peak: consequently it was rich in places of worship catering for every shade of Christian

The new St Mary Abbots Church, built in 1872 by G.G. Scott.

59

observance. A movement towards more ritual and colour in the Anglican service was gaining momentum in the eighties; this was called "High Church" to distinguish it from "Low Church", which was nearer to the form adopted by the non-conformists (referred to as "Chapel"). Marion sometimes attended her local parish church, St Mary Abbots, but her taste leant towards High Church: she went to St Philip's, Earls Court Road, St George's, Campden Hill, and St Matthias', Warwick Road, and sometimes travelled further afield to St Alban's, Holborn and All Saints, Margaret Street, the most "High" of them all. She even experimented with Roman Catholicism, going to the Pro-Cathedral (Our Lady of Victories) in Kensington High Street. The sermon seems to have been the part of the service that attracted her most, as she nearly always wrote a brief comment in her diary, such as "Good sermon" or "Miserable sermon". Sometimes she was more expansive: "Went to early service, beautiful sermon about our failure here, not to be tempted to despair in consequence but to strive harder for great ends." After enjoying another fine sermon she wrote, "Wish I could hear the like every Sunday."

Apart from the Sunday service, Marion did not attend church except for weddings. Christenings are not mentioned in her diary, and when her father died there was nothing about black dresses or drawn blinds, although she must have worn the customary heavy mourning. She did not go to the theatre, or to a party outside the family circle, until three months after her father's death. The only entertainment she recorded during that time was "Dined at Mrs Stone's quietly", and "Canon Harford dined. Thought he would give me some comfort in religion, v. disappointed." Where she did find comfort was in putting flowers on her father's grave. "To dearest Father's resting place, put roses there" she wrote soon after the funeral, and she always made a point of visiting the churchyard whenever she was staying at Westwood: "March 13th 1885. First anniversary of our dearest Father's gain and our loss, took flowers."

Marion loved music. In the days before gramophone or wireless it was very difficult to hear good music, which was one reason why so many people made their own. The unpleasant noise made by the numerous street musicians was often commented upon, and Linley had a particular vendetta against them. For Marion one of the pleasures of going to a seaside resort was hearing the town band playing in the park or on the parade, and she greatly enjoyed the musical diversions so often provided at parties. "At home, 10 o'clock with music" was a popular form of invitation, and hostesses vied with one another to provide the best entertainment. "Delightful dinner at Mrs Powers, delicious food. Magic lantern & music" she wrote, and "Mrs Luke Ionides at home—picturesque Spaniards singing & dancing." Sometimes the music was the best part of the evening, "To Mrs Parish' at home, v.slow there. Capital music but heavy company." Wealthy people invited famous stars to sing or play, and Arthur Burnand (Frank Burnand's brother) was well known for his

An itinerant street musician Linley had a particular dislike of these mendicants, but here he has used one as a model. Stafford Terrace forms the background.

patronage of foreign musicians: Clara Schumann used to stay at his house whenever she came to London for a recital. The painting entitled *Hush* by James Tissot shows a lady violinist about to perform in a crowded room full of chattering guests, and the Sambournes must often have been present at just such a party. Once when Marion was away in the country Linley wrote to her: "You lost a treat last night. 24 to dinner, Piatti and Joachim, Trebella, Santly, Marie Rossi etc etc." Though she wrote "Lovely music" after these evenings, Marion never gave any details; the performer rather than the composer seemed to be the main attraction. "Joseph Hofmann played most exquisitely", or "Heard Henschel play" is as much comment as she allows.

On a more modest level, it was natural for family and friends to gather round the piano after dinner to sing duets or part-songs. Not many middle-class Victorians performed on any instrument other than the piano, but to play this a little was expected of every well brought up young lady. A gentleman with an attractive tenor voice was as much in demand as a pretty soprano, and many courtships were forwarded by a sentimental ballad. It was customary for guests to take sheet-music to a party, concealing it in the hall until pressed by the hostess to contribute to the evening's entertainment. Marion often wrote "Sang & played all evening", obviously thoroughly enjoying it. Sadly for her, Linley does not seem to have been musical

and avoided going to concerts if possible. He did not join in at family gatherings when the Herapaths all made music together, and sometimes he embarrassed her by going to sleep during a performance: "Mr Blunt sang, Lin snored aloud". Spencer, in particular, liked to sing with his sister and would call at Stafford Terrace with new music for her to try, "Spencer came to dinner, jolly evening, sang & played." It was Spencer who took her to the opera, and to the latest musicals. "Saw *Dorothy*" wrote Marion, and later "Spencer brought music of *Dorothy*, tried it."

Several of her friends shared Marion's fondness for music and she would go with them to the Albert Hall (which had been opened in 1871), leaving Linley to follow more congenial pursuits. "To Albert Hall, heard Albeniz & new tenor splendid voice", she wrote, or "To Albert Hall, heard Patti, hall beautifully lighted electric light." There is quite a lot of printed music left at Stafford Terrace. Among the bound volumes of easy classics is one stamped "Marion Herapath" in gold, which has her pencilled fingerings above the notes. There are also loose sheets of works by contemporary composers, Grieg, Paderewski, Heller and Wagner. Several of these are marked "Marion Sambourne" with dates ranging from 1886 to 1894. Marion very seldom made any reference to filling the idle hours by playing the piano, nor is there any difficult music here, so she was probably not a really serious musician. In the 1877 Inventory a "pianette" was listed in the dining-room and some time later the Broadwood grand piano in the drawing-room was purchased. Clara Schumann always used a Broadwood for her English concert tours and as a result every Victorian lady of musical pretensions wished to own one.

There is nothing in the diaries of the 1880s about music lessons for the children. Marion and Miss Penn between them must have instilled the rudiments, though it was probably clear from an early age that Maud had inherited Linley's ear, as well as his facility with a pencil. There is one piece of music in the cupboard at Stafford Terrace marked "Maudie", where the notes have been violently scribbled over by a childish hand, perhaps signifying Maud's revolt. Roy must have shown more interest in the piano, as Marion wrote "To see Mother, Roy played her all his little tunes", and in later life Roy amassed a fine collection of song sheets from all the popular musicals and burlesques.

The 1877 Inventory lists the books at Stafford Terrace. Quite a number of these were antique leather-bound volumes (mostly poetry) collected by Linley, which are now in the glass-fronted bookcase in the morning-room. There were also "240 volumes on the shelves", unfortunately unspecified. Apart from the bound volumes of *Punch* and the books illustrated by Linley or written and autographed by his friends, there is a surprisingly small collection of contemporary literature left in the house, but both Marion and Linley enjoyed reading. Considering how much time and energy Linley put into work, sport, and entertainment, it is quite surprising that he was able to read widely as well. He listed each book in his diary as he read it, and reveals himself as a man of intelligent and catholic taste. Marion's choice was more frivolous; she especially liked romantic novels by lady writers. "Finished reading *The Shadow of Ashlydyat*, Mrs Wood, most exciting" she wrote, and she was very disappointed when she missed a party at which Linley was introduced to that

celebrated author. There are other entries, "Afternoon read favourite novel", "Stayed in bed read *Belinda*", and "Finished *Under Which Lord* by Mrs Linton, don't care for it." Linley did not like his wife to air her views on modern novels too trenchantly: "Lin gave me lecture on self-opinion, must try to correct this" wrote Marion humbly after a dinner party at which lady writers had been discussed. Most books were borrowed from the circulating library: "Remember to borrow from Mudie's" was one entry in her diary, and "*The Mill on the Floss* from Wades, 2/6d deposit, 3d a week." was another; in comparison with the prices of other commodities, this seems rather expensive.

Marion was fortunate in being able to read easily in French. Not only were writers on the Continent very advanced in their thinking, but the "Naturalist" school produced many powerful novels with sexual passion as their major theme; these contrasted sharply with the moralising fiction so popular in England at the time. Even though she wrote, "Read horrid book, Zola", her reading list contained most of his books, as well as those by other French and Russian writers of the same school. In later life her tastes matured and she read fewer sentimental novels, making instead long lists of biographical and historical works in the front pages of her diaries. One curious omission is any mention of books for the children, nor are there any left in the house. This is a pity, as surely the works of Walter Crane and Kate Greenaway would have been just the thing for the Sambourne nursery.

The theatre played a very important part in London social life. Marion and Linley had none of the puritanical views held by some Victorians; they and their friends went to the latest entertainment as a matter of course. Plays, musicals, pantomimes, concerts, circus and conjurors were regularly and enthusiastically attended. The Sambournes knew most of the famous actors and actresses of the day, and though they were not the sort of friends one could ask to dinner, they were much admired. Marion and Linley were out of town for so much of the year that they had to make up for the theatrical deprivation by going several times a week when they were in London. As a certain number of complimentary tickets were issued to the *Punch* staff by theatre managers, going to every play in town was not such an extravagance as it might seem. Marion always noted whom they saw at the theatre, and who came round to their box in the interval to have a chat. The theatre provided an opportunity to watch the interesting and famous— "Prince & Princess of Wales directly opposite our box"—and was the place to wear one's best clothes and jewels. Opera glasses were more for looking at the audience than at the players, and to sit in a box meant that one was in full view of everyone else. In fact Marion often thought it more important to write "Had stage box" than to give the name of the play or the actors, and her comments on the actual performance were always brief: "Sad piece", "Capital performance", or "Play bad", while "Enjoyed it exceedingly" was her highest praise.

Punch had been founded by men with strong theatrical interests, and always carried reviews and articles about the London stage. Burnand had first made his name as a writer of burlesques. His most successful pieces had been *Box and Cox* (in collaboration with Arthur Sullivan), and *Black-Eyed Susan*, both of which had very

PUNCH'S FANCY PORTRAITS.—No. 5.

Linley's drawing in Punch *of Arthur Sullivan. Some of his best work was done for this series of "Fancy Portraits".*

long runs in the 1860s. He continued writing for the stage for many years, and in 1881 produced *The Colonel* which was the first play to have sets and costumes in the Aesthetic style. Although much praised by the public and admired by Queen Victoria, its success was overshadowed a few months later by Gilbert and Sullivan's *Patience* which had a similar theme. Burnand was so annoyed by what he considered a direct plagiarism that he refused to allow a review of this to be printed in his paper.

The Savoy Theatre was purpose-built to stage the Gilbert and Sullivan operettas, so that whenever Marion wrote "To Savoy", it was Gilbert and Sullivan that she saw. The Sambournes went to every production mounted there, but Marion never said what she thought of a performance. *The Mikado* especially was very popular and had a long run: "April 4th 1885. Went to Savoy, v.full, had to sit on dress circle steps" was one entry—a position very different from the usual box. One cannot help feeling that the topsy-turvy wit of the operettas would have had more appeal for Linley than for his wife, who was more likely to comment favourably on serious plays, and especially admired those which moved her to tears.

CHAPTER FIVE
SERVANTS:
FOOD & DINNERS:
HORSES & GROOMS

 CENSUS HAS BEEN TAKEN in Britain every decade since 1801 and this has proved an invaluable document for the social historian. On a certain night of the year every man, woman and child in each household in the country must have their name entered on a form, with details of their age, occupation, and place of birth. In 1871 Spencer Herapath, stockbroker, aged forty-nine, and his wife, Mary Ann, aged forty-eight, were at their residence in Upper Phillimore Gardens. The census shows that they employed a housekeeper, cook, housemaid, nursemaid and under-nursemaid to look after themselves and their eight children, who then ranged in age from twenty-three years old (Spencer John) to six years old (Mervyn). Ten years later, in 1881, when the three eldest children were married and the others were nearly grown up, the composition of the servants had changed to a cook, two parlourmaids, a housemaid and a lady's maid. In Stafford Terrace where the houses were smaller (and not finished by 1871) the 1881 census gives three servants as the usual number to be employed. At No 18, Linley Sambourne, artist, had a wife, two children, a cook, a housemaid and a nursemaid. From Marion's diaries it is clear that they usually kept a fourth servant (either a parlourmaid or a second housemaid) who must have been away on the night the census was taken.

A large part of Marion's diary is taken up with the trials and frustrations of being an employer. The running and controlling of a household, even one the size of 18 Stafford Terrace, was no easy task, as good servants were very difficult to find and seldom stayed for long. Marion was always worrying about temperamental cooks who had to be replaced at short notice, or slatternly housemaids who did not fulfil the rigorous daily schedule of cleaning and polishing. Housemaids were usually young country girls who needed a great deal of training and discipline before they could give their mistress much satisfaction. The census shows their place of birth: a high proportion of them came from Norfolk, one of the counties hardest hit by the agricultural depression and where there was no work for women. They were always called by their christian names: Emma, Elizabeth, Jane, Sarah, Mary and Kate—

good eighteenth-century names then so out of fashion that they were only used by the lower classes—and they came and went with bewildering rapidity. 1883 was a particularly bad year for Marion: a string of housemaids did not last the month before being sent packing. She was constantly having to cope with the tedious business of finding replacements, a task which in a more affluent home would have fallen on the housekeeper.

Personal recommendation was the most satisfactory way of engaging a new servant, but Marion was not often able to use this method. The middle classes had expanded rapidly and were employing more servants than ever before. Demand was beginning to outstrip supply, and all her friends were having the same difficulties. Country girls who came to town had little choice of employment; in the early part of the century most of them went into service, prostitution or starvation being almost the only alternatives. By the 1880s jobs had become available in shops and factories, and, as these gave the girls more personal freedom than service, they became increasingly popular, thus draining away the housewife's supply of labour. Marion usually went to an agency for her servants, or advertised in the daily paper. "Put advertisement in paper again for housemaid—saw four only" she wrote. The candidate then had to produce a reference or "character", which would not only describe the girl as clean, honest and so on, but by implication whether she was likely ever to have engaged in prostitution. Much time was spent in interviews: "Saw two maids, one 7 years one 5 years character." These "characters" then had to be checked, and Marion either wrote to the previous employer or called to see her if she lived nearby.

The parlourmaid was superior to the housemaid and her status was emphasised by the use of her surname. From 1881 to 1883 Marion's parlourmaid was called Reed, in 1884 she was called Groves, and from 1885 to 1889 she was called Laurence. Her main function was to wait at table, but she also helped her mistress with other jobs and seems to have acted more like a companion than a servant. She was mentioned almost daily in Marion's diary: "Put away china with Reed", "Tidied back-yard with Laurence", "Laurence and self packed all day", and so on. She was also expected to help Nurse with the children: "Laurence took chicks out." When, after several years service, she left to get married Marion was unable to find a satisfactory substitute and had to make do with a second housemaid instead. Even that was difficult: "Wish I could get a good second girl, Edie no use whatever", was a typical complaint.

The search for a new cook followed the same procedure as for a maid and it was even harder to find someone satisfactory. In January 1882 Marion wrote, "Sent advertisement to Daily Telegraph for cook", and two days later, "Saw 10 cooks, only two at all likely." After a fortnight it was "Don't think much of Mrs T as cook", and "Spoke to Mrs T", followed inevitably by "Mrs T gave notice." Every few months the pattern was repeated: "First order with new cook, don't like her" was the prelude to "New cook going, impertinent and lazy." Occasionally there was success, only to be followed by regret: in 1884 Marion wrote "My nice cook Fanny leaves." Fanny (who came from Ramsgate) was said to be "Not strong enough for

London." Once again the hunt for a good cook began, and this took up a lot of time in the first few months of 1885: "Saw hideous old cook", "Saw 6 cooks, 5 very old things", "Saw 2 cooks, old and ugly", "Character of cook bad, can't take her", until one feels thankful that the cook problem is now almost extinct.

Cooks were generally given the courtesy title of "Mrs", but there was never any provision made for a married couple. Marion once had a cook called King, and wrote "King goes home at night", as if this was quite unusual. Her most successful cook was one called Emma, who stayed for four years, went away for a time (presumably to raise a family) and then returned on a temporary basis when the Sambournes had a spate of entertaining. She had a very troublesome husband who several times got drunk and came round to the house to create a disturbance. "Awful row with Emma's husband, kicked door, smashed window." Emma herself was fairly rough, "Emma in fearful temper about milk, wish she would not take everything personally", but she had a good relationship with her mistress and was in and out of the Sambournes' employ for over twenty-five years. Marion was always pleased to have Emma back after a period of absence, and was happy to leave her in charge of the household when they were away.

In the gaps between cooks the housemaid and parlourmaid were expected to produce the meals. "Girls very good doing their best during inconvenience of having no cook" wrote Marion, but this state of affairs was never tolerated for long. The cook only "came up for orders", her position being definitely below stairs. She and the housemaid would have slept in the back kitchen and the parlourmaid upstairs in the little room next the nursery, or perhaps both maids were expected to share the bed there. "*Parlage avec Laurence a cause du lit*—tiresome we have not more room", was not the only time that there was trouble with the servants over the sleeping arrangements. The maids were never expected to have husbands, and "followers" were frowned upon: once when Marion discovered that one of the girls was pregnant she dismissed her at once. However marriage was recognised as the right and proper goal for every girl; all the maids who were employed for some length of time and gave satisfaction only left because they were getting married.

Most servants went home for two weeks' holiday a year, and an afternoon and evening out was allowed once a week. Marion did not always write down when or how much she paid her employees, but there are a few entries in the diary, "Gave Kate her three month wages, £5", or "Paid Sarah her wages £1.10s in gold." Although it seems by modern standards that the servants were overworked and underpaid, it must be remembered that they were warm, dry, and well fed, in contrast to the family which they had left behind in rural poverty. Those who found themselves in a well ordered house with a kind mistress were lucky indeed, and many girls sent the whole of their wage packet home to help feed and clothe their little brothers and sisters.

Marion sometimes wrote crossly about the servants, "Vexed drawing-room not properly cleaned", "Found top of house very dirty, spoke to Minnie and Nurse", or "Cook does not see dirty plates", but she expected the staff to carry out their various tasks without much prompting. The list of housemaid's duties which survives, and

looks so onerous, was probably an ideal schedule that was hardly ever carried out in its entirety. There was still plenty of opportunity for the girls to giggle and gossip in the kitchen, as Marion often deplored this and wished that they might be quieter and better behaved. She very seldom went down into the kitchen quarters, but she quite enjoyed dusting the drawing-room if things looked too dirty, and always washed the delicate ornaments in the cabinets herself. In later years Maud (who as a child was often scolded for being untidy) would tease her mother about her "eagle eye for dust", and her "beautifully polished little corners".

Some servants were engaged on a temporary basis: Marion mentioned a char-woman, and a man to do the garden (there was not much growing there except the virginia creeper which had to be cut back every year) as well as extra helpers whenever they had a dinner party. All the laundry went out, and there was the usual trouble finding a good laundress. "Paid three weeks washing, very heavy, £3.6.11" she wrote, and "Saw new washerwoman for Lin's shirts", but she was quite able to cope when an emergency arose: "No shirt for Lin! Borrowed one from Mr A, washed Lin's nightsuit in my bath." It seems strange that in the Stafford Terrace Inventory there is no equipment at all for home washing: no copper, mangle, irons, ironing table, clothes horse or airer. One would have expected Nurse to wash the baby's clothes, even if nothing else was done at home. Some of the omissions can be put down to the fact that a great number of household necessities were transported to holiday lodgings each year, and it is quite possible that the house was let in December 1877 when the Inventory was taken.

Household shopping took up quite a lot of Marion's time, and most of this was done locally. During her childhood the village of Kensington had grown and prospered mightily. Kensington Palace, built by King William III at the end of the seventeenth century as a country retreat far from the unhealthy smoke of London town, was the most important of the great houses in the vicinity, though Holland House was a close rival. The main road to Bath and Bristol passed the gates of both and by the middle of the nineteenth century the section between the two had developed into a thriving High Street. At the junction with Church Street the narrowness of the roads and the crowds of busy shoppers made Kensington notorious for traffic jams, so that a scheme of street widening and rebuilding was put in hand in 1868. The new shops, coupled with the opening that year of a station for the Metropolitan Railway, established Kensington as the latest fashionable suburb. The eighteenth-century houses further west along the main road were slower to change; those on the north side were four storey dwellings, known as Phillimore Terrace. The Sambournes' rear windows looked directly on to the backs of these houses, which were not pulled down and replaced by the present big blocks of shops and flats until 1931.

Kensington High Street in 1868. This was the Kensington Marion knew as a child: by the time she was married the road had been widened and a new range of shop property built. Marion did most of her household shopping in Kensington.

Marion's daily entry often began "To stores morning." By this she meant a visit to John Barker's and the other shops in the rebuilt part of the High Street. "Walked to Kensington, bought brushes & dusters" she wrote, and sometimes she treated herself to a few fresh flowers at the same time, "Bought pot of tulips & two bunches Lent-lilies." Kitchen necessities were ordered by Cook on account and Marion only had to "pay books" every so often, but she liked to be responsible for any extras such as the luxuries needed for dinner parties: "Went to stores, bought crayfish, chicken, cherries, ordered ice." She would not have carried these purchases home herself, but had them delivered. Except for special occasions, she was very careful with the housekeeping money, and constantly worried about over-spending. "Books very heavy" she wrote quite often, or "Books fearfully heavy, so many dinners & company this week and last." It was a relief when she was able to write, "Paid books morning, very low thank goodness." She was always trying to find ways of economising, and was quick to notice any over-charging. Sometimes she got really indignant, "Paid bill at Millers only owing since 23rd of last month & they charged 1/- extra on small account of 3/6d never felt more angry—meanness of supposed swell west-end shops—pity they do not follow example set by Barkers."

69

Next to the employing of servants, Marion found ordering meals the most difficult of her household tasks. To help her she had a useful cookery book, *Family Fare or the Young Housewife's Daily Assistant*, written by a lady who used the awkward pseudonym "Cre-fydd". It was first published in 1864; Marion's copy was from the seventh edition which came out in 1874, the year she was married. It is similar in layout to the slightly earlier and better known book by Mrs Beeton, and is full of the sort of advice that a newly-wedded housewife, intent on making the best show with the least money, would need. A list of meals for each day of the year is included, and twelve dinner party menus, with prices. For example a dinner for eight, of six or seven courses, would cost from £1.19.0 to £2.11.6. A normal family dinner was four courses, while the kitchen staff were expected to subsist on one course (occasionally two) though presumably they ate up the left-overs as well. After the recipes there are detailed instructions for the care and cleaning of the house, and hints for the mistress on how to command servants. There is also a list of things to be kept in the store cupboard and another for the medicine cupboard. The book has been well used, with several favourite recipes marked in pencil. The instructions for the servants are particularly fascinating, and give a very comprehensive picture of life below stairs as it must have been during Marion's rule.

As well as this volume Marion had the little notebook which was filled with recipes (always called "receipts") and dinner party menus, both her own and other peoples'. "Sophy's rice cake", "Mrs Evans' chocolate pudding", "Mrs Coward's caramel pudding", "Midge's potted cheese", "Mrs Stone's Russian salad", "Mrs Boëhm's cheese straws", all sound delicious, and there were several utilitarian entries too: "Beef tea for infants", "Barley pudding for baby", and "Receipt for furniture polish". The first recorded dinner party is at the Burnands': "Monday 23rd April 1877. Soup with chopped spinach, soles au gratin, pigeons stewed with mushrooms. Leg of lamb, potatoes, salad. Ducks, potatoes, asparagus, iced pudding fruit etc." Mrs Stone gave very good dinners, and there are more of her menus in the notebook than anyone else's, as well as several of her recipes. "Mrs Marcus Stone dinner of 8, Friday July 20th 1877. Clear spring soup. Sole au gratin. Cutlets & whole beans. Ducks, watercress, potatoes, green peas. Cold raspberry tart & cream. Souffle or omelet. Anchovy & chopped onion. Very good." Again "Thursday January 24th 1878. Charming dinner Mrs Stone's. Spring soup. Filleted soles, brown gravy. Filet de boeuf, thimble potatoes. Goose pieces in tomato sauce garlic & parsley. Saddle of mutton, artichokes. Rice meringue, mince pies." Fanny Fildes also gave good dinner parties, though not so many as Laura Stone: "Mrs Fildes dinner 19th December 1879. Crécy soup. Fillet soles white sauce. Sweetbreads stewed. Fillets of beef in brown gravy. Lax, watercress. Mince pies." Several other entertainments are listed: Mrs Twiss ("most excellently served"), Mrs Arthur Peto, Mrs Hensman, Mr Colin Hunter, Mrs Boughton ("very good"), and so on.

Naturally Marion had to give equally good dinners in return, and her menus are

just as lavish: "4th March 1879. 8 to dinner. Artichoke soup. Fillets of salmon. Leg of lamb, salad, new potatoes, stewed celery. Wild duck, watercress. Aldershot pud, plum pud. Soft roes of herring, biscuits etc.", or "Dinner of 8, 18th June 1880. Kippered cod's roe, capers, bread and butter. Julienne soup. Cold trout, sauce piquante. Pigeons with asparagus. Forequarter of lamb, mint sauce, tomato salad, potatoes. Beans aux francais. Ducklings, green peas. Coffee savoy, plum tart, cream. Anchovies, parmesan cheese, etc." Nowadays, lectured as we are on the dangers of over-eating and made conscious of starving millions all over the world, this catalogue of over-indulgence seems rather shocking. The Victorians had no such inhibitions. Like other civilisations before them who had revelled in wealth and ostentation, they felt that to keep a good table—and to be seen to be doing so—was the hallmark of success.

As the Sambournes were out of London for so much of the year their entertaining was done in short bursts. In June 1880 they were very busy: "June 15th, Pelegrinis, Hensmans, Eykyns, Freres. . . . June 18th, Stones, Winslows, Bradburys. . . . June 20th, Burnands and Stones. . . . June 22nd, Fildes, Caldecotts, Boëhms. . . . June 26th, Edgar, Spencer, Mr and Mrs G.Agnew." After that no more dinner parties were held until March the following year. "March 18th, Mr Frith, Mr Holland, A.Blunt, C.Keene, Dr and Mrs Morell Mackenzie", and then "June 4th Mr C.Hunter and Mr T.Ellis". By this time most of their close friends had been entertained, and Marion began to go through the list again.

The grander the dinner, the greater the number of courses provided, though Marion never went as far as some of her richest friends. "Fourteen courses!!!" was her note after a dinner with the wealthy Messels. Meals were accompanied by many different wines, champagne being the most popular drink. Providing the wine was Linley's department, Marion never mentioned it. Nor did she say how much instruction or help she gave the cook, apart from doing the more exotic shopping. Such meals meant an enormous amount of extra work in the kitchen, as well as a high degree of skill. No wonder cooks were temperamental, and a good one a real treasure. Apart from the cook's difficulties, the parlourmaid had to be well trained to serve a dinner of so many courses and the washing up afterwards would have been a formidable task.

It is quite a relief after the elaborate dinners in the first note-book to turn to the more mundane family fare which Marion began to write down when she started her diary in 1881. There is a slight problem here deciding where breakfast ends and lunch begins, as the lists all run together: "Jan 9th 1882. Bacon corned beef cold leg mutton milk pud castle ditto scalloped fish curried fowl genoese pastry cods roe", or "January 28th. Sprats hard boiled eggs watercress roast beef 2 milk puds fish minced mutton fillet of beef & beetroot three cornered tarts scotch herring", and "February 9th. Bacon and boiled egg, steak pud, milk pud, fresh herrings small leg mutton, artichokes potatoes jelly cods roe." Fresh fish could be bought all the year round and was very popular; a joint of beef appeared about once a week, but it was mutton (roast, boiled, hashed or curried) which was put on the table almost every day, sometimes twice a day. Milk puddings or numerous versions of steamed pudding

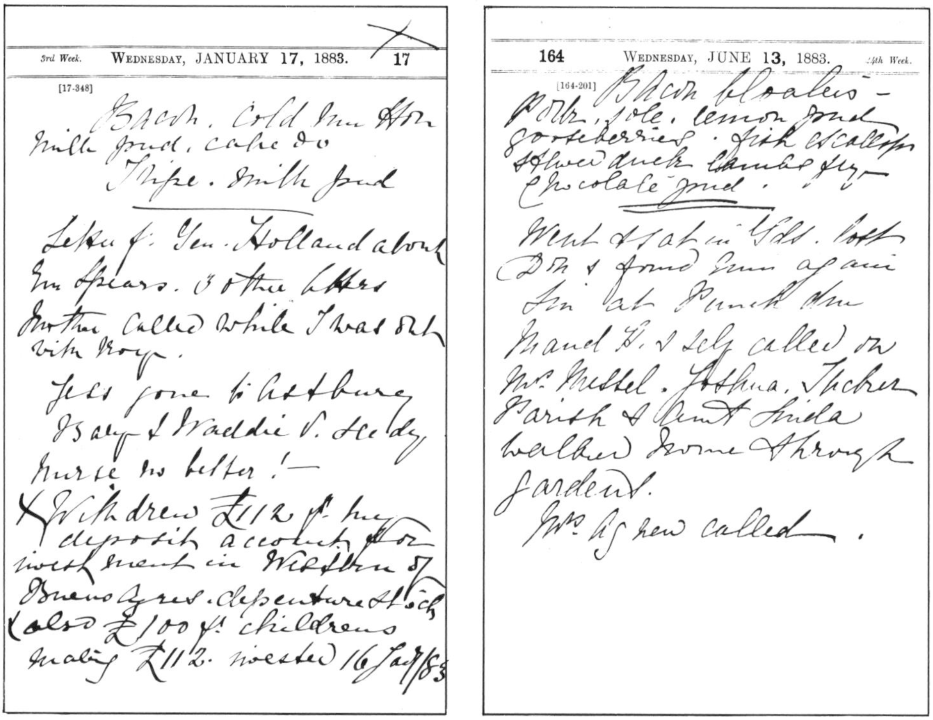
3rd Week. WEDNESDAY, JANUARY 17, 1883. 17
[17-348]
164 WEDNESDAY, JUNE 13, 1883. 24th Week.
[164-201]

Two pages from Marion's diary for 1883. In later years she wrote much more on each page.

were served at all family meals; fresh fruit and ices were dinner party fare only, as was roast lamb. (Nowadays everyone eats lamb, and mutton is a forgotten flavour.) Bacon for breakfast was an unvarying rule, and a savoury of some sort was always served at the end of the evening meal. Bananas, pineapples, oranges, grapes and peaches were only available at certain times of the year and were very expensive. "Never seen so much fruit on any table" Marion remarked after one grand dinner.

Summer was the best time of year for entertaining, when salmon, lamb, strawberries, eggs, cream, and other delicious things were all in season. Catering was harder during the winter months when there was little variety available. In the country, where shops were few, getting in enough provisions to feed a household could still be a problem, especially for the poor. The town dweller was better off, with ample choice from shops not only well stocked with staple foods, but offering hot-house delicacies and exotic imported fare for those who could pay the price. Methods of preserving eggs and salting meat, or making jam from surplus fruit appear in every Victorian cookery book, but the welfare of a middle-class family no longer depended on the housewife's managerial skill in making precious food last through the winter. Most shopping, storing and preserving could safely be left to the servants, and the mistress of the house had little more to do than give cook the orders for the meals each day.

Apart from the formal dinners at Stafford Terrace, there were many evenings when friends or relations dropped in and were pressed to stay for a meal, so the provision of any number of extra servings at short notice must have been quite a problem for the cook. Sometimes the staff were kept up very late: on Fridays, when Linley was hard pressed to finish the cartoon, he often did not dine until ten or eleven at night. Keeping food hot would have been difficult, and keeping it fresh for another day even harder; although the Sambournes owned a "refrigerator" (mentioned in the Inventory), this would only have been a patent form of icebox. Marion often complained of bad food: "Bad fowl", or "Bad mutton at lunch", or even "Very late dinner, duck bad, had to send out for lobster & steak." As there was only a coal-fired range in the kitchen, the expression "slaving over a hot stove" really had some meaning, and cooks were notoriously short-tempered. They were thirsty too, and expected plenty of liquid refreshment. Marion only once found this a problem. The unsatisfactory Mrs T not only drank heavily herself, but must have pressed it on her friends as well. "Spoke to Mrs T about beer, 29 gallons went in a fortnight!" Although a compromise was reached, "Arranged with Mrs T to have £25 a year and *no beer*", it comes as no surprise to read "Mrs T gave notice", only two days later.

Besides their four indoor servants, the Sambournes also employed a groom to look after Linley's horse and to do heavy jobs about the house. He (with his wife and children) lived above the stables in Phillimore Place, just behind Stafford Terrace. A map of eighteenth-century London shows a maze of mews and stable yards behind every elegant street façade, but the pattern was very different in the third quarter of the nineteenth century and the new Phillimore Estate had very little provision for horses. Londoners had come to rely on public transport: there were plenty of cabs for hire as well as horse-drawn omnibuses and the Metropolitan Railway. The well-to-do felt that the noise and unpleasant smell of stables and the inevitable rough characters associated with them should not be located near their clean and comfortable new houses; those who really needed to ride could hire from nearby livery stables, rather than go to the expense of keeping their own horses and grooms. Although Mr and Mrs Herapath kept a carriage, they would have had to send out some distance for it, as there were no stables close to Upper Phillimore Gardens.

The Sambournes themselves did not begin married life with a carriage. Marion had to make all her social calls on foot (which accounts for so many of her friends being Kensington dwellers). Once or twice she wrote, "Mother sent carriage for me", as if recording a special favour. Only after Mrs Herapath retired to Westwood, did Marion and Linley feel it necessary to have their own carriage, and it is unlikely that they would have gone to this expense if they had not already been renting stables and employing a groom. Owning a carriage was a definite step up in the social scale and Marion made a point of using it when she went to her grand

dressmaker, but the fact that she usually took a cab for her shopping expeditions shows that this was an easier method of getting about than ordering the horse to be harnessed and the carriage brought round from the stable. Linley also used cabs rather than the carriage: he would walk to the *Punch* office, and then take a cab back, and the Sambournes always came home in one after a party or the theatre. The hansom cab, with the driver sitting high up at the back, was an excellent conveyance, smart and quick, but if more than two people travelled together it was necessary to take a slower and rather old-fashioned "four wheeler".

A working horse in Victorian England had a hard life. *Black Beauty*, the first novel to have a horse as its main character, had been published in 1877. Marion may well have read this, and she often reacted angrily when she saw horses suffering ill-treatment or neglect. Contemporary photographs show the main roads crammed with unwieldy vehicles, much less orderly—and with their iron-shod wheels far noisier—than traffic today. Accidents were common; once Marion had a narrow escape in Kensington High Street when a horse bolted across her path. It was not unusual for horses to die in harness: "Mrs Messel called at mother's, their horse fell dead", was one diary entry, and another, "Our cab horse fell at Knightsbridge." Cab drivers were sometimes surly and rude, "Took cab, uncivil man" or "Drunk

Linley (right) with John Tenniel, his senior colleague at Punch. Both were keen horsemen and often spent the whole day riding together.

cabman", and Marion complained constantly about the way her own coachman handled the horses. Bad driving made her nervous and irritable, and if the weather conditions were poor she fretted even more — "Roads *dreadfully* slippery" — and it is easy to imagine the horses, so often overloaded and underfed, slipping and straining on the cobbles.

In 1882 the Sambournes owned only one horse, appropriately called Punch, which Linley rode daily. When they bought a carriage a second horse was necessary, so Linley purchased a smart young one for riding called Pippin, leaving Punch to pull the carriage. Pippin was a disaster from the first, always lame or ill, and his treatment cost a lot of money. After a year of worry and exasperation the struggle was abandoned, and a good reliable replacement was procured. This was Folkestone, a faithful friend for several years. In 1886 old Punch was sold to Marion's brother, Conrad, and another horse was bought. This one proved to be the greatest success of all Linley's mounts. Never called by her name, Dolly, but always "the mare", she was put into honourable retirement in 1901 and died the same month and year as her master, August 1910. One of her hooves, mounted in brass, is in the drawing-room at Stafford Terrace. Although good for riding, the mare was not much use for driving: "Very slow in harness, whip going all the time", so it was usually Folkestone who pulled the carriage. It was a perennial problem to find an animal that could be used for both riding and driving — those rich enough to possess a string of horses would never attempt to combine the two.

The horses were nearly all bought and sold at Tattersall's famous auction rooms in Knightsbridge. The Sambournes sometimes went there with Spencer or one of the Hamiltons on a buying spree. Linley got on well with his brothers-in-law, and talking horses was a great bond. Marion took an interest in the horses too: "Con & Lin try new horse in harness, goes very well, handsome", and sometimes gave her opinion on their treatment — advice which Linley and the groom usually ignored, much to her annoyance. A good horse was an important and very expensive part of a gentleman's life, and it seems probable that in this, as in some other ways, the Sambournes lived rather above their station. In the country the equivalent of a cab was always called a "fly", while the Herapaths had their own "cart" in which the coachman would do errands and fetch guests from the station, as well as a carriage for going to church and making formal visits. Marion often drove the cart herself along the country lanes and the children soon learnt to do so too. Even here there were traffic problems. "Accident with cart — brewers' van rushed out at us" wrote Marion, and another day she saw a little boy run over in Margate.

The first groom mentioned in the diaries was called Cave. He was succeeded by Waters, and then for a short time by Crane. In 1887 Jolly came and stayed with the Sambournes until 1891, when he was replaced by Otley. Marion was very critical of the grooms and their careless slipshod ways. It was Linley's job to correct them, but he took little notice of his wife's complaints. "Waters making near shaves again, wish Lin would tell him", she wrote crossly, "Waters drove abominably", "Waters utterly ignores my orders", and "Very angry with Waters, doubt his ever driving well — punishes his horse for his own stupidity." In spite of all she said to Linley,

Waters was not dismissed for some time. At last it was "Saw coachmen, awfully difficult to decide among so many" and it is clear that choosing a new groom was just as troublesome as finding a new cook. At first Marion thought well of the replacement, "Crane drove, much better than Waters", but her satisfaction did not last long: "Crane drove *most* carelessly." The next groom was just as bad, "Jolly drove v.recklessly, wonder if he drinks", "Mare nearly fell, Jolly drives too quickly, told him so." When Jolly finally left Linley's service Marion had one small moment of triumph: "Mr Soames, Jolly's present master, coming to see Lin—does not like Jolly's driving, frightened wife & daughter v.much."

The Sambournes always had a dog, sometimes two, and dogs often featured in the family photographs. They were much loved but their lives were short, as discipline was poor and death by one accident or another occurred every two or three years. In 1882 the current dog was called Don. Marion took him for walks: "Went for short walk, lost Don", and "Went into gardens, took Don, lost him twice." Another time, "Don's leg bad, had to take a cab to come home." In 1885 "dear little Don died" and was replaced by Crum, who began life badly: "Roy bitten by Crum, very anxious." Marion had reason to be nervous, as rabies was not extinct and Kensington residents had recently been issued with a warning notice about a mad dog.

By the end of the 1880s the complement of pets at Stafford Terrace had grown considerably. Besides two dogs Marion had a cage-full of birds to which she devoted much time. She cleaned the cage herself, dosed the ailing birds with cod-liver oil and whisky, grieved when they died and rejoiced when they laid eggs. Linley wrote to her in 1899: "Tony, Ella, the Birds, Tortoise Frog and Beetle are all 'at home' and well. All hungry though, what a lot I have to keep!" Roy had a passion for spiders and other creepy-crawlies—Marion, rather surprisingly, did not seem to object, writing "Out hunting for spiders with Roy." Other creatures were less welcome. The presence of so many horses made fleas a common pest; more than once the diary records "Bad night, flea!" and when moving into a rented house for the summer Marion wrote "Spent all day cleaning house—consumed with fleas—caught bug on curtain!!!" When she was staying at Westwood alone with Mrs Herapath in 1886 it was "Mice in drawing room evening, slept with Mother in consequence." A century earlier no housewife would have expressed shock or surprise at the sight of mouse, bug or flea, but standards of cleanliness in a middle-class Victorian home were very high. It is unlikely that black beetles were tolerated in the kitchen at Stafford Terrace.

CHAPTER SIX
MONEY:
RIOTS: WEATHER:
CLOTHES & SHOPPING

NE PROBLEM which Marion did not have to contend with was a rise in the cost of living. Her father, with luck and skill, had made his fortune during the twenty year period of expansion and inflation which had begun in the mid 1840s. The tide turned about 1864 and from then until the end of the century there was a long, slow decline. Although few people in the 1870s and 80s realised it, England was sliding into what would later be known as the Great Depression. On the surface all seemed well. The Empire was at its peak of power and prestige, overseas trade was prospering and manufacturing industries flourished, while the population of the country had doubled in the last fifty years. For a town-dwelling housewife this was all good news. Marion was able to choose from a wide range of cheap imported food, hire labour for low wages, and purchase manufactured luxuries such as had never before been available in such quantity and variety. That the poor were getting poorer, the plight of sweated labour more desperate, and agriculture on the verge of collapse was hardly noticed in comfortable Kensington. The aristocracy and landed gentry were also suffering badly from the difficulties of farming and the decline in land values. The new money was all in trade, commerce, manufacturing and banking, so that it was the industrial barons who were now commissioning vast country houses and filling them with works of art. This last was a problem, as it was no longer possible to buy Italian Old Masters with ease. A spate of forgeries and inferior copies began to focus attention on contemporary artists as suppliers of large scale works: thus oil-painters of the second half of the nineteenth century found themselves riding the crest of a wave. Ease of reproduction meant that art of all kinds became important to a far wider public than in the previous century; to be a painter was now a passport to wealth, gentility and fame. A black and white illustrator like Linley Sambourne was on the periphery of this success story (the hub of which was the Royal Academy) with his social position not clearly defined. As an employee of *Punch* he just escaped the stigma of being in "trade", but at the start of his career he only narrowly came into the class of "gentleman".

In 1884 Marion wrote, "Dear Lin worried with bills, wish he could be less extravagant, so difficult to make him understand *absolute* necessity." One gets the impression that Linley did not really worry very much, and was quite happy to spend what money there was, leaving his wife to sort out any little financial problems. Marion had inherited more of her father's financial acumen than some of her brothers and sisters, although she was better at saving pennies than taking risks. She had a nest-egg invested in shares and her diaries are full of notes about buying and selling, with memos about certificates and allotments and reminders about when money should be paid into her account. From 1885 onwards (the year after her father's death) the end-papers carry detailed lists of her assets and various other financial jottings. At the end of the year this was all totted up: "Received during 1887 from allowance, interest & presents £182.8.10*d*. Spent in 1887 on dress etc £81.1.1*d*. Invested in 1887 including commissions £127.0.0." (The allowance was part of her marriage settlement and was paid every quarter. It came directly from her father when he was alive, "Papa sent my cheque," and was paid from his estate after his death.) For most of her life Marion relied on the South American shares which had made Mr Herapath's fortune: Central Argentine Railways, Venezuela Bonds, Buenos Aires Tramways, Buenos Aires Great Southern Railway, and many others were good safe holdings in the 1880s, but had her father been alive to guide her during the next decade he would surely have advised her to diversify. The Sambournes' bills were usually paid by cheque, though it is not clear whether there was any distinction between what Linley paid for and what Marion's investments supported. But it does seem as if hers was the careful restraining influence and that her husband, if left to his own devices, would have let the money run through his fingers. Linley's prospects of promotion were not good, as those above him in the *Punch* hierarchy showed no signs of wishing to retire early. No pension schemes or medical insurance existed in those days, so it was essential to save money for old age or infirmity. There were other calls on Linley's earnings; he had his mother to support, and annuities ought to be provided for the children. Maud especially would need money if she did not marry; the lot of a genteel spinster with no private income was dreary indeed.

The Sambournes did not move in political circles, though of course Linley's work for *Punch* meant that he was well informed on all the political problems of the day. Marion seems to have had little interest in world affairs, and very few events of history-book importance were recorded in her diary. Naturally enough, it was things like civil disturbance—or anything which might pose a threat to the home—which concerned her most. Although the middle classes were extremely comfortable and self-satisfied they were not totally unconscious of the poverty around them. Concern about the condition of the poor was often voiced in the press: poverty was recognised as the greatest social evil of the age; not only was it the cause of

Kensington Market Court, slum property on the south side of the High Street.

intolerable suffering and premature death, but it threatened the health of the whole nation and undermined the stability of the state. The novels of Charles Dickens, issued in a constant stream from 1836 to his death in 1870, had directed attention to many areas where reform was urgently needed, while Mayhew's survey *London Labour and the London Poor*, published in 1851, was a shocking indictment of the way society neglected its poorest members. By 1865 the philanthropists William Booth and Octavia Hill had begun their pioneering work to relieve suffering, but it was a long struggle before they gained much support from the wealthy. Although *Punch* often campaigned for reforms, its liking for cartoons in which ragged or ignorant characters were the butt of the joke seems callous by the standards of today.

Europe had suffered its "Year of Revolutions" in 1848, and England had only narrowly escaped the general turmoil. There had been a huge public demonstration in London that year which had caused panic among residents and shop-keepers, but the crowd had dispersed peaceably on being promised reforms. These were very slow in coming and twenty years later research into the inequity of the social system led

Marx to publish *Das Kapital*. This was widely considered to be an incitement to anarchy, so that even dwellers in the pleasant new suburb of Kensington feared that they might soon be called upon to defend their homes from mob violence. According to the 1877 Inventory, Linley kept "a case of revolvers and the ammunition" as well as "a rattle and staff" in the bedroom at Stafford Terrace, but he was never obliged to lean out of the window in his nightcap to call the watch—that Hogarthian image belongs to a different age.

Marion and Linley do not appear to have had any sympathy with the Socialist League, organised by William Morris in 1884, or even with the less extreme Fabian Society founded by George Bernard Shaw the same year. Linley had hung a reproduction of Luke Fildes' powerful painting of wretchedness *Applicants for admission to a Casual Ward* in the dining-room at Stafford Terrace, but more because Fildes was a friend than to show his interest in social problems. Marion did not mention the subject in her diary, nor have anything to do with the sort of charity work which was beginning to occupy the time and energy of many upper class ladies. Not until near the end of her life (by which time a great change in public attitudes to poverty had taken place) did she make a sympathetic comment on the number of "poor men, idle", sitting on the benches in Hyde Park.

The first mention in Marion's diary of unrest among the poorer sections of the community was in the early part of 1886. The winter weather had been exceptionally severe, bringing high unemployment and mounting food prices; as always it was the lowest levels of society that suffered most. Political agitators organised meetings, insurrection was in the air, and the situation in the capital grew very tense. "Monster meeting in Trafalgar Square—dreadful damage to property" was Marion's entry on 8 February. Next day a thick fog descended. The Sambournes stayed indoors—"Did not go out on account of fog & afraid of riots"—and for three days Londoners waited with bated breath for an attack to be launched from the East End. But the fog made organised protest impossible and by the time it lifted tempers had cooled. Although sporadic outbursts of violence continued through the spring, "Row in Hyde Park again, more windows smashed", it seemed as if revolution had once again been averted. In the autumn Marion wrote, "Went shopping morning, plenty of roughs about", but there was no more open violence until the following year. On 13 November 1887 (later to be known as Bloody Sunday) it was "Riots, 4000 military out, 200 people wounded, awful row," and a week later, "Special constables called, expect great row in Trafalgar Square tomorrow." For the second time thick fog saved the day: revolutionary fervour was extinguished and civil disturbances were never mentioned in Marion's diary again.

On the international scene Marion was even more reticent and references to important events are few and far between. In February 1881 she wrote, "Sad news from the Cape. General Colbey killed, great loss among our troops." Nearer home she was shocked by the trouble in Ireland: "May 8th, 1882: Heard fearful news of Lord F Cavendish' & Mr Burke's murder." Other events that year were "July 11th: British guns fire on Alexandrian forts", and "September 14th: Good news from Egypt, battle of Tel-el-Kabir." The next two years passed without a hint that

anything was happening in the world outside, but 1885 was more newsworthy: on 5 February Marion wrote, "Fearful catastrophe at Khartoum!!!" followed a week later by "Terrible news from Khartoum" as the details filtered through to England. Ten days later, "General Buller's retreat" marked the end of her interest in the Sudanese war.

In 1886 there were two important pieces of news at home. High society was scandalised by the notorious Crawford divorce case, and Marion read the newspaper reports as avidly as everyone else. "February 12th: Crawford & Dilke case on" and "February 13th: Long account of Sir C. Dilke, co-respondent in Crawford case." Next month she wrote, "Talked over Sir C. Dilke's affairs", and four months later it was still news, "July 21st: Read Dilke case, astounding facts." For the respectable middle-classes sexual deviation was deeply shocking, and the details of the Dilke scandal make startling reading even today. The painful aspects of divorce were well known to the Herapath family, and one wonders whether the public airing of the Dilke affair helped Marion to feel more sympathy for Annie. The other burning issue in 1886 was the question of Home Rule for Ireland. Gladstone, who had been returned to the office of Prime Minister pledged to promote Home Rule, and made an impassioned speech in Parliament on 8 April advocating this cause. Marion wrote "Great day at House of Commons!" and on 9 April "Read Gladstone's speech to Lin." Unfortunately there is nothing in either diary to tell us

Liszt gave a concert on the same day that Gladstone spoke on Home Rule for Ireland. Linley has imagined them performing together in the drawing-room at Stafford Terrace.

THE TWO GRAND OLD MEN, WHO DIVIDED THE HONOURS OF LAST WEEK BETWEEN THEM.

what opinions the Sambournes held on the Irish question, nor anything to indicate whether they were pleased or disappointed when Gladstone's bill was rejected and his party defeated at the polls.

The most interesting happening in 1887 was the Queen's Golden Jubilee, and Marion wrote about this with much more enthusiasm than she ever showed for politics. "June 21st. Great Jubilee Day! Lin Roy & self to Piccadilly, Mr Watkins' chambers, to see Procession from there. Lord Lathom sent Lin a ticket for the Abbey. Magnificent sight, never to be forgotten. Drove at 7 in brougham by Bayswater to Half Moon Street. Terrific but orderly crowd. Most splendid view. Effie & Con came in after, eggs & cocoa, servants all out. With Roy to see lights." Next day the festivities continued, "Crowds everywhere, swarms of children going to park, Queen in park to see children."

The Sambournes had a very British interest in the weather, and both mentioned it almost every day in their diaries. Marion's spirits, always responsive to beauty, were easily cheered by fine weather. "Lovely day" she wrote many many times, and often, "*Most* heavenly day". Even when she was ill or in bed she never failed to notice a fine day. Adverse conditions also were often commented on, and she suffered very much from the cold: "Bitterly cold, had to keep shawl on all evening." Coal fires in every room were not enough to keep even a wealthy family comfortable in sub-zero conditions, and the Sambournes economised on coal by very rarely having a fire in their bedroom. The first year that Marion kept a diary was very cold: "January 13th, 1881: Lin & self breakfasted in bed. Snow and freezing hard, Lin's bath frozen for first time . . . January 18th. Fearful gale, snow & ice, never remember anything like it, snow 2 or 3 feet deep against front door. . . January 19th. No *Punch* dinner on account of severe weather. . . January 26th. Still bitterly cold, fortnight since Spencer's wedding, snow on ground from that morning till now."

Marion's diary notes on the London fog are interesting. This was much less frequent than one has been accustomed to believe, and the "pea souper" immortalized by Dickens was sufficiently rare to be a matter for especial comment. Owing to the prevailing westerly wind, conditions were not usually so bad in Kensington as in the east end of town where most of the noxious trades were situated. There would have been, however, a constant haze and murkiness from the smoke of the inumerable fires and kitchen ranges. If a fire were lit in every room on a winter day, each house in a street like Stafford Terrace could have twelve chimneys smoking. The Sambournes would probably only have had four or five fires burning at one time, but this figure multiplied by hundreds of thousands makes it surprising that there were any clear days at all. Only exceptional climatic conditions forced the smoke downwards to create dense fog, which came in two types: yellow (sulphorous) and black (sooty). On bad days it was literally impossible to find one's way about the streets at night and difficult even at noon; indoors a layer of greasy

smuts would be deposited on every surface, tainting food, clogging net curtains, and besmirching white collars and cuffs. It was no wonder that the wealthy preferred to winter abroad.

The winter of 1886 began early: "October 19th. Dense black fog", was Marion's first intimation of the hard season to come. On 22 November she wrote "Dreadful fog all day," and on 23 November, "Fearful fog!!! third day. Lin started for *Punch* dinner but had to return." There was a respite until 17 December, but then it was "Dense fog" followed on 20 December by "Bitterly cold" and 26 December "Tremendous deep snow storm". In January the weather was just as bad: "Bitterly cold, fog & hard frost", and so it went on all through the spring up to 15 March, when Marion wrote, "The blackest fog I ever remember, bitterly cold, heavy fall of snow." In most years conditions were not so extreme, with only two or three days of fog recorded and very little snow, but entries like "With chicks to circus. v.v.foggy, returned home safely", "Fearful fog, could not go out", and "Dense black fog, darker than night", are reminders of how bad conditions were. Even during the summer it could still be foggy, as the kitchen ranges smoked just as much as they did during the winter. On some July days Marion would write, "Thick yellow fog", or even "So dark, had to have candles for breakfast." The acrid smell of fog mingled with the smell of horse—both so typical of Victorian London—was even more unpleasant in hot weather than in cold. Nobody stayed in town after the Season was over if they could possibly avoid it, and a visitor to the capital in August would find whole streets of houses shuttered and deserted. Not until gas and electric fires came into use between the wars did this type of fog lessen, and it only became rare after the passing of the Clean Air Act in 1956.

Marion was always interested in how other people looked, but she does not seem to have had much vanity herself. Her poor health was probably responsible for the early loss of the rather indeterminate prettiness of her youth. Nearly all the photographs which Linley took out of doors in the 1880s and 90s show her looking plain and thin, with sallow complexion and heavy bags under her eyes. Her light brown hair darkened over the years and she wore it more severely scraped back with a tiny fringe in front, a less flattering style than the thick plait wound round her head which she had had as a girl. At the turn of the century hair began to be puffed out round the face which suited Marion much better. She also put on a little weight and professional studio photographs taken at this time are more successful, though she still managed to look self-conscious and uncomfortable in front of a camera.

Style of dressing, as in earlier times, was a sure guide to the wealth and social status of the wearer; people in Victorian England did not pretend to be poorer than they were. Thus a visit to the dressmaker was an important event. Appointments had to be made: "Carriage at 11.30 to Madame Bocquet", and smart dressmakers were

Marion posing for a cartoon. The wretched condition of seamstresses, overworked and underpaid, was another of the social evils which Punch attacked.

not only expensive but haughty too. "To Madame B, waited an age" was one of Marion's entries, and "Madame cross & getting dearer" was another. More than once she was obliged to change her appointment, "Madame B too busy, must go Thursday." Elegant dresses were extremely costly, and a lady expected to spend a higher proportion of her income on clothes than her modern counterpart. "Sent cheque £22 to Madame B" and "Went to Madame B's, paid her £38 for making me blue evening dress" meant that Marion's quarterly allowance of £25 was quickly swallowed up. After writing "To Madame B, asked ridiculous prices, ordered nothing", she tried employing a seamstress to come to the house for a few days: "Napper here, don't think dress will be a success, shall never fancy myself in any but Madame's dresses." Her sisters, Midge and Tabby, also patronised Madame Bocquet, so though Marion might have wanted to escape from her dependence, she was probably unwilling to admit that such expensive clothes were beyond her means.

Only a few important outfits were ordered from the dressmaker each year and from the size of the cupboard in the bedroom at Stafford Terrace Marion cannot have owned very many dresses at one time. More disappointments than successes were recorded in the diary: "Expect black dress to be utter failure", "New dress arrived, bad", "Tea gown came, don't like it", were all typical entries. Perhaps it was

the thought of the dreadful bills, or just a lack of confidence about her own appearance, which spoiled Marion's pleasure. She never sounded excited about new clothes, nor ever paid herself a compliment or recorded anyone else's comments. Only once in all the years of diary-keeping did she write down what she wore to a party: "Very jolly dinner, wore red velvet." It may have been the success of that evening which prompted her to write the following year, "Ordered best walking dress and blue cotton, red velvet to be done up." Ten years later the old red dress was being taken to be re-modelled yet again.

Marion had the reputation of being a good needlewoman. Her early diaries are full of notes like "Worked on pink cotton", "Mended dresses & finished home-made black", "Bought frilling and altered silk skirt". She did not own a sewing machine, "Cut out flounce, Judy took it away to machine", but made clothes for herself and Maud by hand, "Finished Maud's blue dress, will wear it Sunday." She would make an occasional trip to the Royal School of Needlework to buy materials but she does not specifically mention any embroidery, although it is said that she made the cushions now in the morning-room. Lamp-shades were quite a speciality of hers and "Worked at new shades" is a frequent entry. Candle flame and gas jet gave shades a short life and the elaborate lace confection over the lamp on the piano is the only one of her shades to survive. Marion also made other things for the house: "Busy all morning cutting out sofa cover", "Hard at work on covers", "Very busy with drawing room curtains, did three sides." Other entries like "Trimmed bonnet & read to chicks", or "Finished mother's pincushion" show that her hands were seldom idle. In later life she did much less sewing, writing regretfully, "Am so slow with needle these days."

Home sewing or going to a private dressmaker were not the only ways of getting new clothes. The department stores had begun stocking ready-made clothes by the 1880s; these would be altered on the premises to fit, or their tailoring departments would make up special outfits to the customers' choice. As time went on, Marion and her contemporaries turned more and more to the shops instead of to private dressmakers, although it was another two generations before "off the peg" garments became standard wear for all classes. Marion went to places that are still—or were until very recently—household names, and she was prepared to travel quite a distance to find a shop which suited her. The Metropolitan Railway, which ran from Paddington to the City, had been opened in 1864 and was so successful that the line was extended to South Kensington in 1868, with a stop at Kensington High Street. Marion used it for going to Whiteleys in Westbourne Grove, to the Baker Street Bazaar, to Maples or Shoolbreds in Tottenham Court Road, or to Gamages at Holborn, and these shops owed much of their great success to the railway. Harvey Nichols (her favourite shop in Sloane Street) and Marshall and Snelgrove in Oxford Street were only an omnibus ride away, and of course Barkers and Pontings in Kensington High Street were within easy walking distance. The shops were not always very clean: "To Harrods—dirty place though cheap" was one of Marion's entries. When she was tired she usually treated herself to a cab home—an extravagance, but much less of an effort than "Om" or "Metro".

The entrance to the Metropolitan Railway, Kensington High Street, opened in 1868. Marion often used the "metro" for her shopping expeditions.

The shops which Marion patronised were not in the buildings that we see today. The late nineteenth-century shopping empires were all founded by energetic and ambitious young men who had started life as lowly haberdasher's assistants. They had graduated to owning small premises and by degrees had bought up neighbouring properties. They prided themselves that they could meet all their customers' needs under one roof, but behind the new plate glass windows the original shops remained a warren of little rooms and staircases, not only inconvenient but also a great fire hazard. By the 1860's the wealth of the expanding middle classes inaugurated a building boom and the old shops were all pulled down and refashioned. John Barker opened in Kensington High Street in 1870 and Marshall and Snelgrove built a fine new shop in Oxford Street in 1876, but the big purpose-built department store did not reach its apogee until Harrods was rebuilt in the early years of the twentieth century.

Marion was a very fussy shopper: "Sent back grey dress to Snelgrove, promised to send credit note", "Ordered hat which Lin doesn't like so returned it", "Changed jersey at Marshalls, fits so badly" are all typical entries. Only sometimes did she mention prices, but "Brown velvet dress £2.19.6*d*, shoes 7/7*d*", "Blue serge dress £4.0.0*d*", or "New winter dress £7.7*s*" show that the £38 which she paid Madame Bocquet for an evening dress was a great extravagance. Not all shopping was for dresses. Less stressful was a morning's outing to buy little things: "Walked down Sloane Street, bought feather, gloves, lace & stamps", "To Barkers, ordered 4 pairs of stockings for Roy at 2/6*d* a pair, pair of trousers 4/6*d*." Shopping could be exhausting, so little breaks were necessary: "To Bond Street, had cup of chocolate at

Charbonnels' ", or "To Gunters for ices." Sometimes she met Linley or Spencer in town and had lunch with them, "Lunch at Rules, expensive" was considered a great treat. But her most regular companion on a shopping expedition was her mother-in-law: "Walked & shopped with Mrs S, bought purse, sachet, & umbrella." A trip to Whiteleys in Westbourne Grove—"Mrs S & self to Grove, bought dresses china etc"—could be combined with a visit to Marion's relations who lived nearby. She was very fond of her Uncle Edwin, "so like dear Papa", and she often visited Uncle John or Aunt Leigh. In April 1884 she wrote, "Mrs S & self went by metro to see Uncle & fire at Whiteleys, found them v. upset." Whiteleys was quickly rebuilt, only to suffer another disastrous fire three years later.

Public health had improved dramatically after Sir Joseph Bazalgette constructed a magnificent new sewerage system for London in 1865. Until then the Thames had acted as a main drain and when the cholera germ had arrived from the East the results had been terrible. In 1849 14,000 died, in 1854 10,000. But once the Victorians grasped the importance of good drainage, they became fanatically keen on cleanliness and hygiene, and by 1870 the cholera death rate was reduced to almost nil. Houses on the Phillimore Estate were all built with internal plumbing; there were three water closets in the Sambournes' house (instead of one earth closet in the garden), but the new technology was not perfect and Marion fretted a great deal about cracked pipes and inefficient waste traps harbouring germs and smells. She never liked the wash basins in the bedrooms at Stafford Terrace and more than once wrote "Sore throat, convinced basin in my room cause." The house had a bathroom (though not a W.C.) on the top landing, and Linley, as was customary for gentlemen at the time, took a cold bath there every morning. No geyser is mentioned in the Inventory and it is unlikely that hot water was piped up from the kitchen range in the early days; water for washing and shaving was carried upstairs in cans by a toiling housemaid. Roy also used the bathroom but Marion and Maud would not have done so, taking instead warm water sponge-baths in front of the bedroom fire. Apart from the fact that it was not customary for the sexes to share a bathroom, Linley had annexed it for another use. He took out the original bath and replaced it with a deep flat-sided marble receptacle in which he could rinse his photographic plates, adding a wide shelf alongside to take bowls of chemical solutions. Everything here was ideally arranged for his hobby.

If anyone in the family was ill, the doctor would be called at once, and he came two or three times a day if the illness was severe. The Victorian family doctor was a much respected figure, but the range of medicines at his disposal was very limited. A healthy diet, careful nursing and (especially for his wealthy female clientele) plenty of rest, was the best he could prescribe, and simple remedies based on plant material were used for most afflictions. In spite of her preoccupation with illness, Marion's diary contains remarkably few references to medicine; castor oil was taken for any

kind of stomach pain, oil of turpentine was used for sprains and mustard plaster for chesty colds. By far the commonest ailments in the Sambourne household were frequent coughs and colds, which were usually started by Linley and then passed all round the family. Mrs Herapath sent Marion some good advice in 1880: "I am so sorry dear to hear poor Lin and chicks have colds, for I know when Lin has a cold there is no mistake in it. You should give him some gruel with milk and a nice lump of butter in it as large as a walnut and two tablespoons of Rum in it taken when he is in bed. . . ."

General standards of health were low and life expectancy was much less than today. Hospitals were places where the poor went as a last resort; those able to afford it employed home nurses and hoped to die in their own beds. Laudanum (tincture of opium) could be taken for acute pain, but aspirin and other efficient pain-killing drugs did not make their appearance until the very end of the nineteenth century. Operations, even major ones, were performed at home, using ether or the newer chloroform as anaesthetics, and fees from a fashionable surgeon could be enormous. Marion suffered very much from tooth-ache, and so did other members of the family—extraction was the only recourse: "Up all night darling Roy in agony with tooth. Mr Herbert came, gave gas & took it out. Quite exhausted!" Linley was plagued with frequent painful boils which Marion poulticed; in the days before antibiotics this type of affliction could drag on for weeks. Constipation was considered the root of all evil, and some enterprising chemists (in particular Beecham and Carter) made vast fortunes out of advertising and packaging laxatives—Linley took what were euphemistically called Liver Pills rather often. In fact his diary contains almost as many complaints about his various ailments as Marion's does, though he adopted quite a different attitude, refusing to cosset himself and insisting that hearty outdoor exercise was the only cure.

Marion's diary never mentioned sex, and pregnancy was usually referred to in an oblique way: "Midge told me news of herself" or "Tabs looking wonderfully well." One feels that she rather disapproved of babies—certainly she thought large families a mistake, "Tea with Mrs D, expecting another baby!!! No 6." Marion's mother had borne nine children and raised eight; her grandmother had brought eleven children to maturity. These would not have been considered exceptionally large families in their generation, but by the 1870s things had changed. Birth control, though never openly discussed, was certainly practised among the middle classes, so much so that large families had become a subject for jokes and pitying glances. Only one of Marion's seven brothers and sisters had more than three children, and she herself never wished for more than two. When in 1885 she thought she might be pregnant again she was in despair: "No little friend, dreadfully afraid, had hot bath", and four days later "No little friend, too awful." Her fears were not allayed for another week, but at last, "Went to early service. *Petit ami a l'eglise. Dieu soit beni!*"

By 1886 Linley had been working for *Punch* for nineteen years and was well established as one of the paper's leading lights. A journal called *The World* published a long article about him in that year under the heading "Celebrities at Home", which gives a good description of the interior of 18 Stafford Terrace:

> Mr Sambourne's drawing room is decked with artistic taste. It is mainly Louis Seize in style, and contains some very handsome pieces of furniture of the brass-bound mahogany period, some marquetrie and a handsome clock and commode of the rococo style. A few pieces of good porcelain, genuine oriental and mysterious Lowestoft and some fine bronzes supplement the decoration. . . .

Perhaps spurred by this appreciation, the Sambournes embarked on some fairly extensive alterations and improvements in 1887 to make their house even more interesting. From Linley's diary we gather that there was work in progress from the end of August until the beginning of November, though he does not make it clear what was actually done. Marion was away in the country most of that time, so there should be a packet of letters giving progress reports but unfortunately these have not been preserved. All we can glean is that, just like ten years earlier, Nash, the builder, was employed to do the alterations, and that Linley again had dealings with Jacksons, as well as with Edwards and Roberts, the furniture makers, though the painting and odd jobs were done this time by Maples of Tottenham Court Road. The only improvements specifically mentioned in Linley's diary are the brass nameplate on the front door, a fireplace tiled, a stove ordered, a mantelpiece painted and a fender fitted. Marion returned home briefly in October: "To Stafford Terrace, workmen all over house. Lovely fire in our room & all very cosy. Felt as if I were on a visit to Lin, most comical." A fortnight later she was back again: "Returned home. My room lovely, everything beautiful in it. Slept in it, Roy in spare room. New stained glass window there, & two stained glass panels on staircase. Unpacked everything, nothing broken."

In the face of this meagre evidence we can only guess at what else was done. We can assume that Marion's bedroom was redecorated and that the fireplace was altered, as the painted wooden chimney-piece with its blue and white tiles and patent slow-burning grate is no longer (as it was in 1877) the same as the fireplace in the spare bedroom. The stained glass in the spare room is similar in style to the glass in the drawing-room, so it seems almost certain that the big bay window there was part of the 1887 improvements. This bay is the same shape and size as the one in the morning-room just below it, but the glass it contains is more elaborate, in fact the most remarkable feature of the whole house. It would surely have been mentioned by the reporter from *The World* had it been in place when he paid his visit, but it was not until the publication of *Kensington Picturesque and Historical* in 1888 that there is a drawing of Linley at his easel in front of it. Each of the side panels contains sunflowers in a blue goldfish bowl; across the top of the window the rising sun throws its beams over a colourful jungle and singing birds welcome the dawn. The

centre panels are filled with a diaper pattern made up of motifs taken from the heraldic crests of the Herapath and Sambourne families. The Victorians were fascinated by the subject of heraldry and went to great lengths to establish a right to a family crest. Linley (even though he was not able to prove kinship) adopted the arms of a Somersetshire yeoman called Samborne who had flourished in the seventeenth century. The crest was a five pointed star: it appears on a brass panel fixed to the drawing-room door (where it makes a pair with one showing the Herapath arms) as well as in the window. In fact Linley used this star as often as he could, having it embossed on all the Stafford Terrace writing paper, and engraved on the table silver and drinking glasses.

Linley took several photographs of the drawing-room in the early 1890s, which show it looking almost exactly as it does now. Although time seems to have stood still, the original fabrics have perished: the curtains and chair-covers we see today are probably all post-1900. It is sad that none of Marion's early handiwork survives, as through her choice of colours and patterns we could have got some idea of her taste. References made in her diary to Mrs Herapath's rooms always looking "so dainty fresh and clean" make one think that she may not have cared for the darkness and heaviness of the decoration at Stafford Terrace, but it is not easy to guess what she would have put in its place. She does not mention going to shop at Liberty's (that fount of the Aesthetic Movement) to buy silks or furnishing fabrics. She did not approve of the craze for all things Japanese, nor think much of Oscar Wilde's house in Tite Street, which had been decorated in pale colours by Godwin in 1884. Photographs all show her in ordinary Victorian dress, never in the mediaeval robes of the Pre-Raphaelites nor the soft drapery favoured by the Aesthetes. In matters of taste—as well as in most other areas of her life— Marion liked to follow the normal conventions of the day rather than strike out in an attempt to be original.

In spite of their possible differences in outlook, Marion was very proud of her artistic husband and delighted with the beautiful home which they had created together. On returning after even a short absence she seldom failed to remark on how nice everything looked, and how glad she was to be back. The rather severe type of furniture which Linley bought was soon covered with the multitude of ornaments, family portraits, embroidered mats and sentimental keepsakes that were cherished by most Victorian ladies. The Queen, as photographs of the royal apartments show, led the way with her love of clutter, and her subjects had been quick to follow her example. Visitors express astonishment at the number of objects which fill the rooms at Stafford Terrace, but they can be sure that there would have been many more a hundred years ago.

PART TWO
1888-1894

Linley's coachman posing as the Duke of Westminster; Spencer as Mr Gladstone. Everyone must have enjoyed seeing themselves in Punch the following week.

CHAPTER SEVEN
RAMSGATE:
ROY TO SCHOOL:
SPENCER

HE EXPERIMENT which the Sambournes made in 1884 of renting a house close to Westwood had been a great success. The following year they decided to look for somewhere in the centre of Ramsgate and chose Townley Castle which, though it had now rather gone down in the world, was the house where Queen Victoria had stayed when she visited Ramsgate as a girl. Marion described it as "Pretty & bright, only five bedrooms, poor china & glass" and the Sambournes lodged here from the beginning of September until the middle of December 1885. They continued to patronise the town (bringing their own servants from London and renting a different house each year) until 1893. For twenty years thereafter Marion came down intermittently for shorter visits, so that Ramsgate was as much an integral part of her life as Westwood or Stafford Terrace.

During the 1820s Ramsgate had developed into a fashionable resort to rival the Prince Regent's Brighton. Several elegant crescents and squares were built, but by the 1880s the town had passed the zenith of its popularity and was becoming a suitable place for middle-class retirement. It had always attracted a better class of visitor than Margate, and though the leaders of fashion might now be going elsewhere—to European spas or the South of France—the Sambournes did not wish for anything better. It was quite smart enough for them. Many of their London friends (among them the Messels, the a'Becketts and the Burnands) went there as well. There were the local people too, like Mrs Pugin (widow of the famous architect), Lady Rose Weigall, Mrs Buckmaster, and Mrs Evans, whose aquaintance it was a pleasure to renew each year. "Met all Ramsgate" was a favourite phrase of Marion's after she had been for a Sunday morning stroll along the front.

There were many advantages in having an autumn break from city life. During July and August holiday-makers in their thousands flocked to the coastal resorts.

Left: Linley. Country tweeds or riding dress were his favourite clothes, a point often commented on by his contemporaries. He seldom wore a town suit.

Ramsgate beach in the 1890s. The seafront station, opened in 1863, brought crowds of holiday makers to the town.

Marion never remarked on the state of the beach, but it may have been to avoid the crowds (as well as to take advantage of cheaper lodgings) that the Sambournes favoured the autumn. The train took less than two hours to reach Thanet from London, so it was possible for gentlemen to commute in quite the modern manner— probably with fewer delays and more comfort than they can today. November was a bad month for fog in London, and many people were enjoying hunting and shooting at their country seats so that there was not much social life in town. Also Marion could recoup expenses in Ramsgate: there were not many tempting shops or theatres, no entertaining on a lavish scale, and no expensive dressmaker to visit.

The great virtue of Ramsgate in Marion's eyes was its close proximity to Westwood, but a special attraction was the presence of the Burnands who spent much of the year at their house in Royal Crescent, on the West Cliff. Frank Burnand had married twice and his first family were nearly grown up, but the three eldest children of the second marriage, Mary, Ethel and Cuthbert, were just the right age for Maud and Roy to play with, while Winifred and Wilfred were a little younger. Rosie Burnand had been an actress before her marriage and still enjoyed appearing occasionally at Ramsgate Theatre. She must have been a most charming person, full of fun and energy and overflowing with good ideas, so that the Sambournes were caught up in a delightful whirl of activity. The families met almost every day, and the adults dined together constantly. "Very jolly evening at Burnands" was a phrase repeated over and over again; indeed it seemed impossible not to be jolly in their company. "Lin & self to Burnands, laughed immensely, all in good spirits", or "To Burnands after dinner, Mr B most amusing." If by any chance these friends were away, Ramsgate lost half its charm. "General emptiness without Burnands" was the diary entry after one happy busy period, when Marion was reluctantly forced to think up entertainment for the family on her own.

Plans for Roy's future had been anxiously discussed during the autumn of 1887 and by the following spring the Sambournes had made up their minds. "Spoke to Miss Penn about Roy's going to school" wrote Marion in February 1888. Albion House, Margate, was chosen for his first school, conveniently close to Westwood and Ramsgate. Marion went to inspect it in April: "With Mother, went over school, saw Matron", and it was arranged that Roy should start there in September. Everyone hoped that school would be good for Roy as he was becoming increasingly boisterous and difficult to control: "September 12th, 1888. Darling Roy to school. Poor little man broke down as I left, hope he will soon feel better, awful to leave him", wrote his mother. She felt the parting almost as much as he did: "Awake most of night thinking of Roy, hope to hear soon how he is."

Roy had just passed his tenth birthday, and was thus older than many little boys of his class who were often sent to boarding school at seven or eight years old to prepare them for entry into the great public schools — Eton, Winchester or Harrow — at the age of twelve or thirteen. From there they could expect to move into the highest circles of politics, law or City business; thus the "preparatory" schools were the foundation stone of an English gentleman's career, and they all laid great emphasis on the importance of discipline, fresh air, and team sports. Linley himself had not had this type of education: it was a mark of how much the Sambournes had gone up in the world that it was offered to Roy. But like so many little boys snatched from the bosom of an adoring family, Roy found school a dreadful experience. Brief tear-stained missives arrived home begging for release — Marion kept them all. "Letter from darling Roy, wish he would be happier" she wrote on 1 October, and packed him up a parcel of comforters, "Sent cake, jam etc to darling Roy." After a few weeks of misery he settled down, and came home at half-term with a good report. This encouraged his parents, and Marion wrote "Roy seems much improved since he went to school." She went to Margate to visit him in the second half of the term, "Saw Roy, looked rather dirty & has a cold in his head. Horrible idea — only one pocket handkerchief a week! Shall be glad to have him home."

The start of Roy's schooling meant several changes in the Sambourne household. Nurse, conscious that the end of her rule was in sight, had been getting more and more difficult. Marion was reluctant to dismiss her, but at the same time was at a loss to know how to deal with her. Ten days after Roy began school, the problem was solved.

Marion with Roy, probably taken at Prospect Terrace, Ramsgate.

"Nurse left quite suddenly!!! Feel upset in consequence, but think it is better so." As Miss Penn had departed in the early summer, Marion was now left in sole charge of Maud. She made no immediate effort to look for a new governess, but did Maud's lessons herself, "Taught Maud in morning, very good & attentive." Maud was now thirteen, rather shy and awkward, so to encourage her daughter to be more outgoing Marion organised some friends to stay: "Evelyn Coward came, independent little girl, wish M were like her in that respect." The next day "Evelyn and Maud out directly after breakfast with their hoops, met the little Messels."

Early in 1888 there had been the first intimations that things were not going well for Marion's eldest brother. "Spencer called morning, jumpy & jerky, disappointed with horse he bought at Tattersall's", she wrote. A few days later he was again reported "Jumpy & queer", but it was not until a month later that the reason for this unease was apparent. Marion's entry in her diary on 14 June was stark: "Bad news. Spencer failed on Stock Exchange." It was a dreadful blow, but perhaps not a total surprise, as she added, "Nothing more than we expected." Next day the news, with all its implications, sank in. "Spencer declared on Stock Exchange — disgrace — Lin awfully upset about it." Linley might be upset, but the Herapaths were devastated. The firm which old Mr Herapath had so carefully built up was ruined, the honourable name of its founder besmirched, his eldest son "hammered" — declared bankrupt and dishonoured — at a public meeting. Marion and Edgar hurried down to Westwood to support their mother in the crisis, leaving Linley to discover what details he could about the disaster. Marion's distress was compounded with severe toothache. "Face all swollen up, so painful, no sleep. Spencer's failure — disgraceful — £45,000 said to be amount, besides bills."

The newspapers that week were full of the tragic death of the Emperor of Germany. All England sympathised with his widow, Queen Victoria's eldest daughter, but there was still room for an article on the Herapath bankruptcy. "Account in Observer of Spencer's failure" wrote Marion on 17 June, adding "Face perfect sight, so painful. Eased it with laudanum." Linley kept the family at Westwood posted about each fresh development: "Two letters from Lin — bad news" and "Letter from Lin, very worried about Sp, had interview with him, as bad as can be." Apparently Spencer blamed his partner, Delmar. "Cling to hope it's all Delmar's fault" wrote Marion on 22 June. Another letter from Linley sheds some light on Spencer's past:

> I caught sight of Sp. and Delmar in a hansom looking awful yesterday, but they did not stop nor has Spencer been here at all and we have heard nothing more. Curiously enough I went to the directors' dinner last night, and the first word that the director on my right said was (loud enough for the whole table to hear) how's Spencer Herapath? He said S. used to go to them before he was married. . . . Spencer told him at that time that as he could get no more money out of his father he was going to marry for money. The director knew all about Spencer being sent to the Cape and the bother and trouble he gave, so I could not contradict it.

Marion returned home on 29 June, and on 9 July wrote, "Letter from Spencer, can't think he realises awful nature of failure." After this nothing more was said about the affair until November, when there was another article in the paper, "Spencer's failure in Times — no idea such failure, over £135,000!" It was a staggering amount, and Spencer was left to bear the blame alone: Delmar, who may well have been juggling money behind his partner's back for some time, disappeared abroad and was not heard of again. It seems that Spencer had been idle and careless rather than dishonest: he simply had no head for money. Marion was badly shaken by the whole affair. Although "Dear Papa" was not mentioned, it is easy to imagine that the family thought of him turning in his grave. Mr Herapath had suffered much disappointment from his eldest son, but the bankruptcy was far worse than any previous escapade, bringing shame on the whole family. When Marion came to add up her own money she was not pleased to find that some of it too had disappeared in the crash: "Invested £136 during year 1888, £18 of this lost through Spencer." Always scrupulously careful herself, this rankled more than anything else, and the lost £18 continued to be noted in her accounts for several years afterwards. The spectre of poverty and ruin began to haunt her, and she was more than ever

concerned about where every penny of the housekeeping money went. "Dreadful worry never having enough money in bank, must put by for children" she wrote. The end papers of her 1888 diary contain a digest of her financial affairs, with comparative tables for 1886, 1887, and 1888, under the headings "Money spent", "Money invested", "Spent on dress." It looked very neat and businesslike, but there was no way to increase her income except by saving. Rash speculation led to disaster—rigid economy was the only hope. Luckily the trusts which her father had set up for his children were not affected by Spencer's catastrophe, so Marion still received her allowance, but not much Herapath money could be expected to filter down to Maud and Roy. At the bottom of the page she added their Post Office savings: "Roy's book, £17.1 11. Maud's book £11.8.1." It was a pathetic sum, and she must have closed the diary that day with a heavy sigh.

The Sambournes stayed in Ramsgate until the middle of December. Marion had had a difficult year: Spencer's bankruptcy, Roy's unhappiness at school and the departure of Nurse all weighed on her, and she relapsed into ill-health. "Feel v. poorly, strange derangement inside. Wonder what I will have wrong with me next" she wrote plaintively. Worst of all, Mrs Sambourne had spent the whole of the autumn with them in their lodgings. The old lady had been, as usual, a thorn in the flesh, and Marion was sorely tried. "Mrs S does depress me awfully, so sorry for her & *myself* too." She unburdened herself to her friend, "Walked to Mrs Burnand's, expatiated on discomfort of having Mrs S here", but at once felt guilty of disloyalty, adding, "Wish I could keep my worries to myself."

By the time the Ramsgate visit came to an end Marion was feeling very unwell. The packing up was a great effort and she could hardly cope with the journey. On reaching Stafford Terrace she went straight to bed, obviously feeling in need of care and attention. Unfortunately Linley was too busy to respond, and on his wife's first day back in London went out with three different sets of friends: in the morning, the afternoon and the evening. Marion was hurt and angry at this neglect, and for the first time openly critical in her diary of her husband's behaviour. It is quite a shock to the reader, used to brief jottings with little emotional content, to come suddenly upon the following: "December 21st. Feel awfully done up. Often think it a pity Lin ever married—only cares for his home as a sort of warehouse for surplus furniture— our lives drifting apart." The next day she felt worse, "Lin home at 2.30 this morning. Did not sleep after 12.30 & feel v.ill—would be glad to die here if not for my poor children. Lin loving but intensely selfish would not give up a pleasure were I dying—I doubt if he would care after the first hour. Spencer came in, was amusing, he too cannot feel much or this terrible bankruptcy business would worry him."

Perhaps it was during this illness that Marion filled a back page of her diary with a rough draft of her will. The writing is swift and bold—certainly not that of a dying woman—and the intention is quite clear: "All money invested by me & in my name should be divided equally between my two children." The bottom quarter of the page has been neatly clipped out with scissors, so something may have been written here which she later regretted. There is no knowing if Linley ever read what she wrote and tried to make amends, but it does seem that he was soon forgiven. Two

days later, though "Still seedy in bed", Marion wrote "Lin to see about drawing, so sorry he is worried about it." She had had time to reflect that she was in fact a very lucky woman to be able to write, after fourteen years of marriage, "Lin loving". The fact that Linley and Spencer were bracketed together as unfeeling wretches rather mitigates the case against Linley—they were both mere men about whose insensitive behaviour women could do nothing, only suffer. Marion must have felt some satisfaction at being able to will her money direct to her children, which would not have been possible before the passing of the Married Woman's Property Act in 1882, but she was never to show any interest in movements to liberate her sex from other unjust constraints.

By Christmas Day Marion felt much better. "Lin self & chicks to dinner with Mrs Boëhm, Con & Effie there, chicks very happy," she wrote. But there was another blow in store: Tabby's baby boy, born last September, was ill: "Letter from Tabs, diphtheria broken out, baby v.ill, Eveleen & Gwen slight attack." The Fletchers fled from the infection and came to London, leaving their sick children in the care of their many servants. Their attitude seems callous, but had Tabby remained at home there was little she could do. On 29 December Marion wrote, "Baby died today. R.I.P. Ham & Tabs here to tea, very cut up about their dreadful loss." Infant mortality was still high, even among the wealthy, although that other scourge of family life, death in childbed, had become less common. As a family, the Herapaths had not been lucky: first Spencer, then Jessie, and now Tabby had all lost baby sons. Maud and Roy had passed the most dangerous age, but Marion must have felt more keenly than ever a mother's constant dread of sudden disaster. Next day she wrote, "Tabby came to tea and dinner—seems to feel her baby's loss v.much. Very happy quiet day." A curious comment, but perhaps the giving of comfort and support to her sister in this hour of grief was just what Marion needed to put her own troubles in perspective.

Linley went to the Fletcher funeral on 1 January 1889. "Poor baby Hamilton buried at Winchester today. Lin gone with dreadful cold, damp & foggy, hope he will be all right." Hamilton Fletcher in his distress omitted to provide any warmth or refreshment for the mourners. "Lin came back perished, cold v.heavy, made gruel, fire in our room", wrote Marion, and she never reproached her husband for his conduct again. The couple were soon back on the old footing. The diary references to "dear Lin" continue; he was as ever much missed when he was away, worried over when he was at home, his jokes enjoyed and his talents admired. His irritating habits and his masculine selfishness were after all only a natural part of married life; Marion (mindful of her duty as a good wife) did her best to stifle all complaints.

One thing which Linley could have done for her was to make better arrangements for his mother. He may have been too busy or too self-centred to notice the strain imposed on the household by Mrs Sambourne's lengthy visits; perhaps Marion made a great effort to conceal from him how much she disliked her mother-in-law. Both parties in this unhappy relationship are to be pitied. At the beginning of 1889 Marion wrote, "Mrs S rubs me (as I evidently do her) up the wrong way & we both hate each other." Soon after this Mrs Sambourne went to stay with her sister at

Ealing for a fortnight and Marion was better able to face her when she returned, "Mrs S and self made round of calls—12—good afternoon's work! Mrs S bright and well", but such improvements never lasted long.

Roy continued to suffer from homesickness at school, so that the start of each term brought depression and tears. This upset Marion very much; she tried urging him to be brave and put a good face on things, but Roy replied in a letter calculated to wring her heart:

> My own darling Mother. I am almost double as miserable as I was it is no good trying to be happy for the more I try the more I get unhappy. Our meat has worms in it and we have the most horrid bread and butter. I get into most frightful scrapes and about nearly half the school is leaving for not liking the school. Last Monday I had a frightful hard whacking it made me cry most frightfully. I send my best love to you and Papa and Maudie from Roy.

Marion put "Unhappy letter from dear Roy" in her diary, and Mrs Herapath was distressed too. "I wish dear Lin would remove poor Roy, but I am so afraid of making myself too forward", she wrote to her daughter. Fortunately Roy soon discovered that sport was some compensation for the general unpleasantness of school, and his letters began to be full of football matches in winter and cricket in summer, as well as the usual requests for more tuck:

> My darling Mother. I hope you are quite well. Please every day cut all the accounts out of the papers about cricket and send them all to me . . . Please send me some honeycomb and some more potted meat and some strawberry jam please do send them because I want them so very much . . . ever your loving Roy.

The word "tiresome" was not applied to Roy's behaviour for over a year—instead Marion wrote "dear Roy", "darling Roy", or "my blessed boy"—but when this respite was over the familiar difficulties began again. Perhaps she and Linley were too indulgent: they always complied with requests for more sweets and more pocket-money, and the holidays were full of treats and fun.

In contrast Maud was never tiresome, but always happy and good. She and her mother grew very close now that Roy was away at school, and when Marion went on a visit to friends she wrote "Very sorry to leave dear little Maud, do not like going away to enjoy myself without her." One of the great pleasures of having a daughter was making her pretty clothes; these new dresses and their prices were always jotted down in Marion's diary, "Bought Maud's serge & lining for sailor dress 11/-, woollen dress & lining £1.2.9." There was never any suggestion that Maud might go to school. The Girls' Public Day School Trust ran a school in Kensington which she could have attended, but the large part of each year spent at Ramsgate made that an awkward proposition. Anyhow Maud was not of an intellectual bent but a dreamer,

Marion (left) with Maud; Roy, wearing a sailor suit (the uniform of every well brought up little boy), looks bored and restless.

who spent her lesson time gazing out of the window or drawing pretty ladies in wonderful hats in the margins of her exercise books. This did not worry her mother unduly, as she knew that a girl with a charming and lively disposition would make her way in society without much book-learning. "Most delightful evening; Mr and Mrs Crawford, Mr and Mrs a'Beckett, Mr Gillespie and Mr Blunt. All admired Maud" wrote Marion with happy satisfaction when Maud was just fourteen.

However, Maud had to have some education, so Marion set about looking for a governess. After a great deal of worry and hesitation, she chose Miss Gill, who came to live at Stafford Terrace in February 1889. Maud was to have French lessons for two hours twice a week with Mme Alain as well, but this still left plenty of free time for mother and daughter to enjoy themselves together and to go out and about. "Had very happy afternoon with Maud, called on seven people" wrote Marion in March. Miss Gill was not an unqualified success: "Too fanciful & too old, wish I had a younger woman" and "Miss Gill wearies me so with her perpetual chatter" were some of Marion's grumbles, but she could not face the bother of looking for another governess. Besides, there were compensations, "Miss G. did my blue velvet bonnet v.nicely." Miss Gill performed her duties of chaperoning and teaching quite adequately, and Maud seemed to like her; a change might not be any better.

101

There is no mention of the subjects which Maud was taught by her governess, but she grew up well able to express her feelings on paper. This letter was written in February 1890, when she was staying with her Aunt Tabby. It looks very childish, but before the year was out her handwriting and her style had both matured.

> My own darling Mother. I hope you will like the snowdrops I am sending you. I picked them myself. I send you the dear little green leaves that belong to the snowdrops. I always like the proper green, I hate flowers mixed . . . . It is lovely the frost is all on the grass and looks like powder sprinkled over. I draw all day now it is so nice I love it more than ever. I wish you were here, I miss you dreadfully. Give my very best love to darling Papa and Roy and heaps of love to you my own darling mother, I am your ever loving little Maudie."

Like all her early letters, this was bordered with tiny delicate sketches which must have delighted her parents. Marion thought that the time had come for proper drawing lessons, so she asked Blanche Vicat-Cole to be Maud's teacher. It is perhaps surprising that she and Linley between them did not prevail upon one of their better known friends to help Maud, but Linley does not appear to have concerned himself with any part of his daughter's education. Blanche Vicat-Cole's father and brother were both oil-painters who exhibited regularly at the Royal Academy; they are remembered as minor Victorian artists, but Blanche herself, though she also exhibited and had her own studio, is now quite forgotten. Maud had regular lessons with her on Mondays and Fridays for several years, and her drawings were hung on the studio walls whenever Blanche had an open day.

Roy's health had always been a bit of a worry and school did not improve it, in spite of all the fresh air and exercise he had there. Like the rest of the family he had constant colds but he found them harder to shake off and complications nearly always followed. "Up a great deal in night with Roy's ear" wrote Marion after Christmas 1889, and the next day, "Roy very naughty, quite tires me out." It was decided to take him to see a famous doctor, Sir William Dolbey. An operation for "an obstruction of the throat" was declared necessary and this was performed at home. "February 2nd 1890. Dr Brain & Sir W.Dolbey came at 4 o'clock. Operation took about 5 minutes & cost £21! However thankful dear Roy seems much better than I dared hope." Three days later, "Roy down, better. Pity so tiresome to manage." Sir William said that the patient should be out in the air as much as possible; Marion interpreted this very literally, taking Roy out for long walks in the park every day. She did not perhaps make sufficient allowance for the debilitating effect of even a five-minute operation: "Roy tiresome & fretful—no doubt weak—but feel how easily he is spoilt, inclined to be selfish & rude. Wish I understood and knew how to manage him better." Roy was sent back to school only a fortnight after the operation, but it did seem to have done him good. He was healthier and happier, and on his return home for the Easter holidays was reported, "Very well & as lively as ever."

The Sambournes continued to be keen theatre-goers whenever they were in town. They went of course to see the phenomenon of the age, "Lin & self to see Bernhardt—wonderful", but the divine Sarah did not appear very often in London. Much more accessible were the productions mounted by Henry Irving at the Lyceum Theatre. Marion, like most of her contemporaries, greatly admired Irving's partnership with Ellen Terry and the Sambournes were proud to number these stars among their friends. The latter's separation from the painter Watts and her subsequent unconventional life-style were not held against her by her admirers, which might have been the case had she been a lesser artist. Her sister, Kate, was married to Linley's friend, the wealthy and respectable silk-mercer Arthur Lewis, and the Sambournes would probably have met a group of theatrical people at the Lewis's house on Campden Hill. They were often invited to Irving's famous first-night parties, which were held on the stage after the audience had left the theatre. The first night of *Macbeth* in December 1888 became a legendary evening in theatrical history: Marion was carried away by the general enthusiasm, and wrote at length in her diary, crossing the page so that it is almost illegible. "Wonderful performance. Went behind after, great crowd, supper ready. Met many friends. Ellen Terry too womanly & sympathetic for Lady Macbeth, liked her best in the somnambule scene. Scenery perfect, all went off as smoothly as if it had gone a hundred nights. Irving addressed a few words to as enthusiastic an audience as any ambitious actor could possibly desire. . . ." Someone else who was impressed by this production was John Singer Sargent; his portrait of Ellen Terry raising the crown of Scotland above her head is one of his most striking works.

A few months later the Sambournes went to see Irving again in *Richard III*. "Only seeing others do these characters one feels what a great actor Irving really is— notwithstanding his eccentricities" wrote Marion, and after another performance: "First night of *The Dead Heart*. Irving, Ellen Terry & son, & Bancroft. Most wonderful performance, enthusiastic reception." The Sambournes took their children with them when they went to see this play for the second time, "Roy & Maud delighted with Irving & E.Terry, first time seeing them." The other great English actor of the time, Beerbohm Tree, was also a favourite, "Lin & self to see *A Man's Shadow* most thrilling play. B. Tree wonderful & Miss Neilson v.beautiful."

From the end of the eighties through the nineties the pace of entertaining gradually increased as the *fin de siècle* fever took hold. Bank of England stock stood higher than ever before, income tax was only a few pennies in the pound, and the London Season grew ever more glittering and frenetic. Among the Sambournes' friends the musical evenings and parties with some special feature continued popular: "To Lady Hardman's. Edison's phonograph. Interesting but cannot see to what use it will be put, to hear *once* is enough, *more* than enough!" was Marion's entry for 23 March 1889. In June that year she spent some time at Westwood and was obliged to miss some engagements; Linley sent her the usual daily letters full of

news. There was hardly an evening when he was without entertainment. "I looked in at the Drabbles after dinner," he wrote, "Lots of people I knew—Colin Hunter and wife, Barker and wife, Davidsons, Hendersons, Sterne, Fahey, Lowes, Bartlett and others . . . a good party. Lots of diamonds, and everyone seemed to have too much money. . . ." When Marion returned to London she found herself much in demand: "Endless invitations to answer—fourteen!"

The Sambournes were being asked around more than ever before, but there is a discernible change in the type of party they attended. Old friends were being mentioned less and less, and some disappeared altogether. Up until 1888 Marion was constantly visiting Laura Stone. In May there was the usual "Jolly little evening, lovely dinner", but after that all reference to the Stones ceased. As they did not move away from Melbury Road there must have been some quarrel, but the diary gives no clue as to what might have happened. The Fildes were still mentioned occasionally, but that friendship seems also to have cooled a little. The Sambournes remained on good terms with the Boëhms, and were delighted when Joseph Edgar Boëhm was made a baronet in 1889, though sadly neither he nor his wife were to live to enjoy the honour long. All through the nineties new names were constantly appearing in Marion's diary; whether by chance or careful management she and Linley were being drawn into a different kind of social circle, less artistic than the old one, but definitely smarter and richer. As Linley's fund of humour and bonhomie was discovered he became more in demand than ever as a dinner guest. Except for "Gentlemen Only" affairs, Marion was, of course, asked with him. Being such an enthusiastic party-goer herself, she too was probably very good company and it is a great pity that not a single memoir has survived which describes her social gifts.

In 1889 the *Exposition Français*, marking the centenary of the French Revolution, was held in Paris. Linley and several other members of the *Punch* staff went over to make up a special number on the Exhibition. The Eiffel Tower had been specially built for this event and was considered one of the modern wonders of the world. Linley wrote to Marion,

> June 17th. Eiffel Tower amazing. We lunched on the *premier étage*. Paris crammed . . . Shall try to get your gloves tomorrow but you must not be disappointed if I cannot get them as my time is so short. We leave early on Wednesday morning before the shops are open. . . .

Linley was so enthusiastic about Paris when he came home that the whole family decided to go there the following spring. "April 24th 1890. Started for Charing Cross en route for Boulogne. Pleasant passage. Roy v.brave but finally ill, Maud & self on deck all the time, felt ill but were not." They rested a day in Boulogne before

going on, "Roy much impressed with Paris and Tour Eiffel. Our rooms overlooking Tuileries." The family had three hectic days sightseeing, going to all the famous places as well as to the Private View of the Salon. Paris was a revelation— "*Tremendous* crowds, *wonderful* dresses" — but Marion took careful note of all the expenses: "Delicious lunch 24 francs, cab 6 francs, to Panorama 5 francs", and so on; perhaps the holiday was paid for out of her own money. On the last day of the visit she wrote, "50,000 troops in Paris on account of demonstration. Left Paris by 10 o'clock train, crowds of English leaving for fear of row." In spite of the panic the Sambournes had no difficulty travelling and reached home at 7.30 that evening—a journey time that is hardly bettered today. "London looking so small & dingy after beautiful Paris" wrote Marion, adding, "Cost of week abroad all told £40."

This holiday was so much enjoyed that the Sambournes went to France again the following year. This time they did not go as far as Paris but stayed at the Hotel Royale in Dieppe. From there they had a day trip inland: "Took train to Rouen, passed Lin's station, Longueville." In 1873 (before his marriage) Linley had gone with three friends for a rowing holiday on the Seine. Their boat had capsized in a sudden storm and they had been pulled out of the river at Longueville by fishermen. Later the friends put up a plaque in the church there giving thanks for their rescue. Linley probably retold the story to his family as they went past in the train and Marion must have wondered how different the course of her life would have been had he drowned that day. As it was, they all had a very happy outing: "Delighted with Rouen, saw cathedral, good shops. Bought M hat, 35 francs. Had splendid lunch." Three days later they returned home. "London looking dirty & commonplace as usual after clear aspect of Dieppe. Beastly coffee & bread & butter too, could not eat or drink either, disgrace to our country nothing to be had fit to touch for love or money travelling" wrote Marion in disgust. This point of view was shared by most visitors to London: the French in particular found conditions shockingly bad.

CHAPTER EIGHT

CRUISE TO THE BALTIC: PROSPECT TERRACE

INLEY HAD BEEN asked to go to Scotland in 1886 for a fortnight's shooting by his friend Vernon Watney. The wealthy Mr Watney, chairman of Watney and Co, the brewers, was fifteen years younger than Linley and seems at first an unlikely companion. Both men were members of the Garrick Club, but it must have been a love of sport which first drew them together. It was to be a long-lasting friendship and on this first visit to Tressady, forty miles north of Aberdeen, Linley joined a party made up of Vernon Watney, his brother Claude, and several other keen sporting men. When they returned to London Mr Watney kept up the acquaintance and this came to include Marion also. They often met at the theatre, "Mr Watney came to our box", and he would ask the Sambournes to join him at a restaurant for an after-theatre meal. He continued to invite Linley up to Scotland each year, but in the summer of 1890 Marion had a pleasant surprise: "June 1st. Letter from Mr Watney asking us to go to Norway in yacht," and a week later "Dine at Mrs Watney's to meet party for yacht". It would seem that the cruise was arranged for the benefit of Mr Watney's mother; he himself was not going, but must have thought that the Sambournes would be amusing company for her. The other guests were an odd assortment: "the Admiral" to match Mrs Watney in age, Mr Barker, Mr Goldie, and Miss Clarke. As it turned out, Mrs Watney was ill almost the entire cruise, so that Marion was thrown very much into the company of Miss Clarke, who though congenial at first, became rather tedious to one used to a large circle of amusing friends.

Arrangements were speedily made for this exciting trip. Linley got special leave of absence from *Punch*, though he still did his weekly cartoons all through the voyage and posted them back to London. He also made a number of pencil sketches (in quite a different style from his usual work) which now hang in Roy's room. He

Left: Roy, aged fourteen, wearing his Eton uniform. His parents were pleased and proud to have a son at the best school in England.

A view of the Baltic. One of Linley's pencil sketches done from the deck of the Steam Yacht Palatine: *"11.30pm, Tuesday July 8th '90".*

and Marion both enjoyed the holiday enormously, and crammed their diaries with information. Linley had the sense to glue extra pages into his diary, but Marion squeezed her normal sprawling hand to half its usual size and crossed the pages too, so that much of what she wrote is illegible. The cruise took them north to the Shetlands, across to Norway, down to Copenhagen and right up the Baltic as far as St Petersburg—a fascinating journey not often attempted by English travellers at that time. The Sambournes never missed an opportunity of going on shore to tour the local sights and to look at the museums and art galleries. These selections from Marion's diary give some idea of what a treat she found it all:

> June 23rd. Left Kensington in yellow fog 8.30. V.pleasant journey to Portsmouth Harbour. *Palatine* lovely yacht 450 tons all newly painted lovely fittings. Shall never forget how beautiful she looked as we came round her. Had luncheon & unpacked, all settled comfortably in. I have large cabin with bath let in floor, large hanging closet & endless drawers. Luxuriant hangings of pale blue & buff satin damask. Lin has cabin to himself.

The first part of the cruise was up the east coast of England, calling at Harwich and Edinburgh before crossing the North Sea to Bergen:

> July 3rd. Approach to Bergen thro' fiords exquisitely lovely. One side mountains covered in snow & on other side trees & grass most lovely green & some red tiled cottages, grandest sight I ever saw. . . .
> July 9th. Trondheim. Lovely warm day. Went in dinghy at 10 o'clock to explore town, charming place, nice square buildings of

wood, broad streets, v.good roads & paths, trees on either side like boulevards. Cathedral most interesting building. Lunched at 2 at Britannia Hotel. Walked, saw shops, Lin bought me lovely silver belt, designs from old Viking boats.

The yacht steamed on down the coast, Marion delighting in the scenery all the way, then called at Copenhagen:

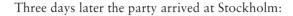

> July 20th. Copenhagen in sight about 1 o'clock. Flat looking coast, picturesque fortifications entering harbour. Lunched & all went ashore. Took carriage to Hotel Angleterre, dined at 7. Most excellent dinner & service, after took carriage to Tivoli!!! Classical entrance to wild dissipation in the way of little theatres, music, merry-go-rounds & a switch-back in which 8 persons can sit which is turned round gently at first then violently & goes off twirling round down incline and back again. . . . then 6 large balloons with cars for 4 into which Mr G, Admiral, Lin & Miss C got and were carried off—cried with laughing. Back to yacht, rough & dark, glad to be on it. Copenhagen delightful mixture of Dutch & French, fine wide boulevards & buildings etc excellent.

Three days later the party arrived at Stockholm:

> July 24th. Lovely day. Just entering Stockholm at 10 o'clock, passing number of islands with charming houses & thickly wooded. Went ashore at 12. Bright city with beautiful large square blocks of buildings. Royal palace standing out prominently like Pitti palace at Florence. Took carriage & drove to palace. Apartments distinguished only for bad taste, carpets hangings etc atrocious. From there walked to Biddenholm where tombs of Kings of Sweden are, also all the colours taken during the 30 Years War. Lunched at Rydberd restaurant, luncheon bad, service tortoise-like. Went in tram to charming garden with 2 theatres & a band. Had coffee there excellent tho' dear. Returned to yacht dined at 7.30. Stockholm looking charming by grey evening light, electric lights like diamonds along the water's edge.

The *Palatine* stayed another two days at Stockholm before steaming up the Gulf of Finland to St Petersburg:

> July 31st. Just anchoring, St Petersburg wonderful, number of exquisitely gilded domes & cupolas. Went ashore, fine large streets magnificent buildings. Russians quite different to any people I have yet seen, Slav or Tartars, morose stern-looking big and broad. Coats all blue & v.long & v.full look like my blue dressing-gown tied in at waist with leather belt. Much struck with great beauty of St Isaac's cathedral, columns of malachite & lapis lazuli, bronze gates silver

sarcophagus exquisite jewels, gilded cupolas & capitals. Entrance like St Peter's Rome. Very devout people men & women prostrate themselves many times before pictures of our Lord & Virgin. From here to Guards Cathedral, uniforms in glass cases of Emperor Paul Nicholas I and Alexander II with the sword he wore when killed blood still on it. . . . August 3rd. Pouring wet morning. Today great fete at Peterhof, Empress' birthday, great illuminations. Steamers going off crammed every five minutes to Peterhof an hours journey from St Petersburg, built by Peter the Great 1720. . . . August 4th. Off at 10 o'clock with Lin took 2 droskeys to Hermitage, the beauty of which surpasses anything I have ever seen. The armoury too beautiful to describe. Saddle cloths exquisitely laced with a design entirely in brilliants another in blue cloth with red & gold fringe & a lace pattern in huge diamonds, sabre, belt & all to match. Pictures — Raphael's Madonna, Titian's Danae exquisite. Rooms of Teniers, Rubens, Reynolds Van Dyck Rembrandt most wonderful collection. Lunch at Hotel de France, excellent. Took 2 droskeys to cottage of Peter the Great, heard service in chapel, Peter's original bedroom. Saw Ikon covered in jewels & on to Cathedral of St Peter & Paul in fortress. Back at yacht 9.15, v.tired.

The yachting party stayed for another week at St Petersburg, going sightseeing every day. They went out to Peterhof (which they thought "tawdry") and another day to the Winter Palace, as well as a second time to St Isaac's and to the Hermitage. On 10 August they drove out to the country where Mr Wishart, the vice-consul, and his wife entertained them.

Drove 15 miles through fairly pretty scenery, flat, passed 7 bridges. Charming large low long house with pretty grounds on quite a mountain for Russia with winding river below. Any amount of lovely flowers & large oak tree in centre of lawn. No carpets but well washed boards. Mr W has four little girls, nice German governess, Russian maids & menservants. Lin took photos. Glorious golden sunset for drive home.

The next day Linley had his first proper exercise for weeks, "Lin to play tennis with Mr Wishart's cousin, enjoyed game immensely."

In spite of all the fascinating things to see in Russia, it was quite a relief when the *Palatine* finally weighed anchor on 13 August and left St Petersburg. Everyone on board had begun to tire of constant movement and sightseeing, and were finding the company of their shipmates rather wearisome. When they got back to Copenhagen on 19 August Linley suddenly decided that he had been away from home long enough. Marion was rather cross at being obliged to pack everything up in great haste and take a crowded train all across Europe, "Slow tedious journey. Reached Flushing at 10 o'clock. Great rush of people onto enormous but horrid steamer, had to sleep in a sort of kennel with four berths, most uncomfortable." The Sambournes

St Petersburg. St Nicholas' Bridge over the Neva with the Winter Palace in the background on the right. Marion and Linley spent a week here seeing all the sights.

finally arrived in London early on 22 August, after an absence of exactly two months. "Reached home 8.35, *delighted* to see dear chicks", wrote Marion.

Maud was equally delighted. While her parents were away she had written to them regularly:

> My own darling Mother. Oh I do miss you so terribly the days seem to me to be weeks. Let me know as soon as possible whether I may go to Uncle Con's. I long to get away I get so dreadfully tired of the stuffy air. . . . Do write soon I look out for your letters so. Your ever loving solitary little Maud.

Another letter had the same theme,

> Never will I let you go on a voyage without me. It seems a year since you have been away and the house is miserable. My chief occupation now is reading at the little back garden door, it is so nice and cool there. . . .

Plenty of exciting things had been happening for Maud to write about too: "The garden party at the Foundling was very nice indeed. We had lots of strawberries and cream but *no ices*. . . ." or "We went yesterday to the French exhibition with Mme Alain and Dora it is a charming place every sort of amusement you can think of so

111

like the French." But the most interesting event was the wedding of Effie's sister, Flossie Boëhm. Maud sent her mother a full description:

> Floss looked very nice but so hot. She had a lovely white silk dress with a sort of muslin sleeve you could see her arm through and orange blossom on her shoulders and her head. The bridesmaids were in white muslin with lace round the bodice and sweet hats with pink roses exactly like your little black straw only white and the loveliest bouquets of pink roses and pink ribbon intermixed. Aunt Effie had a very pretty fawn dress with pointed embroidery and looked very nice indeed. Lady Boëhm looked so ill. . . .

On 8 August Maud wrote again, "Lady Boëhm is ill, very ill again. Aunt Effie was going to a dance and now she cannot go." The very day that Marion returned to London she had to write in her diary, "Poor Lady Boëhm died at 6 o'clock this morning, Con & Effie there, Floss not back from her wedding tour. Called at 3.30 on Eff, poor girl very upset." It was a sad loss for the Sambournes too, but Lady Boëhm had been ill for many months and her friends were well prepared to accept the inevitable.

Mrs Herapath must have been in some financial difficulty ever since her husband's death, as there was much discussion amongst her children about the mis-management of her estate. Mr Herapath had named an old friend (a partner in the legal firm of Welch and Chapple) as trustee, with responsibility to pass to this friend's son in the event of his death. Edgar was another trustee, but he was slow to realise that the family money was not being well handled after old Mr Chapple died in 1877. By the end of the 1880s Mrs Herapath was finding herself in rather straitened circumstances. She decided she would be better off having a permanent base in London again and letting Westwood for the summer months. Early in 1890 she took a flat at Albert Hall Mansions, within easy walking distance of Stafford Terrace. Here Marion was able to visit her nearly every day, though it grieved her to see her mother's increasing frailty, "Lunched with dear Mother, weak & poorly, but cheerful & light-hearted as ever, so different from Mrs S." Other members of the family came round too: "Tea & dinner at Mother's, Con & Mervyn there, v.wild, played sang & danced & at ten o'clock went out together" was Marion's report on a typical lively gathering of the Herapath sons and daughters. Edgar was absent that day; he was the only one not to have inherited their mother's gaiety, but liked to hold forth in moralising tones, making pointed references to the virtues of thrift and common sense. "To see Mother, Edgar there, more Edgarish than ever," wrote Marion with a touch of exasperation, but this was rather unfair, as in the end it was only due to Edgar's persistance that the Herapath affairs were put in better order.

One member of the family who never called on his mother was Spencer. He does not appear to have mixed with any of his younger siblings except for Marion, and after the bankruptcy she saw much less of him than before. In January 1889 he had been the cause of another worry: "Spencer here, dreadfully afraid he and Ada will separate." To have a legal separation was almost as bad as a divorce and would have completed the couple's social downfall, but eventually they decided to stay together in disharmony rather than part. One cannot help feeling sorry for poor Spencer. His life at home must have been wretched, as he was probably dependent on his mother-in-law's charity for a roof over his head. He could escape to Stafford Terrace to tell his woes to Linley and Marion — "Spencer called, everlasting rows with Ada, wonder where it will end" — but their patience was not inexhaustible: "Lin hard at work, many interruptions. Spencer called, same old complaints, wonder he does not see how wearying they are for all alike." Marion had never had much sympathy for lame ducks or lost causes, and Spencer's latest trials were too much to swallow on top of all his other failings. Her relations with Ada had always been strained, and for some time were broken off altogether. Nearly two years passed before Marion felt able to call once more on Mrs Oakes and the rest of the family at Derwent Lodge; she found "Spencer depressed, Ada very hard frost with him, but most aimiable to me." Spencer did make various efforts to re-establish himself, but it was an uphill task. Twice in the next few years he came to the Sambournes with wild schemes for making money, hoping for their support. Marion would have none of it: "He must think us fools" she wrote tartly. But gradually Spencer did manage to creep back into favour. He might be the most feckless of her brothers but he was still wonderfully amusing and she could never resist a good gossip.

The Sambournes continued to spend about four months of each year in Thanet, in spite of the fact that Mrs Herapath no longer resided at Westwood. From 1888 to 1893 they rented a house in Prospect Terrace, Ramsgate. This was on the West Cliff, very close to the Burnands' house in Royal Crescent. Prospect Terrace was, and indeed still is, one of the nicest places in Ramsgate for a family holiday. It is high enough above the harbour to be clear of too much noise and smell, but not too far from all the activity; close to the main shopping centre, yet quiet enough for the children to play safely on the wide promenade which runs along the front. This part of the town is very much as Marion knew it, even the harbour is still full of masts and sails, though now it is pleasure craft in the Marina instead of working fishing smacks. Only the big ferry-boat and the cars parked on the quay strike a discordant note.

The move to holiday lodgings was always a great upheaval, and Marion found it more of a strain each year. The rented house had to be thoroughly cleaned before it was fit to live in, an inventory of the existing furniture taken, and quantities of indispensable objects brought down from London to see the family through their long stay. Linley's paraphernalia for drawing had to be carefully transported and set up to his liking, and a man found to fix the gas tube for his special lamp. "Man to fit Lin's tube, very useful, helped bring Lin's chair, easy chair, easel, 2 globes, drawing board, photo lamp, 2 cushions", wrote Marion. Linley left the household arrange-

Ramsgate harbour, 1893. On top of the cliffs are Prospect Terrace (centre, behind the masts) and Royal Crescent (far left).

ments to her, while he worried about getting the horses to Ramsgate, finding them suitable stabling with accommodation for the groom, and hiring a cart for Marion to drive. All this bother was well worth while, as it meant that he could have a gallop on the sands each morning, as well as go hunting with the Thanet hounds. The children could learn to ride too, something not easy for them to do in town.

Once settled into lodgings it was the extra work required for the Almanack—*Punch*'s supplementary offering to its readers every Christmas—which gave Linley more trouble than anything else, and it inevitably cast a shadow over the Ramsgate holiday. "Lin worried with this hateful Almanack" was a theme which was repeated each autumn with monotonous regularity. "Lin at eternal Almanack, beautiful drawings but oh the slavery!" Marion as usual helped her husband through the long days and nights: "Lin v.busy, read *Our Mutual Friend* to him", or "Read *Pitt* by Lord Rosebery to Lin, most interesting. Lin doing beautiful drawing, new idea and design entirely." She longed for his talents to be recognised, and was always ready with encouragement. After the *Punch* French Exhibition number she had written, "*Punch* excellent, Lin's work beautiful—*best*", and another time, "Mr F.C.B. chaffed Lin about his dinner with Sir F. Leighton—wish it meant A.R.A. for him!"

While the Sambournes were at Ramsgate they only kept two living-in servants and dispensed with a proper cook. Young housemaids could be trained to do some of the cooking, but Marion had to be more domesticated than she was in London. "Busy in kitchen", she wrote, followed by "Made pastry & we were able to eat it!" and "Cooked two tarts, pastry better, washed up, busy all morning." Having people

in for a meal meant that she felt rather nervous beforehand and relieved if the occasion went off without a hitch: "Jane waited well & Alice managed dinner very nicely, v. pleased with both." It was also satisfying for the mistress of the house to find that she was able to cope with all manner of strange tasks: "Mended dining room blind & got sink clean both of which Miss G said would require a *man*! poor helpless thing!"

Kent can be one of the coldest counties in England. Prospect Terrace had no shelter from the weather and the winters were often very severe. "Never felt its equal, fearful night, blinding snow and hurricane blowing from the east" wrote Marion in December 1890, "Harbour v.picturesque all grey and misty, basin filled with fishing smacks and all covered in snow." That month the Sambournes heard sad news; their old friend Sir Edgar Boëhm had collapsed and died of a heart attack at his studio in London. Princess Louise had just been coming in for her sculpture lesson, when he was found dead. The sudden shock distressed Marion very much. "Too awful, feel v.sad not having seen him since Lady Boëhm's death in August", she wrote on 13 December, and two days later, "Sad letter from Con from studio Fulham Road, too terrible, can think of nothing else. Dreamt of Sir E & Lady Boëhm all night, feel we have lost one of the few friends one makes in a lifetime." By the Queen's wish the funeral service was held at St Paul's Cathedral and attended by members of the royal family, who also sent wreaths with personal messages. The funeral took place on a bitterly cold snowy day and was written up at length in the daily papers. Linley was working hard and did not feel able to make the journey up from Ramsgate in such difficult conditions—inadvertantly causing Conrad great offence—but Marion kept the newspaper cutting among her sentimental relics.

During very cold spells Linley could not ride, but there was an ice rink in the town, as well as a choice of frozen ponds. He and Roy were especially jubilant when the temperature dropped. "Lovely day, went to see Roy skate, does wonderfully well" wrote Marion proudly, but in spite of all the fun and exercise Roy had in the holidays his behaviour left much to be desired. One of the first things which Marion had written in her diary when she returned from the Baltic had been "Find Roy much spoilt & inclined to be very rude in speaking, hope he will alter as I do not like it." Her hope was in vain; Roy grew ever bigger and noisier, and was less and less inclined to respond to parental pleading or scolding. Marion was soon at her wits' end to know how to manage him. "Roy skating, came home soaked. Gave him hot bath, was awfully naughty, made me feel quite ill" she wrote, adding next day: "Slept v.badly as worried about Roy who gets beyond me." In spite of having had so many brothers Marion was quite unable to deal with her own boy: "Very grieved Roy so naughty, don't know how to manage him, & feel v.unhappy as he does not seem to care whether he grieves me or not." Only the thought of the approaching term subdued him: "Looked over dear Roy's suit and clothes—v.good, last day!" was the diary entry at the end of the Christmas holidays.

Marion went over to Westwood several times during the winter to check that everything was in order there, as after the first summer let Mrs Herapath had not been able to find another tenant. "Drove to Westwood with Maud, got laurestinus

& celery. Took wreaths to place at dear father's grave." The grave, with all its reminders of the happy past, was an important focus of Marion's life and she never neglected to see that it was well cared for. A month later she was writing, "Ordered box wreaths for dear father's grave", and again, before returning to London, "Maud & self to Westwood, took basket of flowers."

Of all the places connected with this story, the churchyard of St Peter's is the most sadly altered. If she returned today Marion would find Stafford Terrace, parts of Kensington, Westwood, and most of Ramsgate still quite recognisable; St Peter's itself has changed not at all. This dignified medieval parish church is beautifully kept, and so are the eighteenth-century tombs around it, but the rest of the churchyard is a wilderness. The walls have tumbled down, wild flowers and sycamore seedlings flourish among the broken tombstones, graves gape, pieces of angels' wings and hands litter the ground. The importance which the Victorians attached to monuments and memorials and their emphasis on public demonstrations of private grief are a world away from modern attitudes. The polished granite slabs of the Herapath family tomb have defied time and vandals better than most, but how shocked and grieved Marion would be if she saw the desecration all around it.

Roy was finished with Albion House by the end of the summer term 1891. When he had got over his homesickness he had done very well there and was often top of his class. Although his reports were variable, "attention not always steady", his parents were pleased with his academic progress and decided to send him to Eton, the most famous of the public schools. They hoped that he might get a scholarship, but their aspirations were crushed by a letter from the headmaster. "Dear Mr Sambourne. I cannot advise you to send Roy up for the scholarship at Eton; there is always great competition for them and most boys have special training for some time before. If I had thought that Roy had sufficient ability I should have suggested his competing some time since. . . ." This disappointment meant that Linley had to dip deep into his pocket for the fees, but Roy (with various recommendations from his father's friends) was accepted into Eton and started there in September.

Marion's diary contains a list of the clothes Roy had to have, not very different from the contents of a school trunk today. There was the usual last minute rush after the summer holidays: "Took Roy to stores directly after breakfast, got his things, money going like wildfire. After lunch worked away marking & mending. Next day, "September 23rd 1891. Dear Roy to Eton, looked v.nice in his Eton get-up."

At first Eton was quite congenial to Roy. His parents went to see him at the end of his first fortnight: "Lin & self to Windsor. Had tea with Roy, v.well & happy but idle. For the rest of the year Roy sent cheerful letters home, full of requests for stuff to eat, things for his room, and more money. With schoolboy cunning he had laid in a stock of very small letter-cards on to which it was not possible to squeeze more

than a few sentences. "Letter from Roy, short enough!" wrote Marion, but she was pleased to have anything from him, however brief, and they joined the others in her keepsake drawer. Once again the challenge of a new environment did Roy good and his parents were not obliged to censure his behaviour for some time.

As had happened last time when Roy had gone to a new school, Maud had a new governess. Marion had the usual trouble finding someone satisfactory, "Answered governess advertisements, most difficult to get what I want." Eventually she settled on a French lady, Mademoiselle Jacquenot. Miss Gill left; but though Marion was glad to be free of her chatter, she continued to take a kindly interest in her affairs, just as she had done with Nurse and her former parlourmaid, Laurence. For many years these old retainers received letters and presents, and were invited back to Stafford Terrace to see the children and to talk over old times.

That autumn—perhaps to help with the Eton fees—the Sambournes tried the experiment of letting 18 Stafford Terrace while they were in Ramsgate. This made the change-over even more traumatic for Marion, as the thought of someone else occupying her home sent her into a frenzy of activity. Everything of value had to be either put away or taken with them. "Made lists of silver & put away with Alice", "Busy packing boxes with Alice" and "Packing all day hard" she wrote in the week before leaving. There had to be a thorough clean, too, before she could allow strangers into Stafford Terrace. "Cleaned out cupboard outside nursery, Edie doing Maud's & Alice's rooms with carbolic." There was an unpleasant discovery: "Found awful insects in servants' room. Alice put one on table, horrible. Feel very worried just as we are going to Ramsgate." Eventually all was ready. "November 12th 1891. Maud, Mrs S, Mlle, Alice & self go to Ramsgate by 12.15 train. 19 large boxes, 17 small, 2 dogs, & 6 birds. Found all nice here & clean, letter from dear Lin awaiting me." Linley had posted a little note to welcome his wife after the rigours of the journey: "Dearest Polly. This comes hoping you, Mite, my mother, Mamselle, Tony, Mick, Alice and the birds have had a safe and pleasant journey and have got landed in your old quarters. Best and fondest love ever your affec. husband Dickie."

The next day was still a hectic bustle: "Unpacking all morning. Never slept more than 2 hours all night on account of fatigue & gale", and later, "V.busy. Saw cook, won't do. Put up curtains, chose piano." Marion then had to return to London to see to a few more things before the house could be let: "Busy all morning emptying wardrobes & drawers. To stores, bought 2 prs large single sheets £1.8.0, 4 yards muslin for curtains 5/2d." She went back to Ramsgate thoroughly tired out: "Found no dinner laid, all lamps smelling & nothing ready. V.much annoyed, not been so angry for years." A fortnight later she was up in London again to hand over the house to Mrs Robb for three months. "December 16th. To town by 9.30. Shopped all afternoon. To Whiteleys, found glass cheaper than at Barkers. Ordered sherry port & champagne tumblers to make up dozen of each, 2 new brooms, 6 kitchen cups & saucers, 2 pie dishes, 2 basins. Mrs Robb called with cases."

At last it was all done and Marion could relax in the wonderful healthy air of Ramsgate. Men were expected to be strong enough to cope with London in the winter: Linley continued to travel regularly up to town, no matter how bad the

weather, and the reports he sent back made his wife more glad than ever that she had escaped to the country: "Lin not seen the sun since he left here" she wrote with some satisfaction after he had been away for three days, or "Lovely day here, dense fog in London."

Maud was now sixteen, and enjoyed taking on the role of her mother's protector. When Marion was rushing up and down to London organising the move she wrote:

> My own darling Mother. I was so pleased to get your dear little letter. I am so sorry that you were faint for want of something to eat, I cannot think how I can have been so thoughtless to let you go without some sandwiches and wine. I have been very good in practising: two hours yesterday and one *aujourd'hui*. The curtains were put up this morning and they look very pretty. I do miss you so much, you cannot imagine what a blank the house is without you, and your poor little wing (me) feels lonely. Mademoiselle is playing on the tin kettle (piano) that is its new name. There is an F# that is dreadful and quite puts one out. I went this morning and got one or two little things for Granny at Hawkins and then we went on the pier where I was nearly blown away. Oh it wasn't a strong wind, only a slight breeze, but you know what a wafer I am becoming. . . . I feel so much better this morning, quite my little self again, you will be pleased.

Marion for her part was getting to depend on Maud's advice, and was even grateful to have a fault pointed out, writing, "Spencer dined here. Maud tells me I was snappish to Sp. at dinner, v.sorry had no idea or intention of being so." She also noted with pleasure how much drawing her daughter was doing, and felt that it showed real promise. Linley helped Maud a great deal and allowed her to sit with him while he worked, but it was always Marion who nourished the idea that something might be made of her talent. She was encouraged by the comments of various kind friends, "Everyone says how pretty Maud is, Mr Fildes much struck with her drawing."

The Sambournes and the Burnands remained firm friends, and at Christmas time Frank and Rosie Burnand were jollier than ever, dispensing hospitality in a most generous way. For five years running they invited all the Sambourne family to eat Christmas dinner with them in Royal Crescent and everyone enjoyed themselves hugely. In 1891 Marion wrote "Mrs Burnand sent after lunch to ask us to dine there all four. Delightful evening, no end of presents, wonder how it is done. 5/- for Maud in new money, 3/- for Roy". The next day the two families again spent the evening together to see the show which their children had been rehearsing for several days beforehand. "To Mrs Burnand's. V.pretty little play written by Rosie. 'A little

*Maud with a sketchbook,
posing for her father.*

breeze' for Winnie & Wilfred. 'Nigger Song' by Roy & Cuthbert, 'Folly Dance', Maud in that, & 'Neapolitan Song' by Mary & Ethel, v.pretty."

Two months later the Burnands put on a play at Ramsgate Theatre. "Maud & self walked to theatre after dinner. *Meg's Diversion* and *Marquis of Mince Pie* by Mrs Burnand. Mrs B excellent in both, Mr Hardy v.good, Winnie charming. Mr Warren (Maud's music master) as Marquis, fat & comely." Maud made a sketch of Mrs Burnand wearing her shepherdess costume, which she gave to her kind friends. Two days later Marion wrote delightedly in her diary, "Mr and Mrs F.C.B. to dinner. V.pleasant evening, all in good spirits. V.happy about Mr Burnand saying Maud's drawing of Mrs B should go into *Punch*!!! Seemed charmed with her drawing." Frank Burnand was as good as his word, so on 16 May 1892 Marion was able to write, "Maud's first drawing in *Punch*, looks charming." Three more were published in that paper during the next eighteen months, a most satisfactory début for a sixteen-year-old artist.

One less pleasant feature of the winter holidays in Ramsgate was the annual epidemic of influenza. This was an old disease which appeared in a new and virulent form in Europe at the end of the eighties. The first mention of it in Marion's diary was in December 1889: "Bitterly cold, hard frost, talk of influenza coming from Russia." The threat died away, but the following January it was "Mrs Hood's dance put off, all down with Russian influenza." In 1892 all England was shocked to hear

119

of the sudden death of the Prince of Wales' eldest son, The Duke of Clarence. "January 14th. Prince Edward of Wales died of influenza this morning" wrote Marion, and the next day, "Everyone talking of Duke's sad & sudden death, made doubly sad by his approaching marriage with Princess May." Later it was "To church with Maud, prayers for Royal Family in present sorrow & for cessation of plague of influenza." Many of the Sambournes' friends were also stricken: "Lin called & saw Mr Burnand, v.shocked to see how ill he looked", and "Terrible news of Mrs Warre's death from influenza." In spite of frequent bad colds and sore throats the Sambournes did not catch the disease, but it continued to take its toll each year, among rich and poor alike.

Marion arranged for Maud to be confirmed into the Church of England at St George's, Ramsgate in March 1892. Her own interest in Roman Catholicism was on the wane by this time, and she did not appear ever to have urged the children in that direction. Her doubts had probably reached a peak at the end of the eighties when she had written, "To Pro, fearfully crowded, Cardinal Manning preaching, wish I could believe & understand." Manning, like John Henry Newman, was an Anglican divine who had advocated High Church principles and then moved across into the church of Rome. Those who found the High Anglican liturgy attractive were often tempted to step over the boundary into Roman Catholicism. Frank Burnand was one such convert; he and his family must surely have had some influence in the Sambourne household. In London Marion went sometimes to the new Oratory at Knightsbridge: "Music beautiful, sermon commonsense which is more than can be had in our churches!" but satisfaction with her church at Ramsgate ("Very good new man") deflected her from Rome. Her comments on Maud's confirmation service were purely secular: "Darling Maud confirmed 3 o'clock by Bishop of Dover. Mrs S sat with me. Very pretty sight, Maud looked sweet in her dress, but all v.tired, took over 3 hours so many communicants."

The packing up and return to Stafford Terrace at the end of the winter holiday was another major effort. "March 24th, 1892. Busy packing all morning" wrote Marion. "March 25th. Alice & self to London with 6 boxes. Unpacked at Stafford Terrace in 1¾ hours. Found all much as usual, no more dust than if house had been empty. Brass evidently never polished & velvet on Cromwell chair spoilt but £80 is £80 and will cover small damages." She then went back to Ramsgate to finish packing up, and on 31 March wrote, "Return to London en masse by 1.15 train with 36 boxes! Lovely day, grand escapade with champagne in carriage. Dogs having battle royal under our skirts, had to drag them away from each other. Unpacked & nearly everything in place same night." But the family must have decided that the £80 was not worth all the effort involved, so the experiment was not repeated.

CHAPTER NINE
THE LONDON SEASON: FAMILY AFFAIRS

 N THE AUTUMN of 1890 the Sambournes heard that their friend Mr Watney was to be married. "Vernon Watney engaged !!! and v.happy" wrote Marion. The bride-to-be was Lady Margaret Wallop, daughter of the Earl of Portsmouth. Mr Watney's wealth made him an acceptable candidate for the hand of an Earl's daughter, but the thought surely crossed Marion's mind that this marked the end of a pleasant friendship. Mr Watney would have new acquaintances to entertain, and would distance himself from the more humble Sambournes. They were not invited to the wedding in February 1891, but the following June Marion received a letter from Lady Margaret asking them both to Tressady that September. Flattered and delighted, she hastened to invite the Watneys round to Stafford Terrace. On 13 July they came to dinner: "Very successful dinner, all went well & they stayed late. Lady M charming & full of fun."

It was eight years since Marion's last holiday in Scotland, and she must have been envying Linley his annual draughts of Highland air. Maud and Roy were sent to stay with Conrad while their parents caught the night mail to Scotland. It was an exhausting journey, via Perth and Inverness. "August 31st, 1891. Arrived at Tressady at 6, *very tired*. Lady M most kind." The Watneys had not laid on a proper house party: Vernon had invited the same sporting friends who had so often joined him before and Linley seems to have been the only one of the group to be married. Thus Marion found herself the sole lady guest. To begin with she was rather overawed by the aristocratic Lady Margaret and kept remarking on how kind, how sweet, how thoughtful, her hostess was, but she soon overcame her shyness and a very happy relationship was established. As the men were out shooting all day and Lady Margaret was expecting her first baby, Marion had a quiet time and her diary entries were not very exciting—"Took little walk round grounds with Lady M" or "Sat all morning talking & working with Lady M"—but she enjoyed herself very much. One day they went for a drive: "To see crofter's loom. Most interesting, wonderful the materials turn out so well, as the cottages are not clean!"

The following September the Watneys again asked the Sambournes to join them at Tressady. This time several other couples were also invited, so there were more people for Marion to talk to and the evenings were enlivened by games of whist and dumb-crambo. The men as usual were out all day, though the ladies sometimes joined them in sporting activities: "All played golf except Lady M & self." Marion and her hostess were now firm friends, with the extra bond of a baby to talk about. Lady Margaret was still considered "delicate" so the time passed pleasantly as before, sitting talking, going for drives, and meeting some aristocratic neighbours. "Had tea at Lady Fitzhardinge's. Lord F v.cross; Duke and Duchess of Wellington, Lord & Lady Westmorland & Mrs Antrobus there. House not nearly so large or as pretty as Tressady." A few days later another guest joined the Watneys' house-party: "Lady Frances Fortescue, v.pretty & charming manners" who brought with her a new occupation: instead of the usual sewing (always referred to as "work") it was now "knitting much in vogue".

These holidays in Scotland with the Watneys were an important stage in Marion's social career. The idea of the house-party, long familiar to the aristocracy, was filtering down to the *nouveaux-riches* and the comfortable middle classes. Though an earlier generation had considered a month the minimum length of time for a visit, the increasing speed and comfort of travelling meant that a fortnight was now quite long enough, and soon the weekend break was to become the height of fashion. The ingredients for successful entertaining were simple: a big house in the country, a convivial host and several appreciative guests; sport all day for the gentlemen, gossip for the ladies, and jolly games in the evenings for everybody. The house-party was a delightful way for the wealthy to display their possessions, and an essential part of the ritual was to invite people who would repay kindness by being either beautiful or witty. In the melting pot of Victorian society there were always those ready to swim to the top, and the Sambournes were more than willing to mingle with their betters. When they returned to London it was most gratifying to find that Lady Margaret continued as hospitable and kind in her town house as she had been in Scotland; she called several times at Stafford Terrace, invited the Sambournes to dinner to meet interesting people, and most important of all, took a great fancy to Maud.

Marion and Linley had always been busy on the fringes of smart society, but during the nineties they became more than ever involved in the London Season. The Private Views of the leading art galleries were the first events of importance each year, so at the beginning of May a typical entry in Marion's diary would be "To Academy & Grosvenor, met everyone!" In 1890 she wrote "To New Gallery, *crammed*," and "To Academy, exceptionally good, met endless friends." At these assemblies the elegant clothes which were to determine the look of each season had their first airing; in 1892 it was "Many pretty dresses, striped all the fashion, long skirts full sleeves & sashes to bottom of skirt."

Though May was a busy month, the Season did not reach its peak until June and July when all smart fashionable Londoners were caught up in a hectic round of entertainment. The Sambournes usually had a good choice of invitations to accept,

being asked to three or four parties each day. They made a point of attending at least two of them: "Delightful lunch at Mrs Boughton's about 24. Josephs, Dicksee, Cheeseborough, Grossmith, Ponsonby Chapmans etc etc. Only got up from lunch 4 o'clock & had delightful evening at Joshuas. Justin McCarthy took me in, Hunter, Laboucheres, Boughtons etc etc, home late" was one very typical day. Another was "To Windsor, delightful lunch with Hensman. Back to dinner Miss Rose-Innes, to Savoy, had double box close to stage", or "Lovely dinner Mrs Fagans, 8 o'clock. Mrs Moulton's at home 10 o'clock, lights all over square giving the grounds a vast appearance, splendid German band." It was of course impossible to accept every invitation, but one wonders how the less popular hostesses felt when they found that all the world had chosen to go elsewhere.

Besides all the at homes and dinners, the Sambournes were also being asked to a number of grander parties and receptions. Each season had its highlights: in 1890 it was "Mrs de la Rue's fancy dress ball, 10 o'clock. Prettiest ball I ever saw, costumes lovely. Returned 1.30, v.tired." Marion had chosen a yellow and black dress from Wittons (the theatrical costumiers) the previous day and wrote, "Mr Irving kindly sent dress & paid cab, unheard of kindness." Another big event the same year was "To Duchess of Sutherland's at home to meet Mr Stanley." The journalist Stanley had been a hero since his famous meeting with Livingstone at Ujiji in 1871. His latest exploit had been the rescue of Emin Pasha by the shores of Lake Albert, so all London was eager to meet him. "To Stafford House. Magnificent; hall, galleries & staircase lovely." Though Marion was delighted to see Stanley — "Dear little face" — it does not seem as if she was introduced to him.

In May 1891 the Marchioness of Salisbury held a reception at the Foreign Office. "Saw Prince of Wales, Prince Arthur Edward, Princess Christian, Princess Maud etc: on staircase each time they went up and down. Duke & Duchess of Portland, Sir R.Webster etc. Mr B.Tree only actor there, saw no other artists but ourselves." In July there was another grand function: "Marchioness of Salisbury's Garden Party, Hatfield House. Special train to & from Lady S's. Charmed with Hatfield, lovely old Elizabethan building with beautiful grounds. Saw Prince of Naples, Prince Edward of Saxe Weimar, Princess Louise etc. Millais, Tadema, Burne-Jones, Bosanquet, Sir F.Sullivan, large number of MPs corps diplomatique and nobility!" Marion was obviously very pleased to find herself in such distinguished company. Another notable event that year was the visit of the Emperor and Empress of Germany. Marion saw them at the opera on 8 July: "Emperor handsome, Empress plain & older looking, flowers exquisitely arranged in festoons all round house", and again on 9 July when they were at the Albert Hall. Two days later the Sambournes went to spend the day with Linley's cousin, Fanny Barker, at Wimbledon to watch the Emperor reviewing the troops on the Common.

The Sambournes' own entertaining remained on a fairly modest scale. The soirées, garden parties and weekend house parties given by so many of their acquaintances were quite impossible for them to emulate, but it is very noticeable from the diaries that the hospitality they dispensed fell very far short of that which they received. They did not attempt a big at home party themselves, even though the

drawing-room at Stafford Terrace was quite large enough to hold one. Fortunately it does not seem as if equal return was ever expected: those rich enough to put on lavish entertainments were happy to brighten the lives of the less well endowed. The Sambournes' regular dinner parties could, however, be made more impressive. The octagonal dining-table was satisfactory for fairly informal entertaining, but eight was too small a number of guests for an important dinner. Linley had a removable false top made for the table, so that twelve people could sit down in comfort. These larger dinners were very special occasions, needing a lot of thought and only taking place a few times in the year. Linley drew a seating plan in his diary each time, listed the wines, and made comments on the guests and the carefully chosen menu. The feeling in the air was that the Sambournes had at last "arrived".

Marion's dinner menus did not alter much over the years, the same type of food being served in the nineties as had appeared on the table in the seventies. Clear soup, cold salmon, roast chicken and roast lamb were the staple fare, and it is interesting to see that pork, or beef in any form except soup, was never offered, and they seldom appeared on other people's menus. Marion still occasionally wrote down what she ate when she went out: at Mrs Clarke's on 6 March 1893 it was "Oxtail soup, beautiful piece of salmon, cucumber and delicious sharp sauce. Saddle of mutton, jelly, potatoes and sprouts, quails well done, meringues, fruit salad, peaches red

Linley's photograph of the north end of the drawing room in 1892. Except for the piano, moved to the other end of the room in 1899, nothing has changed.

cherries and oranges, devils on horseback, etc all well served by one maid." She was always ready to admire other peoples' skills when it came to entertaining: "Most charming dinner at Col. Welbey's, silver, furniture, dinner all *perfect.*"

"Gentlemen only" dinners continued popular, and Linley held quite a few of these at Stafford Terrace during the nineties. On 11 July 1893 Marion wrote, "Out stores morning, spent £2.14.6. there. Arranged table etc. Caviare. Clear soup, cold salmon, chaud-froid pigeons, tomato salad. Roast lamb, peas etc. Haricots verts. Roast chicken, salad, Russian salad. Jelly, macedoine of fruit. Anchovy savoury cream cheese. Ices—pineapple cream, raspberry water. Grapes cherries greengages etc. All stayed till 2 o'clock, peals of laughter. 2 men waiters, Mrs Birley & girl." Linley noted the wines he had chosen in his diary: "12 bottles Ayala '80, 5 Geister '74, 2 Sauternes, 3 Burgundy." Later he added: "Very good dinner, 15 bottles champagne drunk. Slight bilious headache which lasted all day." The modern reader can only be surprised that the after-effect of such a meal was no more than a slight headache. Though Linley could work off excesses by hard exercise, he still became very stout in middle age, and his less active friends were probably even more portly. Many of them died young by present day standards—over-eating and heavy drinking must have been a contributory factor. From the late 1880s onwards Linley pasted cuttings from the daily papers into his diary; most of these are death and obituary notices of people that he knew. It was a very rare occurrence for any of them to have passed their sixty-eighth birthday; many died in their forties or fifties.

The beginning of the nineties ushered in a golden age for the theatre. Burlesque and other forms of light entertainment were flourishing with a new generation of actors and writers coming to the fore. The Sambournes, encouraged by their theatre-loving children, went more often than ever to the play: "Took chicks to see *English Rose* after dinner. Roy enjoyed it immensely, did us good to see him laugh." When Roy came home for the half-term weekend two visits to the theatre could be fitted in on the Saturday: "Dear Roy arrived 1.30, all to Court Theatre to see *Guardsman,* excellent. Roy & Lin to *Prodigal Daughter* after dinner 6.30." On another occasion Roy managed to go to three theatrical performances in two days. Marion's diary entries became more expansive than they had been in the early years: "April 15th, 1891. To Haymarket, *Dancing Girl* by H.A.Jones. Charming & original wonderfully well acted by B.Tree & Miss Neilson, enjoyed it immensely, lovely box. Not quite the piece to take young girls to see." (Implied moral disapproval like this is very rare in the diary.) Not all plays were uncritically enjoyed: "Lin & self to Criterion *Fringe of Society* awfully stupid came out early", and "Roy, Maud & self to Daly's Theatre saw *The Hunchback* but oh so dreary and dull, were densely bored." Henry Irving at the Lyceum was the most successful of the actor managers. His Shakespeare could always be relied upon: "Most delightful performance of *Much Ado about Nothing,* Irving & E.Terry better than ever, both looking

younger!" but his modern productions were not always so good, "To Lyceum, dull play very." However Irving had a big success with a new play in 1891: "Lin M & self to Lyceum, saw *Charles I* v.good, cried copiously!" and an even greater one in 1894, "Lin & Roy to first night of *Faust* & behind scenes after. Roy v.excited, Irving most kind to him, not home till 3."

The occasional foreign oddity gave spice to London theatrical life. Bernhardt was of course a great experience: "*La Dame aux Camelias*, enjoyed it immensely. La Sarah more wonderful than ever", and Marion was always eager to sample anything new: "To *L'enfant Prodigue* at Prince of Wales, dumb show with music, wonderful performance by French people *most* pathetic, could have cried heartily. Came away thoroughly satisfied having understood whole thing, wonderful." Most of the dramatic works mentioned in the diary are now quite forgotten, but it is interesting to read Marion's comments on plays which have stood the test of time. Wilde, Pinero and Shaw were beginning to write a new kind of domestic drama which delighted sophisticated London audiences with its wit and polish. Oscar Wilde's first play in 1892 took London by storm: "June 18th. To see *Lady Windermere's Fan*, charming piece dialogue excellent & acting as good." 1893 was a vintage year with several classics performed for the first time: "To see Pinero's new play *The Second Mrs Tanqueray*, enjoyed play immensely, Mr Watney took us to supper after at Willis' restaurant", and "Box for Globe, *Charlie's Aunt*, enjoyed play v.much". Wilde's second play *A Woman of No Importance* was deemed "Unpleasant but cleverly written", but all these productions were worthy of a second visit and *Mrs Tanqueray* (with Mrs Patrick Campbell in the lead) was declared "even better than first time".

1895 was another good year. The Sambournes saw two more plays by Oscar Wilde; in February, "Lin Maud & self to *The Importance of Being Earnest*. Most amusing play, smartly written", and in April, "To Criterion to see *An Ideal Husband* with Roy. Liked play immensely." In the autumn Linley's *Punch* colleague, George du Maurier, put his successful novel *Trilby* on the stage: "October 29th. Lin & self to rehearsal of *Trilby*. Delighted with piece, most original & D.Baird sweet & charming as Trilby, so natural & unstagey."

Scenic effects were much appreciated; costumes and lighting had never been better and productions vied with each other to impress the audience. "Lin Maud & self to Haymarket, *The Templar*, time of Chaucer. Piece much more interesting than we expected, wonderful scenery. Mr Guthrie met us there & Mr Tree came to our box. Mr W.S.Gilbert & Mr Goodall in stalls." Marion loved anything with music in it and though Linley would not go to a concert, he did not object to opera. Both of them preferred light pretty pieces, "Lin & self to opera, heard *Orfeo*, Gluck, & *Cavalleria Rusticana*, Mascagni—charming the last." Other pleasant evenings were *La Traviata*, cheerful & good", and "*Manon*, music charming so bright & full of melody, enjoyed it immensely."

The Gilbert and Sullivan operettas continued to be a popular treat for all the family, but the nearest Marion ever got to a comment was "Chicks v.interested in *Mikado*." However she must have enjoyed going to them, as in 1889 she had

A matinée at the theatre, 1899. Linley and Marion often went to a performance on a Saturday afternoon.

written, "Saw *Yeomen of the Guard* for fourth time" and in 1890 she went three times to *The Gondoliers*. The partnership between Gilbert and Sullivan split up after this production and when they got together again in 1893 for *Utopia Limited* the magic was no longer there. Sullivan went on composing for the theatre in the interim, but none of his new partners were thought to be as good as Gilbert. Marion seemed quite satisfied: "To see Sullivan's new play *Haddon Hall*" she wrote in 1892, "Mr Burnand thinks it bad. I liked it, music pretty, scenery charming, and dresses lovely." Frank Burnand was still a great man of the theatre and the Sambournes were among his most loyal supporters. In October 1890 it was "With Maud to Lyric to see Mr Burnand's piece *La Cigale*. House crowded, excellent piece", and some months later "To see *Cigale* for third or fourth time." In 1892 Burnand had another success: "Dined early & went to first night of Mr Burnand's & Le Coq's comic opera at Lyric, *Incognita*. Piece *well* received."

127

The south end of the drawing-room. The open drawers show Linley's photograph collection, all neatly docketted.

There was never any suggestion that Marion and Linley might move to a larger house; their finances were sufficiently stretched already. Besides, Stafford Terrace was very convenient, and Linley in particular had expended so much care on the decoration that he would have been loath to part with it even if they had had the money. Marion would have dearly loved more space as all the rooms had been filled and every surface covered ever since their marriage, but Linley had the collector's instinct and his urge to add yet more things was unabated. The over-crowding inevitably became oppressive: "Every corner in the house now fitted with corner cupboards" complained Marion, "Lin bought new desk in dining room" and "Two new arm chairs, it never rains but it pours with Lin, epidemic of chairs now!" It is disappointing that the inventory taken in 1891 when the house was let to Mrs Robb has not been preserved to enable a comparison to be made with the one taken in 1877, though Marion did make some lists in the front of her diary that year: "Blankets, Silver (counted with Jane), Linen, Glass, Best crested glass, Stable Furniture. . . ." Like everything else there was, by modern standards, more than enough, and it is sad that only a few pillowcases and tablecloths and a couple of dozen crested wine-glasses remain at Stafford Terrace.

Linley loved pottering about re-arranging his possessions, a trait which exasperated his wife who never came to terms with what she considered his time-wasting activities. "Lin putting up pictures on stairs all morning" she wrote, and it is easy to

*The drawing-room door, hung with
heavy draught-resisting curtains. The
upper panels are painted with a design
of sunflowers and butterflies; the lower
panels show the armorial bearings of the
Sambourne and Herapath families. The
pastel portrait on the right is by the
American artist, George Boughton.*

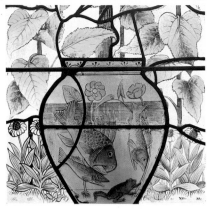

Above: The drawing-room takes up the whole of the first floor. The southern end served as Linley's studio; his easel can be seen at the back, silhouetted against the window.

Left: A detail from the south window: goldfish in a blue glass jar.

(vi)

imagine him spending hours moving them all about to get the close fit (no wallpaper showing) which is such a feature of the house today. Worse still was the amount of time spent on his favourite hobby: "Endless endless endless photography!" scrawled Marion angrily in September 1891, then listed her own good deeds for that day: "Polished two pieces of furniture, watered plants, practised one hour, looked out things for Roy, cut out cloth for armchair." In 1893 Linley had an idea which alleviated Marion's complaint, though it may have worried her in a different way: he joined a Camera Club which provided models for gentlemen to photograph. Artists had always considered the nude model essential for their work, so under this cloak of respectability Linley went once a week—sometimes twice or even three times— to take pictures of pretty young girls in provocative poses. As he did the developing at home and filed the prints in his ever-growing collection, Marion must have known what he was about. She may have decided that it was a harmless ploy which kept her husband happy. It does not appear to have affected their relationship, and she grumbled much less about the time he spent at home playing with his camera.

During the nineties the South American railway shares which were the backbone of the Herapath family's prosperity suddenly ceased to be safe holdings. In August 1890 Marion had written, "Fighting in Buenos Aires, v.anxious about Midge and Dora", and a few weeks later "Accounts of revolution very bad." All through 1891 things went from bad to worse in Argentina. Shares sank lower and lower and Marion had to borrow money from the bank because her securities were so badly affected. "Feel tired & worried no money and can't pay my own bills & yet want so many things, *must* go without" was one entry in her diary. It is not clear where she made the economies. "M & self shopping, 4d hair pins, 1/3 candle shades, 4/3 chemist for glycerine curling tongs and powder. M's shoes 3/11, veils 1/6" all seem much as usual, but perhaps she cut down on the entertaining as later in the year she wrote, "Books better, could afford cab, 1/-." Naturally she was aggrieved when Linley continued to spend lavishly on his own hobbies: "No expense spared in *stables*—carriage worries increase, medicine for horses, harness does not fit !!! etc etc." By October 1891 she was really gloomy, "Wrote to Mr Welch about my quarter, not yet paid. Everything *v.bad* in Buenos Aires, wish I had invested in safe English securities. When shall we ever learn to profit by others' experience!" She asked her bank manager what to do: "Took list of securities to Mr Lowndes, advised me to hang on as all are so low just now." Marion might have done better to follow her inner promptings, as the Langleys (who came back to England for the summer) did not hold out much hope. "Things worse & worse—Ham thinks all South American securities will go below par." Midge and Hamilton went back to Buenos Aires in November, taking Mervyn with them ("Mother very upset"), but by the following summer they were able to send back better reports. Everyone except Edgar began to feel more cheerful: "Edgar came, spent long afternoon, v.austere."

Only the Fletchers seemed immune from financial anxiety. Hamilton Fletcher had inherited his father's shipping fortune and had little to do except find ways of spending it. He bought his first steam yacht, the *Scarf*, in 1890, and the following year he changed it for the larger *Columbine*. Thus yachting was now added to the Sambournes' pleasures when they went to stay at the Fletchers' new house, The Anchorage, near Christchurch. Cruises up and down the Solent became regular treats, though Marion and her sisters really preferred sitting gossiping together on the beach, or going for a little gentle shopping: "With Tabs & Midge to Bournemouth, bought pears 9*d*, honey 1/- buns 6*d*, chiffon 8/9*d*, buttons 4*d*, staybones 1/1*d*, hairpins 2*d*." If they gave way to the men's insistence, it was usually disastrous: "All went on yacht at 11 o'clock for Bournemouth Regatta. Came on to rain heavily, thunder and lightening. Felt v.bad, ill, Maud also, had to go below. Lin brought us ashore & home by rail, thankful to be back again." The arrival of the French fleet for manoeuvres in the Solent that day caused great excitement. Such an event could only really be appreciated from the deck of a yacht, so the two Hamiltons, Linley, Maud and Roy all went off for a long happy day afloat.

Tabby often came up to London for a brief visit, when she and Hamilton always stayed in the best hotels. She would call at Stafford Terrace to see the Sambournes, and go with Marion on shopping expeditions or to the theatre. Tabby was the prettiest of the Herapath sisters, and Marion often wrote, "Tabs looking lovely", or some other complimentary remark. Although young Mrs Fletcher was probably very expensively dressed, Marion did not feel the same compulsion to record Tabby's clothes as she did Ada Spencer's, except on rare occasions. "To see Tabs in her presentation dress. White satin with rich gold embroidery all round, edged with white ostrich feathers, train lined with gold embroidery 4 inches deep" she wrote in the spring of 1891. This dress would have cost Hamilton Fletcher a great deal of money, as must the portrait of his wife which he commissioned Jacomb-Hood to paint the following year. Marion went to sit with her sister to amuse her while the picture was painted, but she made no comment on the portrait itself. Presentations and portraits were not to come her way, but she never gave any indication that she envied the Fletchers their wealth, or felt uncomfortable because she was a poor relation. It was left to Maud to be critical, and in her letters she was surprisingly sharp. She disliked Hamilton and thought Tabby selfish and vain, the exact opposite of her own mother, who in her eyes could do no wrong.

One thing always on Marion's mind was the problem of how to cope with her mother-in-law. It seems that Mrs Sambourne was spending as much, or more, time with the family as ever, but though there was the occasional grumble, "Mrs S v.disobliging" or "Mrs S in bed all day, much nicer in drawing room in consequence!" Marion must have decided that the best course of action was to take as little notice of her problem as possible. A whole year passed without a single

reference to Mrs Sambourne in the diary, other than as a travelling companion to and from Ramsgate. On 1 April 1892, the day after the family returned to London from their winter holiday, Marion at last did something that Linley should have insisted upon years ago: "Went after lunch hunting for rooms for Mrs S. Saw beautifully clean rooms in Edwardes Square, much taken with them, ask only £1.0.0. a week all told." Four days later the transfer was made: "Took Mrs S in cab to her rooms, Maud came later with flowers. Untold relief!"

The new arrangement worked wonderfully well. Marion called regularly at Edwardes Square and was as patient and kind as she could bring herself to be. She sat whole afternoons with her mother-in-law, took her for drives in the carriage, supplied her with little delicacies, and made sure that the children visited her often. When staying with Tabby at the seaside that August she wrote in her diary, "Sent wire to Mrs S for her birthday — 81 — *que Dieu ne m'accordera pas une aussi longue vie!*" In September, back at Stafford Terrace, she wrote, "Mrs S here, is really v.well, pottered up & down", though there were still many bad days, "Saw Mrs S, found her well, but as usual weepy & complaining."

In October Mrs Sambourne went on one of her periodic visits to her sister in Ealing. Marion drove there with her and lunched with Mrs Linley, her son Arthur, and daughter Alice. She went back to London with a light heart, but ten days later wrote in her diary: "November 5th. 1892. Shopping morning. Returning met Maud who told me of telegram received from Ealing, dear Mrs Sambourne passed peacefully away at 10 o'clock last evening after only one day's illness. Lin rode over to Ealing, I drove. Saw Alice & Arthur, stayed some time. Mrs Sambourne looked most peaceful. Her body brought here at 9.30 & now rests in the morning room. Dear Lin terribly cut up." The next day, "Lin slept badly. Poor Mrs Sambourne closed at 11 o'clock", and the day after, "Lin arranged about funeral tomorrow. Kind letters from everyone about dear Mrs Sambourne."

It is ironic that only in death could Frances Sambourne be called "dear" by her daughter-in-law. Linley was genuinely distressed, but Marion found conflicting feelings of relief, guilt, and remorse hard to reconcile. It was "all so sad & sudden" and "the one I wished to be kind to but could never love" had departed so unexpectedly that she felt quite stunned. The struggle to be a good daughter-in-law had lasted eighteen years; now it was all over. If any ghosts haunt Stafford Terrace that of Frances Sambourne is the most likely. A portrait of her as a young woman hangs on the bedroom wall, but it is her ivory walking-stick in the hall which is most evocative. How often, one wonders, must Marion have heard the tap of that stick approaching and steeled herself to be bright and kind — and how often had she failed in her resolution.

The few remaining male members of the family gathered for Mrs Sambourne's interment at Highgate Cemetery. Roy was sent for from Eton, and went with his father to the family grave. There they were joined by Arthur Linley and also by Mervyn Herapath, representing Marion's side of the family. After the brief service Linley took Roy to his club, where, man to man, they relieved their feelings with a good lunch. This was Roy's first experience of a funeral and it naturally made a great

impression on him. The following day Marion wrote, "Darling Roy returned to school, been so dear & good."

On the very day that Mrs Sambourne died Marion had another shock, this time about her mother's money. What the family had long suspected was true: "Letter from Edgar, deficit of Welch and Chapple £12,000 odd. Mother has received £500 a year less than she should have done—they are unable to account for over £7,000." What had happened is not clear. Some time earlier Marion had written, "Aunt Anna told me of Mr Chapple's wicked behaviour" and from other stray hints it seems that there was suspicion of embezzlement, but nobody had realised that the Herapath money was at risk. As soon as Edgar grasped the situation he acted with commendable swiftness and efficiency. He put all his mother's affairs into the hands of Messrs Lee and Pemberton, wrote to each member of the family, and went down to see Marion at Ramsgate where they discussed what should be done next: "Edgar came, talked about affairs, things bad but better than dared hope."

All this was very distressing to Mrs Herapath, who was far from well. "My own dearest Polly," she wrote, " Oh how I wish I could come to see you if only a day or two it would make me so happy but I cannot manage it I fear. I shall not have any money till after Christmas but plenty of paper in my cheque book which can only be used for lighting gas. . . . When do you think you shall be in London again? I miss you awfully this evening. I am trying to finish this scrawl in bed for I have not had half an hour's sleep all night. . . ." On receipt of this letter Marion took the next train up to London to see her mother and try to dispense a little comfort and cheer. By March 1893 things were still not settled: "Long letter from Edgar about estate, unsatisfactory."

Mrs Herapath had used Westwood very little during the last three years. It had proved impossible to find a tenant in 1891 or 1892, and none of the children wanted to live in the old family home. With its servants, its gardeners, coachman, horses and carriages (all essential for comfortable country living) Westwood was a heavy drain on her depleted resources. It was inevitable that the painful decision to sell would have to be taken soon. In the spring of 1893 an auction was held of the contents of the house: Mrs Herapath, accompanied by Linley, went down to save a few sentimental relics. "Sale of all the dear old furniture at Westwood. So passes away one more link with the dear past", wrote Marion sadly on 27 April, adding "Lin has bought goods amounting to over £10." A few days later: "Lin put up barometer from dear Westwood" in the hall at Stafford Terrace. The house itself did not find a buyer for a long time, so that although Mrs Herapath economised on the running expenses, the estate received no injection of capital.

CHAPTER TEN
MAUD GROWING UP:
COUNTRY HOUSE VISITING

 AUD HAD HER seventeenth birthday in August 1892. Her education was nearly finished: next spring she would be "out" and able to taste all the pleasures of the grown-up world. The fairy godmother at her christening had bestowed not only good looks and a happy temperament, but also that other mysterious and not always welcome gift: sexual attraction. Photographs taken by her father during these teenage years show a pretty girl with a sweet expression, not yet a beauty, but graceful in every pose. As a child Maud had been admired and petted by the adults; on emerging from adolescence she soon discovered the excitement of having a crowd of young admirers at her feet. This letter, written in September from Ramsgate where she was staying with the Burnands, shows the awakening of the butterfly:

> My own darling Mother. How I wish you were here, your 'wing' misses you so!!!! I shall be awfully sorry to leave here as I have enjoyed myself so much. Ethel goes to the Convent tonight—how thankful I am I have not got to go to school. How lonely you would be!!!!!! I am waited on hand and foot by all the boys down here—I have only to express a wish and it is gratified at once—like so many little slaves. The night of the dance one boy had my fan another my programme another my little shawl. Mary doesn't see it at all and it makes her cross. . . .

The Sambournes spent the winter in Ramsgate as usual. On 11 April 1893 they returned to London and Marion at once began to prepare Maud for her first season. Short skirts and shoulder-length hair were banished for ever: a sophisticated young lady was expected to replace the scatterbrained adolescent overnight. To complete the transformation a whole new wardrobe was necessary, and for the first time Maud was taken to an expensive shop to buy an evening dress. "Went with Maud to

133

Maud in 1893. One of her Punch *drawings that year was taken from this photograph. Although she used her father's methods, Maud's style was very delicate and her drawings have great charm.*

order her dress at Woollands" wrote Marion and five days later expressed her delight at the success of her daughter's first London party: "April 20th. Lady Reed's dance, 112 Cromwell Road. M looked sweet in her new white muslin, had heaps of partners and seemed much admired. Lin paid M's dress £6.6.0. and gloves 7/11."

This was only the preliminary canter for the big social whirl. Maud needed more dresses, but already Marion had left it a little late. "May 13th. Took Maud to Liberty's. Got material for 3 dresses, green, pink, and white. Manning and Witton unable to make anything for a fortnight!!! Cut out pink dress and worked away at it." She had to work hard and fast as Maud had been asked to stay at the Watneys' country house (Middleton, near Longparish in Hampshire) on 19 May. This was to be her first experience of visiting as a grown-up, without mother, governess or girl friend of her own age, so Marion sent her off with many admonitions to behave well, and much worry about her wardrobe. The Watneys, however, lived simply, the house was not very grand, and Lady Margaret was, as always, delightfully unaffected and kind. It was an ideal introduction to adult manners and society, but even so Maud felt a little homesick. As she had only just recovered from a feverish cold Lady Margaret took great care of her. There was plenty of quiet time in which to write long letters home and these charming artless missives tell us more about the characters in this story than a mature writer could possibly convey.

My darling Mother. I am longing to hear from you, it seems ages since Friday. Lady Margaret is simply an angel so sweet in fact the sweetest woman I know bar you. Every little thing she thinks of. I have hot lemon and water by my bed every night. My cough has gone off my chest and is now ending up in my head which is really much better although not so comfortable. Baby is a duck and Mr Watney is simply devoted to her he is always carrying her about and playing with her. . . . This place is glorious, so pretty! I am entreated to do everything I like and pick the flowers in fact it would be Eden if you and Papa were here too.

My own darling Mother. I am spiritually jumping with delight as I have your letter now. How wicked of 'It' to keep 'Its own' waiting so long!!! My cold is ever so much better in fact quite well now. One couldn't possibly feel nervous with dear Lady Margaret! And Mr Watney is so particularly kind to me! Oh how different from relations one is waited on handsomely from hand to foot all the smallest requirements gratified. . . . Lady Margaret likes all my little frocks so much. I must say myself that the pink evening dress is quite lovely on and so comfortable. I only wish I had another evening frock as warm. . . .

What it is to be rich and as happy as Lady Margaret is! She is always saying how happy she is and how good Mr Watney is in giving her everything and that little gem of a baby you would love it so. Lady Margaret goes about like the spirit of love doing kind things, never on any account saying things that make one feel small. So clever too. Only fancy darling what you would be if you hadn't to worry over books and add up sums and weep at the end of them. . . .

Everyone dresses so tremendously in the evening especially Lady Margaret who looked grand and majestic last night. She wore a lovely striped yellow and white satin brocade with a sweet little spotted muslin front and sleeves and big collar. . . . If you could send me a pretty rose pink sash with ribbon to match for my neck and sleeves I should be so glad. Not a meagre narrow ribbon but a nice wide sash 4 ½ yards long and 2 ½ yards pink ribbon for the sleeves and if 'It' likes 'Its own' to have a small narrow choker and bow at the side 1 ½ yards of narrower than that of the said sleeves. I find it is in evening frocks I am a little short. Everyone wears jackets all day, I ought to have had a black jacket but never mind it is of no consequence.

7 o'clock. I have been strolling in the garden to pick a flower for my dress. How lovely the country is! Darling when we are rich together what a time we will have. You shall have your own little greenhouse to potter in and grape vine to dress, your own room to put tidy as you will. . . . I am sure you want me back to rumple up and scatter

about and make untidy those new-pin rooms. What must the house look like so scrupulously neat, not one hair even left to straggle on the carpet. I can see you now smiling quietly to yourself and turning out the cupboards undisturbed. Goodness knows what has been done, poor me! I hope you are counting the demi-seconds for the time when we shall once more be united. I am in full form, my old colour has returned to my pallid cheeks. Oh darling how I wish you were enjoying the lovely country with me, it's the only blot not having you and Papa. Heaps of love, ever your devoted Maud.

Maud returned from the Watneys' at the end of May and found a string of invitations waiting for her. Marion and Linley were busier than ever establishing contacts and making new friends, and Marion must have worked hard to arrange such a full programme of parties and visits. The word would have been put round that the Sambournes were launching a pretty daughter, so as well as invitations to several dances which were specifically arranged for young people, Maud was asked to all the at homes and weekends to which her parents were invited. "June 12th. To Mrs Cohen's Englefield Green till Wednesday. Mr Cohen met us at Egham, drove to Round Oak, charming place, tea under trees. Maud much noticed by Mr Palmer." There were other outings to ensure that Maud met the right people: "To Mrs Peto's Knowlton Court until Tuesday, house party", and "With Maud to Mrs Ionides for day. Took cab at Reading, charming house."

Marion did not accompany Maud to dances though she often sat up waiting for her to return. "Mrs Holl's dance, Maud going with the Orchardsons. Home 2.30. I let her in." Sometimes she was escorted to a function by one of the maids, or the coachman would take her and wait to bring her back. "Miss Holland's small evening party, Maud had carriage, enjoyed it immensely." Of course Maud would never have gone to a party without her parents unless there was some older lady present who had promised to be her chaperone. Once Marion wrote, "Lin Maud & Mary Nicol to Mrs Henderson's dance. No introducing so did not enjoy it much." Without a kind and efficient hostess to make sure that every girl had a partner, a dance lost half its point, as it was not possible to talk to a member of the opposite sex without first being introduced.

It was not only Maud who was enjoying herself. Marion was busy too and had to replenish her own wardrobe. A big dance given that year by Mme de Souberville at Queens Gate Hall must have required a new gown: "July 19th. Home 2.30 from largest private dance I ever went to. Madame had 96 to dinner first at Queens Rooms and most gorgeous supper served hot & cold at 1 o'clock, perfect everything." In spite of her oft repeated vow never to patronise Madame Bocquet again, Marion could not manage without at least one expensive new dress each season. In 1893 she invested in a black satin evening dress at 14 guineas, ordered a fawn and black dress at 10½ guineas, had a grey dress made over and a black bodice altered. With all Maud's new clothes it was an expensive year: "V.worried over books, expenses seem to increase & I cannot keep them down. Cabs, money for

Maud etc etc, & Lin paying me only bare housekeeping money. Have already overdrawn £3.19.3. from private account leaves me only £21.1.0. in hand" wrote Marion anxiously. She was obliged to resort to a second-hand clothes dealer (called Vieux Habits) who came to the house discreetly, but she seldom got more than a pound or two out of him.

Some welcome extra money came from the exhibition of drawings which Linley held in June. "Lin busy all day hanging his pictures at Fine Art Gallery" wrote Marion, and the next day, "Lin Maud & self to see Lin's drawings. They look beautiful, I was delighted with them. Many drawings already sold." The show opened on 3 June: "Private view of dear Lin's drawings at Fine Art Gallery. *Very* crowded, great success, drawings look charming." The prestige was almost more important than the money; Marion must have felt very proud as the fashionable world flocked to the gallery to admire and buy her husband's work.

That summer the Sambournes were reminded of their old friend, Sir Edgar Boëhm, and his connection with the royal family: "To see the Queen pass by on way to uncover the statue of herself by the Princess Louise in Kensington Gardens" was Marion's entry on 28 July 1893, "saw well, but unfortunate thunder shower came on just as they were passing." The imposing white marble statue of Queen Victoria by her daughter overlooks the Round Pond; its inscription must have been read by thousands, and it is an interesting example of the work of a female pupil being better known than any by the master. Not many people, on seeing the Wellington monument at Hyde Park Corner, or the statue of Carlyle on the Embankment, would be able to name the sculptor as Joseph Edgar Boëhm.

Maud was asked to spend another fortnight in the country in July, a visit which was to have far-reaching consequences. "Maud to Mrs Messel, Nymans, Crawley. Saw her off by 4.20 train with Mr Messel & son" wrote Marion. In London the Messels lived at 8 Westbourne Terrace; the Sambournes knew them well enough to have been asked to dinner there a few times and Maud was quite friendly with Ruth Messel, who was a year older than herself. However from the tone of the letters which she wrote while staying at their country home it does not seem as if she knew the rest of the family very well. The Messels had been bankers and financiers in Darmstadt, Germany, for two generations. Ludwig Messel was born 1847; he and his brother Rudolph emigrated to England in 1871 after the Franco-Prussian war. Both became rich and successful: Ludwig founded the stockbroking firm of L. Messel & Co. which prospered exceedingly; Rudolph made a fortune by improving a process for manufacturing sulphuric anhydride (used in dyes and explosives). The third Messel brother, Alfred, remained in Germany where he became a well known architect. Ludwig married an English girl, Anne Cussans, and had two sons and four

Leonard Messel, taken at Oxford, where he was an undergraduate.

daughters. In 1890 he purchased a country estate for his family; this was Nymans in Sussex, a smallish Georgian house which he enlarged greatly, adding a tower and a huge conservatory. Here he was able to indulge his passion for gardening, carrying out extensive planting of rare trees and shrubs obtained from expeditions, which he helped to finance to distant parts of the world. His eldest son, Leonard, was twenty-one in 1893: he had been educated at Eton and Oxford and was soon to join his father's firm.

Maud found everything about her visit to Nymans quite delightful. The house was situated on top of a hill and the magnificent view — which she admired greatly — was not yet obscured by new plantations. The eldest girl in the Messel family, Ottilie, was away, while Leonard and the second boy, Harold, did not appear until Maud had established good relations with Hilda, Ruth and the four-year-old Muriel. Thus she felt less shy than she had at Lady Margaret's, but she still missed her mother's company and wrote home every day:

My own darling. You see I never forget to write much less think of you which I do always and long for you to be with me. Roy will soon be back to console you for my being away—one chicken at a time. Oh how I wish you were here so much, you would love it just as much as I do! Mrs Messel told me to tell you she was quite touched at your kindness in sending fruit to her sister. Of course I am not surprised as you are so unselfish and sweet. I have never seen any other mother so dear! or ever shall. I only wish your Wing could do likewise and think a little less of her own little self! It does one quite good to be with Ruth she is so good and dear to everyone and has the most tremendous influence over her brothers. They simply adore her and baby also. Mr Lennie is very kind to me and so are they all. Ruth said she would have to get quite jealous because Mrs Messel never likes any girls but her own. I have never enjoyed myself so much in all my life bar being away from you darling. . . .

Only fancy going to Tabs after being here, won't it be beastly to stay in a place where one is always in the way instead of where one is a favourite with the whole house. . . . You have no idea the impression you made at the Messels' dinner party—Ruth told me! They delight my heart by saying I am just like you! So I am, I always said so, its only people with defective sight who won't allow it. . . . I have been dressing dolls for Ruth's Sunday school children. Last night I was finishing the doll's frock and Lennie was so anxious to do it so I let him. He sewed the frill all round the neck and also the sleeves. The garments we made on the lawn were hardly fit for public observation, even on dolls they seem to be rather—!!!. [here Maud drew sketches of frilly underwear.] I don't think I ever stayed in such a jolly house. They won't hear of my returning Monday. They say you may expect me when you see me sometime later, isn't it dear of them. I miss you so much darling and only wish you were here to enjoy the lovely country as I do.

Marion must have been worried that Maud was being spoilt by too much attention at the Messels. An admonitory letter drew the following reply, one of the few in which Maud struck a serious note:

I am sorry you think I am conceited but I see my faults through a magnifying glass—my good qualities are so few, the only one is my love for you and Papa. Some day when I am rich (but not through those beastly South American things) you and Papa and Roy will take up your abode with me.

Maud returned from Nymans on 8 August. "Fetched dear Maud from Vic Station, met Mrs Messel there, M looking so well" wrote her mother. Five days later the Sambournes went down to Christchurch for their usual fortnight with the Fletchers. This time Mrs Herapath joined the party. Marion had been unwell, so "Sat out all

Buscot Park. Maud was enormously impressed with all the luxuries (including electric light) which she found when she stayed here with the Hendersons in 1893.

day with dear Mother & feel much better" was unfortunately followed by "Horrid neuralgia all night, dear Mother seedy too with pain in back. Think we have been unwise in sitting out so long and so late without jackets or hats." However they were well enough next day to go for a little cruise in Hamilton's new yacht, the *Alba*, and, as always, plenty of boating, tennis, and cricket was laid on for the entertainment of the other members of the family.

Maud went back to London with her parents on 29 August and then travelled with them in the train up to Scotland. She stopped off at Aberdeen to stay with Mary Nicol, while Marion and Linley went on to the Watneys at Tressady. Mr and Mrs Nicol were old friends of the Sambournes, and Maud was sure of a hearty welcome there. She wrote to her mother:

> I am having a *ripping* time here, *simply delightful*. I never enjoyed myself more! Today we are going to the Games isn't it splendid every day something on. The Ball is on Friday, only think how excited I am over it. . .

This was Maud's first really grand ball and it more than came up to expectations:

Never have I enjoyed myself so much as last night. We were a party of nine, 6 men and 3 ladies, just what it ought to be. . . . We had an 8 mile drive leaving here at 8.30 and arriving there at 9.30. They had a magnificent tent on the lawn and a band—simply a dream! I had heaps of partners, my program could have been filled over fifty times, there was a rush directly I got there, well its a compliment to you darling as I am your Wing.

As soon as Maud got back from Scotland she was off on another visit. This time she went with her father to stay with the Hendersons at Buscot Park, Oxfordshire. Mr Henderson was a rich industrialist and connoisseur, a great patron of contemporary art. Ostensibly the purpose of the visit was for the gentlemen to have a few days shooting; probably Mrs Henderson had asked Maud to come as well to help amuse her large family of six sons and one daughter. Maud had been to stay with three wealthy families already that year, but she was nevertheless staggered by the standard of living at Buscot Park:

> My own darling Mother. Oh my goodness what a place!!!!!!!! You never saw anything to equal it under the sun—no never because I never have!!!!!!! My room is much too much for me to describe, it makes me think of the Tinder Box in Andersen's Fairy Stories when the poor little common soldier came in for all that enormous fortune and married the Princess. Oh darling their bread's been well buttered, only far too much for the bread. When I'm rich I think I will leave a few things found wanting its so monotonous to have everything one's heart can wish for. Of course the whole thing is wrong—'Lay not up for yourselves treasures on earth where moth and rust doth corrupt' etc. If only the rust and dear little moth were here just a little it would be much nicer. Electric light all over my room, and I have amused myself by turning it all on at once. It's on over my bed so that I shall be able to see to read and no trouble striking a match.

Maud had not done badly for her first ventures into the grown-up world of wealth and pleasure. The transition from child to adult was very sudden in those days and it was quite a strain for a sheltered eighteen-year-old girl to have to cope with the stresses and pitfalls of a social season on her own. Luckily Maud had been used to plenty of intelligent adult company; she had probably enjoyed more freedom in her formative years than many of her upper-class contemporaries, and her lack of serious education was a positive advantage. Her comment on Mrs Henderson's only daughter was revealing: "Maggy I don't much care for. Like most of these tremendously highly educated girls she hasn't much to talk about and is not amusing. The boys are quite nice, all handsome, the girl least good looking of all." It is not difficult to imagine what Maggy Henderson (or all the other plain shy girls) must have felt about Maud's good looks, easy manners, and instant popularity.

There were no more visits arranged that year and the autumn passed comparatively quietly. Some of the young men whom Maud had met on her travels came to

call at Stafford Terrace, Leonard Messel among them. The Sambournes did not go to Ramsgate until 20 December, and there Maud had to deal with another admirer, Bill Weigall, one of the local boys whom she had known for years. Marion did not approve of this suitor and was obviously alarmed by the thought that her daughter might throw herself away on a nobody: "Maud and self to St George's to avoid B.W. Met him on parade, walked with Maud whilst I was speaking to Mrs Hoad. Seems v.fond of Maud, pity as it's quite hopeless." A week later, "Maud showed me B.W's letter to her. *Je crois qu'il aime, mais l'amour ne veut rien sans argent.*" Although Marion herself had chosen love without money she did not recommend this course to her daughter; in fact she must have dreamt of a brilliant match for Maud ever since the child had begun to show promise of being a beauty. The introductions, visits and dances arranged for her education and pleasure all had a serious purpose, and Maud herself was well aware of her mother's expectations. She did not rebel: the advantages of wealth were abundantly obvious. Had she fallen in love with a poor man Marion would no doubt have given in gracefully, but though Maud was flattered by the attention she received from her numerous admirers, her heart remained untouched.

Christmas 1893 was the last holiday that the Sambourne family took all together at Ramsgate. On 8 January 1894 they dined with the Burnands, then returned to London next day, having been away for less than three weeks. Possibly Marion wished to remove her daughter from the vicinity of B.W, and Maud was no doubt eager to continue the exciting round of parties in London, where there were so many people ready to shower her with compliments: "Took Maud to Mrs Joachim's who said she had looked sweet at ball & was much admired", and "To Mrs Thompson's where Oscar Wilde devoted his attention to Maud & was most kind" were two of Marion's entries in the spring of 1894.

Marion was busier that year than she had ever been before. Her regular Tuesday at homes were so well attended that she had to ask Linley if she might take over the drawing-room; what with her own friends, Maud's girl friends who came to stay, and all the young men who clustered round, the morning-room was far too cramped. "February 13th. Fourteen people called", and soon this was a figure taken for granted. In spite of all the activity Maud still found time to work at her drawing, and Marion continued to encourage her. "Maud received cheque £8.8.0. for her four drawings illustrating poem, *Pall Mall* magazine" she wrote in April. (This was double the young artist's previous payment from *Punch* and must have pleased her very much.) Another entry was "Maud & self to call on Mr George Allen at 156 Charing Cross Road about illustrating book." Whether Marion felt that it was necessary for her daughter to have some way of earning a living, or whether Maud was ambitious on her own account is not clear. There seems little doubt that she

One of Maud's pencil and wash drawings.

could have done well as an illustrator, for her drawings were improving and they have a charm and delicacy all their own.

The Sambournes went as usual to all the exhibitions in town, and to numerous dinner parties. "February 19th. To Burlington House Old Masters. 5 delightful Turners 2 Romneys 2 Canalettos 2 Walkers quite lovely, Jan Steen's pleased us most. Saw Blake's mad productions. Lunched at St James's. To New Gallery, Japanese collection interesting no doubt to those who understand, we don't! Dinner at Mrs Leng's, more amusing than usual, Maud much admired." Another evening very much to Marion's taste was 11 March. "To Mrs Joachim's. Dr Joachim played magnificently with Piatti & again with Lady Hallé. Delightful evening, v.crowded. Mr Joachim took me in to supper & amused me vastly grumbling at everything."

As the season of 1894 got under way more invitations poured in to Stafford Terrace, with a peak of seven parties on 23 June. "To Mrs de la Rue's dinner, heard about the Souls" was one entry in the diary. "The Souls" was the name (first given in jest) of a group of wealthy well-connected people who appeared to have mastered the art of truly gracious living. Lord Curzon, Arthur Balfour, the Wyndham and Tennant families, Lady Desborough, Lord and Lady Elcho and Violet Duchess of Rutland were at the centre of this group, but many lesser luminaries circled round them. The men were nearly all outstanding in the world of politics, the women beautiful and artistic, skilled hostesses who entertained lavishly in their great houses

in London and the country. The Sambournes' richer friends and relations were able to adopt a similar style of living, but none of them had the magic touch of glamour which marked the Souls as something apart. Though Marion herself never met the people who had set the fashion, all her reports of grand dinners and house parties can be read as echoes of this ideal life.

At the end of July it was once again time to set off on the country-house circuit. Maud was invited to Buscot Park for "Cricket Week", and from there she went on to visit Mrs Clowes who was hosting another large party of young people at Hitchen. Meanwhile Marion, Linley and Roy set off to stay with the Galbraiths at Ayton Castle, in the Scottish border country. The Galbraiths were old London friends who, as was customary among the wealthy, regularly rented a big country house (complete with staff) for that part of the year which was devoted to sport and country pleasures. "By 10 o'clock train from King's Cross," wrote Marion, "Long journey, train crowded. Most delightful house, v.large standing on a steep hill with exquisite views all round & built in red sandstone with the curious round towers peculiar to Scottish mansions." The next day was Sunday. "To church—sermon on Mercy far better than I hear in London! After luncheon went round stud, saw 29 horses, v.interesting. Sat in garden with Mrs Galbraith, the loveliest garden I have ever seen. Air bracing & I feel already worlds better. Roy playing tennis & Lin wedded to camera all afternoon." The whole visit passed very happily, and the Sambournes returned home on 16 August for a brief spell in London before going to the Watneys again.

This time it was Maud's turn to accompany her parents. After the usual pleasant fortnight at Tressady, they all three went on to the Nicols at Banchory: "Find house most comfortable & cheery, large fires everywhere & flowers most exquisite. Lovely garden & the most marvellous raspberries I ever saw" wrote Marion, appreciative as always of the good things in life. Linley and Maud then stayed in Scotland for another week while Marion went south to join Roy, who had been staying with Conrad and Effie in Sussex. "Roy looks v.well & seems happy with them all, cousins get on splendidly." By now Effie had three sons: Geoffrey, eight years old, Claude six, and a new baby, Fitzroy. Dora was there too, the Langleys having returned after a long spell in South America; she was twelve, so perhaps Roy, who was just sixteen, enjoyed having a band of hero-worshipping little cousins at his heels.

Meanwhile Maud was continuing her progress round the country. In September she went to stay with Mr and Mrs Galbraith at Ayton Castle for a fortnight. Here she found a group of young people (not the older couples who had made up the party when her parents had been there earlier, as the Galbraiths had a long succession of visitors throughout the summer and the mix was always changing). She wrote to her mother:

> I hear all sorts of little tales about you—you are a great favourite
> here darling with both Mr and Mrs Galbraith they say all sorts of
> nice things about you *both* and I can tell you its no humbug for I can
> see very well that Mrs Galbraith is not fond of everyone.

Above: The drawing-room, looking north. The Broadwood piano has an orange silk embroidered cover, on which stand family photographs and a fan autographed with many famous names.

Left: A china model of Punch, a brass statuette and a photograph of Linley Sambourne on a small table.

The morning-room. Sheraton-style furniture and oil-paintings in heavy gilt frames give this room a different character from the others. The stained glass was put in when the Sambournes first moved into the house and is much less elaborate than the later glass in the drawing-room. The original gasoliers in the main rooms were replaced with electric light fittings in 1896.

Ayton Castle. Maud stayed with the Galbraiths here and was courted by Mr Blair. He proposed to her in the little round summerhouse in the kitchen garden.

One of the guests at Ayton was a Mr Blair, a young man from Edinburgh whom Maud had met and liked at a party which she had attended the previous year. Now she had an opportunity to get to know him better, and he soon became her first serious adult suitor. Bill Weigall, Willie Buckman and all the other Ramsgate boys were far too juvenile to be contemplating matrimony and Maud rather despised them: "Oh how I like *clever* men and men who have something in them, not babies. I am spoilt in this I am afraid". A more serious young man, Leonard Messel, was away in Germany learning the ropes at the Messel bank. He also was too young and too busy struggling with an uncongenial career to be thinking of settling down for some time. Maud had been pleased to see him in May ("Mrs Messel's dance, Lennie back, Maud enjoyed dance immensely, home 3.30"), though most news of him came through his sister Ruth. But now here at Ayton was a new and exciting kind of admirer; Marion must have read Maud's next letter with more than usual interest:

> We have had a long day out in the open following the shooters. I stayed by Mr Blair when he was shooting and he didn't miss a bird. I have asked him to come and see us when we are in town. He has a very clever face rather aristocratic looking. . . . I think he and Papa would get on very well together.

Linley and Marion were back at Stafford Terrace before Maud returned. There were plenty of jobs to be done after the long summer break; one call that Marion made was on Mrs Crane, who had just moved in to Holland Street. Linley had known Walter Crane for many years, but as the Sambournes did not share his socialist views Marion may not have met his wife before. She was clearly not a kindred spirit: "Walked to Mrs Crane, what a dirty house, dust & crumbs of weeks, the wonder is people turn out of such houses looking comparatively clean!" There was one more country house visit to make that year, but this was not the usual success: "November 12th. Go to Mr Rider Haggard's for a few days, Bungay, Norfolk. Most uncomfortable journey, end of world place. House party distinctly dull & uninteresting, no doubt found me more so—and certainly weaker, they seem made of iron. Rider Haggard charming as ever, a most kind and attentive host." (Rider Haggard had been a literary lion since the publication of *King Solomon's Mines* in 1885; although Marion found his wife rather dull, they were friends of long-standing.) On this occasion all the famous author's skill could not make amends for lack of sparkle among the other guests: "Had a little walk with Mrs Longman, found her most uninteresting in every way, wonder if my own sympathy is waning as I come across so many more uncongenial people than of old!" wrote Marion, and the visit ended, "Pouring all day hopelessly, not sorry to leave."

PART THREE
1895·1901

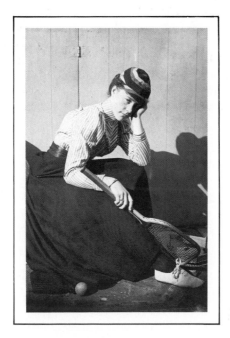

Maud as a tennis girl.

CHAPTER ELEVEN
MRS HERAPATH:
NEW INVENTIONS:
ANNIE

HE SAMBOURNES did not go to Ramsgate in the autumn of 1894. This was the first year since 1881—and probably since their marriage in 1874—that they had not had a long holiday by the sea. The children had outgrown Ramsgate, but another reason may have been Linley's increasing difficulties with the Editor of *Punch*. He and Frank Burnand had always got on well when they were off duty, but things did not go so easily at work. Burnand had never been a tactful administrator, and had adopted the disconcerting habit of sending stiff notes to members of his staff, containing an abrupt order or rebuke. These always came as an unpleasant surprise, and caused much distress in at least one household. "Lin received worrying letter from Mr Burnand" was a not infrequent entry in Marion's diary. Linley would be angry and hurt, and though each time harmony was soon restored, a certain cooling of the friendship between the two families resulted. Marion did call occasionally at 27 The Boltons, South Kensington (the substantial town house which the Burnands had bought in 1892) but after 1893 she saw much less of Mrs Burnand, although the break in their intimacy was less sudden and complete than the one with Mrs Stone had been in 1888.

Another very good reason for staying in town was Mrs Herapath's ill-health. In September 1894 Marion wrote, "Lin & self dined at dear Mother's, everything looking as fresh & dainty as ever, Mother charming in her cap & fichu", but the family soon had cause for alarm. "Dear Mother v.v.ill with her heart, weak & short of breath" was a note in October, and by the end of the year Mrs Herapath's condition was very serious. Midge was able to stay with her mother to look after her at Albert Hall Mansions (Hamilton Langley returned to South America and Dora was sent to Ramsgate with her governess), but little could be done to ease her suffering. Her children watched sorrowfully as Mrs Herapath gradually faded

Left: Maud in the summer of 1895. A studio portrait taken to mark her twentieth birthday.

away and by the beginning of June 1895 it was clear that there was no hope of recovery. "To Haymarket for *Fedora*—no heart for anything, darling Mother always in my mind", wrote Marion. Even her brother Mervyn's announcement of his engagement to Ethel Dale could not cheer her: "Feel so tired and done up—dear Mother what must she feel if only seeing her suffer makes one feel so bad." On 21 June Marion, Midge and Edgar were at their mother's bedside: "Mr Carr Glyn called & prayed with us. The darling seemed comforted but sank into a sleep from which we could not rouse her & passed most peacefully away at a quarter past six to our great grief & sorrow. The dearest & most loving mother & truest friend and adviser—how shall we live without her?"

Marion was quite overcome with grief, "Feel so wretched, could not rest. The reality comes in waves like a hideous nightmare." For three days she, Midge, and Tabby were at Albert Hall Mansions to receive condolences and to arrange the quantities of flowers sent by family and friends. There were sweet peas, roses, and arum lilies, in bunches and baskets; thirty-four wreaths; and each day Edgar brought a fresh armful of red roses. Very early in the morning of 26 June the family gathered round their mother for the last time: the daughters hung the wreaths round the coffin and the four sons and three sons-in-law escorted the hearse to Victoria Station. From there they took the train to Ramsgate, then went on to St Peter's, where Mrs Herapath was laid to rest beside her husband. Marion, Midge and Tabby stayed behind in their mother's empty room to read the Burial Service together; only Annie was conspicuously absent from the scene of mourning.

The days after the funeral were filled with the heart-breaking task of sorting through all Mrs Herapath's possessions. Little packets of mementoes, labelled in her own hand, had been put aside for each of her children and grandchildren, (including Annie and Edith) but as she had not had much money of her own her will was short. She left "£50 to my old and faithful servant George Tassell", and the residue "to be divided amongst all my children except my son Spencer and my daughter Annie." Such a rebuke from beyond the grave might lie more heavily upon the recipient's conscience than a remonstrance face to face had ever done.

There were quantities of papers for Edgar to deal with concerning the final disposal of Mr Herapath's estate, left in trust until his widow's demise. Because there were some ambiguities in the wording of his will, Spencer contested it and this naturally led to family ill-feeling. During the ensuing weeks Spencer's past misdeeds, as well as those of Welch and Chapple, were all dragged out into the light again: the division of the spoils, when each of the sons and daughters found that they would receive less than they had hoped or expected, made everyone uncomfortable and cross. Marion was particularly upset to find that a clause in her marriage settlement meant that she (alone of the eight) could not get her hands on her share of the capital, but would have to appoint trustees to manage it for her. There were other troublesome muddles—each more "monstrous" and "vexing" than the last, but it was impossible to be angry and miserable for ever; normal life had to be resumed and there was no doubt that in future Marion's financial circumstances would be very much easier. A month after Mrs Herapath's death she was writing, "Edgar

quite cheerful over the new flaw in the will—wonder when complications will terminate! To Mme Bocquet, ordered evening dress."

It was decided not to put off Mervyn's wedding, fixed for 14 July, and Marion was kept busy with the preparations. "To MacKay about flowers for wedding, dear Mervyn's button-hole. To Buszards about cake. Midge & Tabby to dinner v.cheery evening" she wrote on the eve of this event, but it was difficult to keep her spirits up for long. "Dear Mervyn's wedding. V.fine morning. In brougham to church, met Dale party there. Felt v.low & miserable so vexed with myself but could not master the feeling. Mervyn looked so handsome & spoke up well & looked v.happy going away. Maud and Hylda followed, threw flowers. All our people came to tea here. After tea went with Midge to Mansions, packed all Edith's and Annie's things. This day felt like a whole week."

Although Marion continued to write at intervals in her diary "miss darling Mother v.much", the succession of summer visits which followed were a welcome relief from the weary months which had gone before, and she began to enjoy life again. Maud went off on the same route as last year: Buscot Park, followed by visits to her Scottish friends, while Marion and Roy went down to Tabby's at Christchurch for a fortnight, up to Ayton for another fortnight, then down to stay with Midge at Earl's Barton, Northamptonshire, for three weeks. All this travelling about was as easy and

Mervyn. Whenever Marion's brothers came to call they stood in as models for Linley.

151

comfortable and very nearly as quick as it is today. The railways were at the peak of their efficiency, with an intricate network of lines spread across the whole country. Marion never seemed to worry about the price of a rail ticket or tried to plan her holidays to avoid lengthy train journeys, though she did sometimes complain about the number of times she had to change trains to get to the more isolated country districts. The visit to Ayton was an even greater success than the previous year. The beautiful weather, the kindness of the Galbraiths and the liveliness of the other guests made Marion go so far as to write, "Never felt better in my life." Only one member of the party was uncongenial: "Mr and Mrs Clarke arrived, owners of 8 children all well planted in life. I find her v.dull & heavy—seems absorbed in the feats etc of her various children—wonder if I too bother people about my family! Think it more than probable and must refrain."

Maud spent a few days at Stafford Terrace between visits. She was on her own except for Mervyn and Ethel who were staying there after returning from their wedding tour. London was as usual empty during August, and Maud wrote to her parents:

Maud and Marion posing. Among the quantities of photographs in Linley's collection there are very few of his wife. She thought posing a great waste of time, but everyone else in the family clearly enjoyed it very much.

152

Neither of you dear things are to worry about me though I should be ever so much happier if you were back. To look out on the dismal Terrace with all its windows carefully papered up and blinds down is a sad sight indeed. It's like a deserted city where there is no-one to breathe let alone making sounds. I had no idea London could be so utterly empty, really its as if some unknown hand had taken a broom and swept away the population. . . . Ethel is quite a dear it is so nice having them both here. Mervyn is sitting racking his dear brain over little accounts, he is worrying over a tiny washing bill of a few pence. So like you darling but I love it for it reminds me of my own dear little mother. I shan't marry until I find someone like Papa, for the more I see of other husbands the more I think how disgracefully you two behave for such an old married couple! I want something of the same order, I couldn't stand quarrelling all day long. To 'chuck up' a happy home and dear little parents would be madness—I mean to keep 'a mere child' as long as possible.

In September Maud was at Ayton Castle again. She wrote to her mother bubbling over with high spirits:

I am getting so excited about the dance that I believe I shall be nearly off my head on the night. I mean to enjoy it like anything, not knowing what will happen amongst all those millionaires. Hardly any of them have less than 7 thousand a year so darling your little own may have a chance of fishing out one of them. Mrs Galbraith wants Mr Walker for me—she says he is an awfully good fellow and though plain has other qualities that make up for his lack of appearance. She is waiting to welcome Mr MacCall and Mr Hall Stevenson who are due at about five to seven. Two men at last! What a grab there will be when dinner-time comes. I have just come in from the garden where I have gathered such a lovely bunch of pink roses to wear tonight with my dress. I am going to be an awful swell at the two balls, I don't think even Mary MacQueen with her Russell & Allen gowns can beat your own, what do you think darling? Fancy Mary has 12 dresses, all her tailor-mades were got at Redferns, ballgowns at Russell & Allens and day gowns at Marshall & Snelgrove but my dresses this year are so very dainty and pretty that not even she can make me envious.

Mrs Galbraith had asked Mr Blair to attend her dance. He had visited London in the spring and had been entertained at Stafford Terrace, and was by now very much in love. Some of Maud's excitement would have been due to the prospect of seeing him again at the party. Next day she wrote another long letter:

The dance was a very great success. On Friday morning early we heard carts and vans driving up to the door. When we came down to breakfast we found the hall all most exquisitely decorated with

palms and lilies. The fireplace was like a fairy garden all one mass of yellow flowers and smilax. Well at last the evening came and with it many more arrivals by the 6.45 train. What excitement when we all met for an early dinner at 7 o'clock! . . . After dinner we all raced up to our rooms and changed. . . . Dancing began at half past 9 o'clock. Although there were several more ladies than men my program was full and extras down on the back page at once, the men stood in a long line and came up in turn. I am afraid you mightn't have liked all that went on that night but still darling I daresay you did very much the same when you were a wild little thing yourself! The dancing was kept up until 4 o'clock and then we all went and had a lovely supper where toasts were called and speeches made. . . . It was half past 5 before we got to bed for it was quite impossible to settle down after an evening like that!

Two days later the expected happened: Mr Blair proposed. Maud told her mother all about the offer, and how she had refused it. "I don't think I like him enough to marry him, and I could not leave you and live far away", was her firm decision.

A year later Maud had her twenty-first birthday. She was staying at Buscot Park at the time and wrote to her mother:

> August 5th 1896. My own darling. I was delighted to get your dear letter this morning and Papa's wire. Thank you ever so much for all the good wishes, I shall indeed be fortunate if they all come true. Thank you again and again for the present that is far too much for me besides a necklace! I don't feel that I deserve it all and surely I shall some day have to pay for all the happiness I am having now. . . .

It was during this visit to Buscot that Maud had a chance to visit William Morris's country house near by, Kelmscott Manor.

> This afternoon I went with Mr Henderson and Mrs MacNaught for a long walk. We went chiefly with the object of calling on the great William Morris. We did not find him at home as he is somewhere in Iceland but his daughter was there and she showed us over the place. The house is lovely for its oldness but oh! *so so* artistic & grubby. The tea was laid out in a barbaric fashion with a loaf on the table and a dirty jam pot that had been broken open through the paper at the top and the spoon looked too sticky to touch. We did not accept the tea but sat in a row in the plain *painfully* plain dining room & stared at Miss Morris and wondered why she dressed in such a sloppy way with no stays.

154

As so often happens, a youthful criticism can provide the perfect antidote to the world's adulation.

All through 1896 Mr Blair did his best to persuade Maud to change her mind and consent to marry him. He wrote her long impassioned letters, but she remained adamant that marriage with him, or indeed anyone, was out of the question. In the autumn she was back once more at Ayton Castle, where she could not help thinking of him and re-living the events of the previous summer:

> I had the dearest and saddest letter from poor P.J.B. Oh mother darling I do feel so sorry for him, don't you? I know the older I become the more he will go on—how I wish I could have my time over again, I would never have let things come to this pass. . . .

But life was far too much fun for Maud to waste time repining, and a fortnight later she was attending another ball in the best of spirits:

> I never enjoyed a dance more, the floor and everything was just perfect and the music divine. Everyone I danced with prayed and implored me to give them more than two dances when I could not even find one for them. I had to say I was so so sorry ever so many times, all through the evening. . . . I shall never be as happy when I am married as I am now. I am free now to say go to one and come to another and to change my mind with the wind and yet keep their love all the same, perhaps the more because I don't bother about any of them. . . .

Maud posing, and the cartoon dated May 1896.

155

Freedom, and power over the hearts of men, was a heady brew which Maud was determined to enjoy to the last drop.

Electric light was installed at No 18 Stafford Terrace in 1896. When the Phillimore Estate had been laid out gas was supplied as a matter of course to all the houses, but this was only for lighting purposes as its value as a heating and cooking agent was not realised for some time to come. Gas lighting was one of the great technological advances of the nineteenth century: Pall Mall was first lit by gas in 1807 and by 1823 London had 40,000 gas lamps along 215 miles of streets. The coal gas which was used gave a bright clean light, and a "gasolier" was soon preferred to the big colza-oil hanging lamps seen in early nineteenth-century pictures. Paraffin (available after about 1860) was a very satisfactory fuel for smaller portable lamps, as it did not smell and gave a good light for reading or working. The 1877 Inventory lists pendant gasoliers in the reception rooms, with wall brackets elsewhere. The gas burnt with a bare flame and gave off a lot of heat as well as the risk of lethal carbon monoxide fumes if not properly lit. At Stafford Terrace a grill leading into an air duct was incorporated into each ceiling rose and these can still be seen: they were not standard fittings, but must have been a special "selling feature" put in by the developer.

The first public building in London specifically designed to be lit by electricity was the Savoy Theatre, opened in 1881. Other theatres and concert halls soon followed suit, and Marion remarked on the electric light at the circus in 1886 and at the Albert Hall in 1887. Cragside, the house built in 1880 by the millionaire William Armstrong, was the first private home to have its own generating station and to be entirely lit by Swan and Edison lamps. Many wealthy property owners were quick to copy: Maud had found the electric light a wonderful novelty on her first visit to Buscot Park in 1893. However it was not until a few enterprising companies set up local generating stations that electricity became available to the ordinary house-holder. Linley had always been keen on new-fangled inventions, Marion lukewarm, so it is typical that when he wrote in his diary "October 21st, 1896: The Electric Light put on this day by the Notting Hill Company" she should ignore the great event. The next day Linley made another entry: "Tried Electric Light in Dining Room for first time", and on 26 October, "Man from Maples to finish the Electric Light", but Marion still did not comment. During November she made notes in her diary about shopping for lampshades—she bought some, returned them as unsatis-factory, and then bought others—but it was all a great nuisance, and on 1 December she wrote crossly, "Hate Electric Light—Electric *dark*, does not give as much light as lamps." It is true that early bulbs were weak, not only in the amount of light they gave, but also physically: Marion later noted down how many "electric globes" were broken by careless housemaids. The system was also very unreliable: "Electric light again blown itself out!" was one diary entry, and men were often called in for emergency repairs and adjustments. Marion probably felt that the old ways were much better: just turning a switch could never be so satisfying as having the lamps carried in at dusk by a maid, who would then draw the curtains, stoke the fire, and settle the family comfortably for the evening.

It is not easy to guess how many fittings were part of the 1896 installation and which were added later. The brackets in the hall still have their gas taps, with the electric wires threaded through the supply pipes. In contrast the hanging lamp on the first landing (which at first glance looks like an oil lamp) is in fact purpose-made for electricity. The brass girandoles on each side of the fireplaces in the ground floor rooms had always held candles, and these were quite easy to convert by using artificial candles and a flame-shaped bulb, a convention still popular today. The morning-room pendant is again like an oil lamp, but the dining-room has a much more modern-looking affair in wrought iron with an elaborate rise-and-fall system, something not possible with gas. The gasoliers in the drawing-room were not replaced: the Sambournes may have decided quite early on that they did not like the overhead lighting here, and the supply pipes have been sealed off. A pair of pendants light the dressing tables in the two principal bedrooms, but whatever was supplied for the other rooms has not survived. The flower-shaped copper shades on the landings are perhaps the most interesting in this varied collection: they are by the firm of W.A.S.Benson who supplied all the light fittings for Standen, the house in Sussex built by Philip Webb in 1894.

Shortly before the electricity was put in, two "incandescent lamps" had been added at Stafford Terrace. A type of incandescent gas mantle had been patented in 1885, but a really practical version was not available until 1893. This was a great advance over the simple gas jet, and had it been introduced a few years earlier less interest might have been shown in the development of electricity for lighting purposes. With hindsight one can say that electric light was bound to triumph, but gas remained for many years a strong contender. Even after the Second World War many parts of Kensington had no electric street-lighting and the poorer sections of the community had not made the change to electricity in their homes either. When evening fell the lamp-lighter with his long pole was a familiar sight up to the mid-1950s, while indoors there were still gas-brackets and lamps, and coal fires burning all the year through to keep the basements dry in terraces where damp-proof courses were unknown.

The Sambournes made various other improvements to their house during the latter part of 1896. "Men putting down linoleum on landings. Mr Galbraith came to luncheon. General confusion, cabinets in hall smothered in dust" wrote Marion, upset at things being discovered in less than their usual pristine condition. Linley had another idea: "Speaking Tube connected to Stables. Spoke to Otley through it." For a busy impatient man the few minutes saved by not having to send one of the maids round to the mews with a message must have been a boon. No trace of this device remains, though there is still a speaking tube, complete with ivory whistles, connecting each floor with the staff quarters in the basement: whether this too was one of Linley's ideas, or another of the developer's desirable extras is not known.

Of all the innovations which took place in the late nineteenth century, the invention of the bicycle probably gave the most innocent pleasure to the largest number of people. The "safety bicycle" (basically similar in design to the modern vehicle) had come on the market in 1885, but it was the introduction of pneumatic tyres in 1888 which made bicycling so immensely popular. Roy learnt to ride a bicycle soon after he had gone to Eton in 1891, and by 1894 he was enjoying long cross-country rides on his machine. In August that year he rode from London to Conrad's house in Sussex, a distance of nearly forty miles, no mean feat on dusty unmetalled roads. Linley was not to be outdone by his son, so early in 1895 he too purchased a bicycle. Always athletic, he must have been very surprised to find how difficult it was to balance on two wheels. A new skill is not easy to master late in life, so the struggle lasted from the beginning of March (when he had the first of a course of six twice-weekly lessons) until the middle of July, when Marion was at last able to write, "Lin rode bicycle, can get on and off now to his satisfaction." After that there was no stopping him; when the horses were put out to grass in August he went for at least one long bicycle ride every day, and over the next few years he used his horse hardly

Roy posing, wearing an outfit hired for the day from a theatrical costumiers.

158

at all. In January 1896 he wrote: "Cycle completed 1,000th mile at gate of Stafford Terrace this morning" and he continued noting the mileage regularly in his diary. By the following October two thousand miles had been achieved, and by April 1899 the total was five thousand.

Linley was in good company: everyone was bicycling and talking about this wonderful new sporting exercise. "V.pleasant evening at Mrs Corbett's" wrote Marion in May 1896, "had long interesting talk with Lord Coleridge on bicycles etc, he has just patented a bicycle mackintosh." Maud was the next member of the family to take up the craze: with youth on her side it did not take her long to master the art. When she went up to Scotland in September a bicycle was hired for her by her kind hostess, and she went off for long cross-country rides by herself or with her girl friends, with no escort apparently considered necessary. The liberty and equality suddenly offered to young ladies was unprecedented. Bicycling was a far less expensive sport than having one's own horse—something which had never been available to more than a favoured few—yet it managed to provide the same exhilarating thrills of speed and power. It was a pity that Marion did not try harder to acquire the knack: in August when the family was staying with the Fletchers an effort was made to teach her, "Tried bicycle again, no progress, am v.awkward & cowardly" she wrote, and soon gave up. Tabby thoroughly enjoyed bicycling: she could ride as far as any man and continued this exercise even when she was pregnant. A son (Gareth) had been born to her in 1894 and she was expecting again in 1896. Marion wrote "Tabs and Mr Guthrie off at 9 o'clock, took train to Winchester. Came home on their bikes, over 30 miles, arrived 9.30." Next day she commented with some surprise, "Tabs none the worse!" Tabby's family was completed on the last day of December that year by the birth of another son, named George Mervyn.

Marion did not go to Ramsgate at all in 1895, and only for a day-trip in 1896. The Herapath children were planning to have a stained glass window put into St Peter's church in memory of their parents: "June 21st. Anniversary of dear Mother's death. Midge & self to Margate by 10.30 train with our wreaths. Drove to Cliftonville Hotel, lunched there. Took fly at 1.30 to St Peter's, found dear Edgar's wreath already placed there, all looking well tended, glorious day. Vicar showed us only available window near organ. To Westwood, deserted and fearfully overgrown, like 20 years growth. To Hotel for tea, returned by 6.15 train." Edgar was in charge of all the arrangements for having the window made, and later informed his sister, "The cost will be about £120, perhaps a pound or two more. I do not think the design particularly original, but of course it will be of best workmanship by Clayton and Bell." He was right in thinking the window undistinguished, but Marion was quite satisfied: "Spencer to luncheon & went with me to Clayton & Bell's to see window to dear Parents' memory. Delighted with it, colour v.good." Presumably it

would have been thought too extravagant to commission a design from one of the Sambournes' artistic friends.

1896 was a year of bereavement for the art world. Frederic Leighton, President of the Royal Academy since 1878, died in February. Linley, along with everyone else who had any interest in art, attended the funeral in St Paul's Cathedral. Millais was elected to the Presidency, but he was already mortally ill and died that August. William Morris, artist, poet and socialist, died in October. Although recognised as a great man, Morris had less stature among his contemporaries than he has today, and was probably considered rather an eccentric outsider by the respectable conventional Sambournes. More distressing to Linley was the death, also in October, of George du Maurier, his colleague at *Punch*. Marion was sorry too, even though they had never been very friendly with the Du Mauriers. (Their house in Hampstead was too far away for afternoon calls, nor were they ever asked to dine at Stafford Terrace.) But for Marion the saddest loss was that of the actor, Arthur Blunt. He had been a close friend for many years, and his charming voice had given her much pleasure whenever guests had gathered round the piano for a session of after-dinner music. "Heard of Arthur Blunt's death, v.sad. Another of our oldest friends gone, aged only 52" was the note in her diary on 17 March. On the day of his funeral she went to the opera and, as always, was moved by beautiful music. "To see Lohengrin, first time I have heard it. It does not do to think or one would feel so sad—in the midst of life we are in death" she wrote, and a fortnight later, "Private view Academy, met endless friends, but missed dear Arthur Blunt & others gone."

January 1897 brought yet another death, closer to Marion and far more painful and disturbing. She had gone to stay with Midge for a few days at a house near Ardleigh in Sussex. News must have come to the sisters that Annie was in trouble, for Marion's diary entry on 4 January begins: "Midge & self sent off £5 each to Captain Powell—alas too late for the one we should have helped", and then goes on: "Drove to Ardleigh & met boy with telegram saying poor Annie passed away last evening." How Annie had died or what part Captain Powell had played in her life we will never know, but all Marion's long suppressed feelings surged up and she was overcome with remorse and sorrow: "V.grieved I did not go or send—shall bitterly regret this to my dying day—poor Annie but why did I not go—regrets useless— ought to have influenced Edgar who would have done anything but for *one*—too late—" were some of the frantic jottings in her diary. More news came a few days later: "Terrible circumstances surrounding poor Annie's death feel most bitterly that I did not go to her as I ought to have done—it is all so awful I shall regret it every day of my life." Edgar, upright and disapproving, dealt with the funeral arrangements. Annie, aged forty-two, was laid beside her parents in the Herapath family vault. "Poor Annie buried at St Peter's Thanet. Edgar went and saw it all."

One cannot help feeling that Marion was right to blame herself, not only for failing her sister at the end, but for all the years of neglect that had gone before. Annie may have refused help from her disapproving family; alternatively there is a hint that begging letters had often been received and that any charity offered had fallen into a bottomless pit. Linley wrote firmly to his wife, "You must always remember that there *was* a provision which was enough with ordinary care to prevent want—if it had been doubled it would have been just the same." It was not so much Annie's spendthrift nature as the sin which went with it that gave her relatives such pain, though once she had set foot on the downward path there was little they could have done to save her. For a girl of her class and station in life there was no turning back—truth mirrored fiction, and as in the sensational novels of the period the punishment for adultery was despair, degradation and an early grave. Whether Annie had also felt proper remorse is not recorded.

To ease their consciences Marion and Midge decided that something must be done to make amends to Annie's children. Edgar reluctantly agreed, and a trust fund was set up for Edith (who was studying music in Germany) and her two brothers, last heard of in an orphanage in Australia. The boys were contacted, and Marion undertook to pay £21 a year into the fund. Like everything else to do with Annie and her disreputable life, these arrangements were deeply distasteful to the whole family. "Had talk with Tabby about this horrid advancement of money for Annie's children—hers very sensible view, wish Edgar's were the same," wrote Marion on 13 February. Annie's name was never mentioned in the diary again, but thoughts of her must often have come unbidden into Marion's mind. Twice in the next year when she met someone to whom she took a dislike she wrote, "Reminds me of William Furrell." Perhaps Annie's husband should have borne the blame for the failure of the marriage; in a just society he would have been the outcast, not she.

Martin Jacolette,

QUEEN'S GATE HALL, SOUTH KENSINGTON & NORTH BROOK HOUSE, DOVER

CHAPTER TWELVE
LENNIE:
ROY AT ETON:
MAUD'S MARRIAGE

T DOES NOT SEEM as if any period of mourning was set aside for Annie and the early months of 1897 were filled with the usual parties and theatres. Marion's vain regrets and painful thoughts were soon submerged in the demanding social round, while Maud's admirers were more attentive than ever. Mr Blair visited London in February; Willie Buckman, Bill Weigall, Mr Carlisle and Leonard Messel all paid court. "Poor Maud kept pretty busy with her lovers!" wrote Marion. She thought Willie Buckman "Not improved", was sorry for Mr Blair ("Seems very much in love") and wrote of Mr Carlisle, "Can understand M's aversion to Mr C, so simple and foolish tho' kind—pity nice men seldom have any money!"

At the end of February Marion recorded a dramatic turn in her daughter's affairs: "Maud home from ball this morning at 3.45. V.unhappy poor child, Lennie Messel proposed & wishes all settled in 3 weeks—cried over it in my room. Mr Carlisle also said unmistakable things but is less unhappy in his love than Maud's other 4!" Maud's first reaction to Lennie's proposal was to refuse outright. Her tears were more of anger than distress—how could these young men be so foolish as to break their hearts and spoil her fun. She only wanted them to stay devoted slaves, vying with each other to satisfy her every whim. Flirting was a delightful game and Maud had no intention of giving up her precious freedom, so she composed Lennie Messel a letter of polite but firm refusal, and went off to stay in the country. "Hope the change & rest will do her good, poor mite—v.worried with her 5 love affairs" wrote her mother.

Lennie was not quite crushed. There were a few parties at which he could meet Maud before he had to return to Germany and once there he bombarded her with letters. Maud took little notice of him, whether he was there or not, and continued

---

Left: Leonard Messel. A very eligible young man.

163

her feverish whirl of gaiety through March and April. After she had been to three dances on consecutive nights Marion wrote with understandable anxiety, "Maud back from ball at 3 this morning, looks perfect wreck." In spite of her mother's remonstrances, Maud would not rest and take things easily, but embarked on another commission for book illustrations, this time for Mrs Willard's fairy story *Cherrywink*. Whenever there were a few hours to spare she shut herself up in the schoolroom and worked away with the same concentration as her father, "Maud hard at work all day long."

None of Maud's suitors could take no for an answer. Mr Blair was more in evidence than ever and seemed determined to capture her before Lennie returned to England, but on 11 May he was obliged to return to Edinburgh unsatisfied. Two days later Lennie was back in London. Maud met him at Mrs Yates' dance, and on 16 May he presented himself at Stafford Terrace to make a formal application to Linley for his daughter's hand. Maud had made it clear to her parents that she did not wish to marry, so Linley sent the young man packing. Marion too was firm: "Lennie spoke to me about Maud. Poor boy feel v.sorry for him, but it cannot be thought of for many reasons."

It is a pity that Marion does not explain what the "many reasons" were. The most obvious was the Messels' German-Jewish background, but the Sambournes had numerous Jewish friends, and at this time there was little prejudice against Germany. Ludwig Messel had renounced the Jewish faith when he married and his children were all brought up in the Church of England. Young Leonard had much in his favour: he was well educated, intelligent, interested in the arts and a lover of nature. He was not as handsome and dashing as Mr Blair, but was short and dark, quiet and serious; someone whose worth would be discovered slowly. His trump card, which none of Maud's other suitors could hope to match, was of course the money. His stockbroker father was extremely rich, his childless Uncle Rudolph even richer. Lennie, even if not rich yet, had great expectations. Maud (with her mother's encouragement) had always vowed to marry a wealthy man; the wonder is that she prevaricated for so long before she finally made up her mind to accept the offer.

Lennie was very tenacious. During the next week he wrote daily to Maud saying how much he loved her, and to Linley begging for another interview. They both refused to see him, so he tried another tack: he sent his sister Ruth to see Maud, and his mother called on Marion. They each campaigned vigorously on his behalf, and Maud was invited to lunch at the Messels' house; there the whole family welcomed her just as if she had already agreed to be another daughter. Wherever she went in the next few weeks Lennie made sure to be there also, and he followed her about at parties like a shadow. But Maud continued to flirt and tease, and to receive love letters from her various swains. Like the bird she so often imagined herself to be, she hopped and fluttered outside the gilded cage, while Lennie stood by patiently waiting. It was Marion who allowed the first crack in the family defences to appear: she asked Lennie to dinner at the same time as she asked Tabby and Midge. They both liked him at once and agreed that he was a much better option than Mr Blair, so Marion was quite likely swayed by their enthusiasm. It is most disappointing for

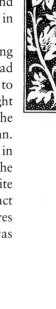

the reader that she puts so little about the affair into her diary, but the impression given by the few sentences that do appear is that by saying nothing derogatory and appearing quite neutral and detached, she gradually caused the tide to turn in Lennie's favour.

In July it began to look as if he might be making headway at last. After watching a cricket match at Lord's Marion wrote, "Lennie & self drove home in hansom, had long talk, afraid Lin won't give his consent yet." On 11 July the young man came to dinner at Stafford Terrace to put his case once again to Linley. What Maud thought is not recorded, but her father seems to have agreed to some arrangement, though he stipulated that no formal engagement should be announced until the autumn. Technically Maud was still free and would have the long summer holiday in Scotland to consider her future. Two days later Linley wrote, "At 5.10 to the Devonshire Club & had disagreeable interview with Mr Ludwig Messel about Mite & Lennie. Lasted 20 minutes—a sort of settlement." Perhaps Linley resented the fact that he was not in a position to offer a large dowry with his daughter, but no figures appear in the diary, so we shall never know how many thousands a year it was suggested that Maud would enjoy.

Nymans, Sussex. Ludwig Messel employed Ernest George and Leonard Stokes to alter his simple Georgian house out of all recognition.

165

All the Sambournes' friends were agog to know whether the match would come off. "Mrs Sington asked if Maud & Lennie were engaged—distinctly said No" wrote Marion. Maud made it plain that she had certainly not said Yes, even though she went to stay for a fortnight at Nymans, where the place was so lovely, the family so kind and Lennie so importunate that she must have felt the net drawing ever closer. At the end of August she went to Scotland with her father; they were to stay at Skibo Castle for a week and then Maud would go on alone to visit her friend Mary Macqueen. Linley wrote to Marion: "Lennie came with us to Euston. He said 'Goodbye darling' and kissed Maud—if that's not engaged, I don't know what is!"

Maud's letters to her mother from Scotland that summer were full of doubt and indecision. As always she wrote quite freely of her feelings, and it is obvious that a great mental struggle was taking place. Her normal cheerful spirits failed her: marriage seemed not a joyful adventure but a prison to be entered trembling, with many a backward glance towards the sunny land of childhood. Yet married she must be: to remain for ever a spinster was unthinkable. All her friends, even the plain dull ones, were finding husbands, and if she played the field too long the eligible young men would tire of waiting and go elsewhere. Among her present suitors only Mr Blair and Leonard Messel were at all possible, and of the two only Lennie was wealthy. How she must have longed for someone quite new to appear and sweep her off her feet—but the days slipped past and nothing happened. She wrote wistfully to her mother:

> I am waiting anxiously for the post to bring me a letter in your dear handwriting. I get a little sad when I think what a time it will be before I can see you, and when I do—well I cannot say that I am so anxious to come back to be engaged. I do so love being free, and it will be a new sensation to be tied to anyone else. . . . When I am alone it is *you* who seem everything to me, I think of *you* always and my own dear home and that is why I have no room in my heart for others. . . . Fondest love your devoted and unhappy Own

The day arranged for Maud's return drew nearer. She was asked to stay for another week, then just a few more days. . . . Finally she travelled south on 18 October, perhaps thinking right to the last that she might escape her destiny. But Lennie and Roy were waiting for her at the station to escort her home to Stafford Terrace, and Lennie was pressed to stay to dinner. Next day he came to dinner again, and this time he brought an engagement ring in his pocket. Maud accepted it: the deed was done. Linley was still not quite convinced, "Poor Mite very upset and not wanting to be engaged." But Marion had no doubts: "Maud formally engaged! V.weepy but will be happy as he is so devoted."

Marion was probably quite right in her intuitive feelings about what would best suit her daughter and make her happy. Maud turned to Lennie more and more as the months of her engagement passed, surprised perhaps to find that she was after all only exchanging one kind of freedom for another. The Messels were most

welcoming and friendly and asked the whole Sambourne family to spend Christmas with them at Nymans. On 30 December 1897 Marion wrote, "Lin and self returned after v.charming visit. Find Mrs M delightful companion & had some good talks. Quiet evening at home with Lin, v.peaceful & happy." It had been a good year: Maud's affairs were brought to a very satisfactory conclusion and even Roy's future now looked quite bright.

Roy's progress through Eton had been far from brilliant, and Linley must often have wondered if the expensive gentleman's education was really worth while. There had been trouble about illicit smoking and general bad behaviour several times, and Roy seemed quite unable to apply himself to any kind of work. Sport was still his main passion, especially cricket, which he played a great deal during the holidays. Even so he was not picked for the school team, though he did succeed in beating all the other boys at billiards. In the spring of 1892 the Sambournes had been distressed to have a chilly note from his housemaster: "Letter from Mr Ainger about Roy's behaviour

Roy at Eton, aged eighteen, "a very great masher".

167

Roy posing as the famous Indian cricketer, Ranji, and the cartoon dated December 1896. Roy was passionately keen on cricket.

making us v.unhappy cannot imagine where he gets his manners which have always made me uneasy" wrote Marion. Linley sent a stern letter to his son which produced a reply by return: "Letter from Roy, v.sorry and promising to do better."

"Darling Roy home from Eton" was Marion's entry at the beginning of the Easter holidays, but his behaviour soon made her quite distraught: "Roy v.troublesome so rude and noisy made me quite ill and had good cry unable to go down to lunch. Lin to Sir A. Hickman's for tennis, refused to take Roy. Think Roy more unhappy at this disappointment than sorry to make me unhappy—hope I am wrong." Linley must have been really firm for once, as next day, "Roy subdued & v.quiet". Term began shortly after this incident and next time Roy came home it was "with excellent report, Lin & self delighted." Maud's letter to her mother in August 1894 gives a picture of her brother which—though it may have amused Marion a little—would have caused her to sigh more: "We were a party of 14 to dinner, all of them Eton boys. Roy seems to be well known amongst them and a sort of chuckle goes round when they speak of him. Mr Fryor says he is the naughtiest boy at Eton! and is well known for doing foolish things and making a row. It's rather fun when I ask if they know Sambourne, "Oh don't I just! He makes more row than anyone at my tutor's'."

By 1985 Roy had grown tall and handsome. In his mother's eyes this was compensation for some of his defects, and when he came home for half term she

wrote: "Roy arrived 1.30 in tails & stick-up collar, a v.great masher with violet button-hole." A year later he had quite established himself in the role of young man about town and Maud wrote: "On our return from Windsor we saw a very smart youth standing outside the house. On closer inspection we discerned it to be Roy arrayed in all his glory and not even the sunflower dared to compete. We spent a very happy day and Roy behaved as a brother of mine ought to. . . ."

The Sambournes enjoyed having a son at Eton, as there were various pleasant social occasions connected with the school which brought them into contact with many new acquaintances. One important fixture in the social calendar was the match between Eton and Harrow held at Lord's cricket ground in the middle of the summer term. Like Ascot and Henley, this occasion was another chance for the fashionable throng to meet and talk, and for the ladies to parade in their best dresses and hats. The Sambournes made certain of attending and enjoyed themselves hugely. "July 14th 1894. Eton & Harrow match, Maud & Roy off early. Lin & self went to Lords about 1 o'clock, lunched at Mrs Steincopff's, very large party there. Joined Mr Hartree after, saw game splendidly from his brake. Excellent tea at 5 o'clock v.crowded." Then there were the annual celebrations of the Fourth of June at Eton itself, when Marion and Linley were very pleased to be invited to go with Mr and Mrs de la Rue on their launch to view the festivities from the river: "Left Paddington 11.30, boys met us at Windsor, went on to launch. Steamed up river, perfect day, lunched sumptuously every luxury fruit ices etc in quantities. Back to see procession of boats, v.pretty. Dined on board & a turn up the river after. V.delightful day."

Roy had a bad report ("Lin v.vexed") at the end of the spring term 1896, and the summer term produced no better results. "Roy's bills heavier than ever, £115 odd, upset Lin, and his report not good, v.lazy." At Christmas it was the same story, "How I wish Roy would try to do better for Lin's sake, it worries him dreadfully." But like many boys who behave badly in front of parents whose expectations are high, Roy got on very well with outsiders. He was asked down to Nymans with Maud in August 1897 and Marion must have been pleasantly surprised when her daughter wrote home, "You will be glad to hear that Roy is immensely liked here and they are all charmed with his manners. Mrs Messel likes him so much and Ruth is delighted with him. I am so pleased because it does him a world of good to be among nice girls in a large country house."

Marion and Linley cherished hopes that Roy would go on to a university career, even though grave doubts about his ability were expressed by his tutors at Eton. He had taken an entrance examination for Oxford in March 1897, which he failed, so it was decided that he should leave school at the end of the spring term and have special cramming before trying again in the summer. Facility in the classics was still the only route to success in almost any respectable profession, but one feels that Roy might have flourished if only he had found something more congenial to do than pore over Greek and Latin texts. He did manage to scrape through one exam in June, but there was another to be negotiated in the autumn; as he did no work at all during the summer the result was not unexpected: "Lin v.upset about Roy's not passing into Magdalen College Oxford after Matriculation exam. Wish Roy were more

earnest about it & serious generally, he does not appear to value all the trouble Lin takes over him" wrote Marion, distressed to see her husband taking it so hard. But all was not yet lost: some strings could be pulled by one of Linley's *Punch* colleagues: "Mr Lehmann kindly doing all he can to get Roy into another college at Oxford." Once again the unfortunate boy sat for an examination. "Feel he cannot hope to pass as he has not worked or exerted himself in any way—feel v.anxious about him and his future", but to everyone's surprise and delight he did finally manage to pass, and was granted a place at University College.

The date of Maud's wedding was fixed for 28 April 1898. The letters she wrote to her parents during her engagement show that she was quite happy and growing in confidence about the future. "The more I know Lennie the more I love him and I have you my dear dad to thank for that. You knew what was best for your little Mite and I owe it all to you and Mother who have been so dear and sweet in guiding me to the gate of happiness when I was blindfolded—you two dear ones how I long to do something to repay you for your love." Maud wanted to settle in Kensington, near her parents, but she and Lennie found nothing suitable and eventually chose a house in Gloucester Terrace, Bayswater. This was just north of Hyde Park, in an area much favoured by City men. The house was very similar in size and appearance to Stafford Terrace, and Maud set about furnishing and decorating it with the same enthusiasm and flair as her parents had done twenty-four years earlier.

Marion felt the strain of the wedding preparations very much. There was so much to be done, and the shopping expeditions for the elaborate trousseau thought necessary for a bride in those days were most exhausting, "Out all morning with Maud—Swears & Wells and Dickens & Jones—nearly *dead*, Maud *so* slow choosing" was a typical entry. Dresses, blouses, underwear, had all to be ordered and made up by favourite dressmakers. The nuns of Kensington Square charged 7/6 each for eight embroidered lawn nightdresses, but Maud's wedding dress and going-away dress were created by the smart dressmaker of the moment, Monteith Young, who had been recommended to the Sambournes by Tabby. To help with all the worry and bother Marion invited a friend, Bee Barrs, to come and stay. Bee did everything which Marion felt unable to manage: she escorted Maud on her shopping trips, went to see the vicar, arranged about the choir, the cake, the flowers, the bridesmaids' outfits, and a hundred other useful jobs. Old Nana also came to help, so that the house must have been full to overflowing. The Royal Palace Hotel, Kensington, was the place chosen for the reception (the Royal Garden Hotel now stands on this site) and the presents were all taken here on the eve of the wedding to be put on show, with the name of the giver on each, a custom which enabled the guests to assess which of the Sambournes' friends had been most generous and which distinctly parsimonious.

At last the great day dawned. "Darling Maud's wedding day. Dull wet morning. Maudie fairly cheerful, pestered by newspaper reporters. Cleared and sun shone a little. Church v.full, darling Maud looked sweet, Nana helped her to dress. Empress Rooms charming & all went off splendidly, Maudie v.brave all bright to the last. Hilda, Ruth & Muriel Messel, Dora, Gwen, Mabel Wallace & Maud Hanson-Walker bridesmaids," wrote Marion proudly. The report from the *Daily News* fills in the details:

> The marriage of Miss Sambourne, daughter of Mr Linley Sambourne, the well known Punch artist, and Mrs Sambourne, attracted a great number of friends to St Mary Abbot's, Kensington, yesterday afternoon. The bridegroom is Mr Leonard Charles Rudolph Messel. The beautiful chancel was decorated with palms and white flowers in great profusion, and the ceremony was fully choral. . . . The bride, who wore white satin, orange blossoms, and fine old lace, had a low bodice and short sleeves, and looked charming. She entered the church on her father's arm, and was followed by several brides-maids, all dressed in white muslin and sky blue sashes with white hats trimmed with ostrich plumes. They carried bouquets of yellow roses. . . .

About two hundred people attended the wedding. From the guest list the *Daily News* gleaned some forty famous names, a stupendous roll-call of late-Victorian worthies. The *Punch* staff of course were all present, as well as many artists, but the worlds of science, literature, law, politics, theatre and industry were also well represented. It was a gathering which would have flattered any bride and groom, and must have made one middle-aged couple feel the greatest pride and satisfaction. The newspaper report continued:

> At the close of the ceremony Mr and Mrs Linley Sambourne held a reception in the Empress Rooms of the Royal Palace Hotel, where refreshments were served, and the presents were displayed. They were numerous and costly. After the reception the bride and bridegroom left for Paris, en route for the Italian lakes where the honeymoon will be spent. The bride's travelling dress was of shot heliotrope voile, daintily arranged with a collar of cream embroidered muslin and point d'esprit net, and a pretty little sleeveless coat lined with heliotrope silk. The hat worn with this costume was of rustic straw most becomingly trimmed with branches of mauve lilac and draperies of heliotrope chiffon.

The whole affair went off without a hitch, a triumph of organisation. When all the guests had finally departed the core of the family gathered at Stafford Terrace and Marion wrote: "Ten to dinner, all off after to Haymarket Theatre. Wire from Lennie and Maud from Dover during performance". Not surprisingly she later recorded that she had passed a very bad night, unable to sleep a wink from exhaustion and emotional strain.

171

Maud's honeymoon was a great success. It was something she had dreaded, but her letters to her mother—headed "Do Not Read This Aloud"—reveal her astonished delight in the married state. Lennie was so natural and kind, so ardent, so generous and so full of laughter and fun that all her lingering doubts and fears were swept away: she really loved him after all. The European tour lasted for six weeks: Paris, Monte Carlo, Florence, Venice, each city better than the last, a dream of beauty and romance. Almost the only moments Maud could snatch for letter writing were in the train, so reams of wobbly ecstatic descriptions were despatched to Stafford Terrace from each halt. Lennie completed the triumvirate of people Maud loved best; over and over again she assured her parents that she could never love them less; indeed her devotion to them never faltered.

The young couple's new house would not be ready by the time they returned, so in the interim they planned to stay at Stafford Terrace. On 11 June Marion wrote, "V.busy all morning preparing Maud and Lennie's room. Brought 3/- worth flowers which died at once. At 4 o'clock broke record of calls in one afternoon—made 17!" (Naturally everyone had to be told the exciting news that the bridal pair were expected home). Next day it was "Darling Maud & Lennie return from wedding trip, Lin to meet them at Calais. Both looking so well." Ten days later Roy came down from Oxford: "Merry little dinner with *all* our children!" wrote Marion happily on 20 June.

Maud and Lennie were able to move into 37 Gloucester Terrace a month later, and Marion was delighted to discover that her daughter was turning into a very capable young woman. "To lunch with Maudie, all her presents unpacked. Stayed & had tea with her, all v.nicely done." At the end of her first week of housekeeping Maud gave a dinner party: "*Very* good dinner, wonderfully well waited on, 9 courses, all served by one maid!" It was a relief for Marion to see for herself that the marriage was patently a success: "Dear M & L so happy together it makes me more thankful than words can express to see them, & he so good & unselfish to her." Lennie's unselfishness extended to his not minding how much time Maud spent with her parents; when they were in London she went round to Stafford Terrace almost every day, and when they were away she wrote to them in the same affectionate manner as always. One of Maud's greatest joys was being able to fulfil her childhood dream of helping her mother through life, and Lennie's money was to provide a constant stream of presents, varying from a bunch of flowers to a new dress or an expensive holiday.

As soon as Maud was set up in her new home the Sambournes decided to make some alterations and improvements to Stafford Terrace. "Very busy arranging drawing room, all parqué'd over," wrote Marion in September. This must have been quite an upheaval; it is surprising that they had waited twenty-five years before putting parquet here to match that in the downstairs rooms. "Drawing room chairs v.nice re-covered" was the next entry, followed by references to new net curtains and green sun-blinds. On Christmas Day Marion wrote, "Drawing room so pretty with new sofa, my extravagant white curtains, & yellow shades." Linley thought there was still room for more improvements: "January 2nd 1899. Lin off on furniture

Linley's studio on the top floor, as fitted out in 1899 after Maud's marriage. This room has since been substantially altered.

hunt after luncheon. Bought 3 new pieces & a quantity of curtains—grey-brown satin—for drawing room." These curtains must have been second-hand as men were called in to adapt them to fit the windows. In this they were rather inefficient. "Awful mess after, I cleared it" wrote Marion, and then: "The huge cornice with curtains at the stained glass end of the room fell with a crash when Emily drew them at tea-time! Only put up yesterday."

Even more pleasing than new curtains was the prospect of getting all Linley's work and photographic equipment out of the drawing-room. Marion had complained about lack of space for years, but now with Maud gone the old night-nursery could be transformed into a study-workroom. It was a wonderful excuse for Linley to go shopping again: "Lin to Maples. . . more furniture arrived. . . Lin v.busy rearranging his room. . . . helped Lin with books etc in his room all morning . . . Miss White here doing Lin's curtains. . . ." wrote Marion at intervals during January. At last all was finished: "In all day sitting in Lin's room, v.cosy." Linley, far from feeling banished, was delighted with what he called his "little room".

Maud became pregnant early in 1899. To give her the essential benefit of country air the young Messels rented a house in Sussex, and Marion spent most of the summer there with them. Linley and Lennie went up to town to work during the week, while mother and daughter spent many happy hours sitting in the garden embroidering baby-clothes, or going for gentle drives along the quiet country lanes. Family precedent decreed that Maud's first child should be born at her parents' home, so everyone returned to Stafford Terrace at the end of August. Lennie and Maud had Roy's bedroom (Roy was sent to Nymans to be out of the way) but luckily there was not long to wait. "August 31st. 1899. Lennie called me at 2 o'clock this morning, Maudie having pains. Emma & self made up bed in spare room, got her there. Lennie for Dr Pollock, came 3.30. Nurse arrived 6 o'clock. Maudie had a little son at 12.10, both doing well. Nurse Millie arrived, washed & dressed baby. Dr breakfasted & lunched here. Mr & Mrs Messel came evening, all so delighted with baby & darling M."

Everything had gone wonderfully well. "Maudie & baby had v.good night, both flourishing. Dr Pollock came once. Mrs Messel came, brought flowers" wrote Marion the next day, and continued to note at intervals, "Maudie & baby doing splendidly." But however easy the birth had been, no lady was expected to put a foot to the ground for at least three weeks; consequently it was 22 September before Marion wrote "Maudie stood up for first time to sofa." Three days later Maud lunched downstairs, and four days after that she was allowed out for a drive, having been "confined" to the house for the regulation twenty-eight days.

It was Maud's idea that the baby should be given her father's name, so the heir to the Messel fortune was christened Linley Francis. As a baby he was called Nonie and his mother thought him the most wonderful being who had ever existed. On 30 October she took him down to Nymans, and her letters to her parents from this time onwards are full of raptures about the joys of motherhood, though what Lennie thought of fatherhood was never mentioned. Maud was fiercely possessive of the baby, writing soon after her arrival at Nymans:

> Nonie grows sweeter every day and he is all the dearer to me because he is like the Dad and Roy. I feel sometimes a wee bit resentful when everyone looks at him here as if they had a sort of connection with him. My little demon prompts me to snatch him up and run right away with him because he is my very very very own and yours and the Dad's own and if it had not been for you he could not have existed. He likes Nymans but he *loves* home—*my home*—and no place will come up to it.

Happy though she might be in her marriage, Maud still struggled to hold on to the freedom which she prized so highly, and it was through her children that she was to find her greatest pleasure and fulfilment. Photographs of Maud with her babies show her at the height of her remarkable beauty, and the glow of love and tenderness persists in later portraits where she is surrounded by her grandchildren.

CHAPTER THIRTEEN
ROY AT OXFORD:
EDGAR

OY HAD BEGUN his first term at University College Oxford in January 1898. His parents were naturally delighted to have their son at such a prestigious seat of learning and were full of hopes that it would be the making of him. Oxford was a romantic and beautiful city, as yet unspoiled by industrial expansion. Marion enjoyed a day's outing there, "Perfectly charmed with Oxford, one of the loveliest places I have ever seen, full of beauty and interest at every corner." Roy's first letter home augured well:

> My dear Papa. I arrived quite safe last night and have exceptionally nice rooms for a freshman, looking over the High Street. I start working tomorrow on Livy. I shall expect to see you on Tuesday, and don't forget the bicycle as it is somewhat necessary to have one here. We have to get up at 8 am three mornings in the week, and also have to attend 24 chapels per term, besides twice on Sundays. I have got my cap and gown and wore them for the first time when I called on Mr Bright this afternoon. With much love to Mother and Maud, your loving Roy.

His parents hoped he would enter the legal profession (for which proficiency in the classics was essential) and the University was still very conscious that it was primarily a religious foundation.

As might have been expected, the first taste of adult freedom was intoxicating. Work took second place and Marion soon had new cause for worry. At the end of the summer term she wrote: "Roy returned from Oxford at 4 o'clock. Looks fairly well, dark round eyes—too much in theatrical set." Roy had always been stage struck, so predictably his first love affair was with a pretty young actress. Photographs taken at this time show several groups of friends: the young men looking very dapper in flannels and boaters, the ladies wearing "tailor-mades" and elaborate hats. Some names are signed on one of these pictures: Jane May, Edna

175

Roy (in the light suit) with the Mays. Edna (right) with her mother (centre) and sister Jane.

May, and their mother Gina May. The Mays were an American family, probably all theatrical, as Edna is known to have made her first appearance on the stage when she was only five years old. In 1887, aged nineteen, she had been "discovered" and offered the lead in the musical *The Belle of New York*. This had a successful run in New York itself, then crossed the Atlantic to open in London on 12 April 1898. How Roy managed to strike up a friendship with Edna and her family is not clear, but *The Belle of New York* was an instant hit and he became the envy of all his fellow undergraduates. He wrote to his mother:

> I am sitting here simply surrounded by photos, chiefly of Miss May
> of course. . . . my room is a topic of conversation throughout college,
> and men keep dropping in one by one to inspect it.

Later Roy put all these photographs together in an album especially devoted to Edna, and the progress of their friendship can be charted by the message she wrote on each one. These move from "With kind regards" to "In remembrance of many

176

bully times", a phrase which at once evokes the new world: liberated American girls from all levels of society were taking Europe by storm at the turn of the century. The sheet music of *The Belle of New York* (with its drawing of Edna on the cover) is still at Stafford Terrace. The catchy tunes from the musical were sung and whistled all over town, and the most popular number "When we are married" has remained in the light music repetoire to this day. Marion and Linley (who had always enjoyed a good musical) went to see it four times, while Roy probably went very much more often than that. It is easy to imagine him persuading his mother to join him at the drawing-room piano to play and sing through the music, even though the star herself was never invited to cross the threshold of the parental home.

Not enough evidence is left to show what effect Roy's infatuation with Edna May had on the course of his life. *The Belle of New York* ran for more than a year, and was followed in 1900 by *An American Beauty* so that Edna enjoyed great popular acclaim. She was already married (though this was probably only a marriage of convenience) and it is unlikely that she would have been swept off her feet by a penniless undergraduate, however handsome and charming he might be. Roy's parents were quite understandably nervous of the company he was keeping. On 25 June 1898 Marion wrote, "Lennie and Maud went to see *Belle of New York*—saw Roy in stage box there with women! Could not recognise him of course. Perhaps Lin will see at last Roy is not the innocent child he seems to think him." This is one of Marion's diary entries which acts like the sudden opening of a window on to another world: the fact that Maud could not even wave to her brother because he was with unescorted females (though they may well have been Edna's mother and sister) shows how different the moral climate was from that of our own day. In matters of social etiquette Maud was just as strict as her mother. There were people one knew and people one did not know: proper introductions were essential. Tradespeople and servants existed as necessary supports to the upper echelons of society—the gap between mistress and maid being well understood—but there was an intermediate level where the boundaries were not clear-cut. The theatre occupied a place on the very edge of respectability. Great stage personalities like Ellen Terry or Henry Irving were people who Marion was proud to know, but even so they were never invited to Stafford Terrace. Girls who sang and danced in musical comedies were outside the pale. They were too close to the darker side of the entertainment business; the gambling hard-drinking sets, the kept women who lived in luxury, or the prostitutes who waited outside theatre doors. This half-world, familiar to Victorian men, was forbidden territory to their wives and daughters. Marion never wanted to explore—or even to mention—those regions where Annie and others like her dwelt, but it must have been an ever-present fear that Roy might slip into the same pit of vice.

Roy had always been adept at returning a soft answer to a parental rebuke. A year after his first meeting with Edna he was writing from Oxford, "Of course I would not like to displease Papa or cause him or you sorrow in any way, but he is wrong about Edna May, who although a burlesque actress and living apart from her husband is as *good* and as *ladylike* as anyone I have *ever* met. You would think the

same if you knew her. . . ." This letter would have done nothing to assuage his parents' anxieties. Even if the association was as innocent as Roy tried to make out, the fact remains that he never found a wife to make him happy in the way that Marion and Linley would have wished. Signed photographs of other pretty young actresses were later added to his collection, but one picture from each was enough, and it is tempting to assume that Edna was the only girl he really loved.

Whenever Roy was at home for more than a few days at a time friction began to build up between him and his mother. She was always pleased to see him—"Dear Roy returned from the Messels looking v.well & so good looking"—but after only three days of his company she was writing: "Roy to Oxford. Sorry & glad as it gets on my nerves to have him idling the precious hours away." Roy's academic career did not prosper, though he may have made some small efforts to please his long-suffering parents. In October 1899 he wrote, "I am doing a good deal of work but it

Edna May. All the photographs in Roy's collection are signed: this one says "With tender regards".

178

is fearfully hard and dull and dreadfully long. . . . very few think it would be possible for me to get a degree next June." This was not good news, but another letter (though it sounds strange to our egalitarian ears) would have given his father more satisfaction:

> I shall be glad when this term is over, it is really getting very dull here now. I find a very great difference between the general class of men at the Varsity and those I used to be accustomed to at Eton. The Etonian one can generally recognise all the world over, but there seems something lacking in the man that comes from another school, something in him that prevents him from becoming a real gentleman. . . .

Some of Linley's trouble and expense had after all been worth while, as there was never to be any doubt that Roy, even if he achieved little in life, was a proper gentleman.

Marion and Linley still went on regular visits to both Tabby and Midge in the country, but they did not go to Ramsgate for a long holiday, or even a short break, for several years. Instead they took to sampling various resorts along the south coast, staying in hotels instead of lodgings. Linley especially liked the channel ports as he could make a day trip across to France. Marion sometimes went with him, but not if the weather looked rough, when she preferred to stay ashore. She liked to establish herself comfortably in a hotel for a week or two at a time, with Linley as usual travelling up and down to London. In August 1897 when he had a whole string of engagements in town he wrote to her anxiously, "My dearest Polly. I feel quite sad at leaving you alone. If you feel in the blues, never again, and you *must* come up on Saturday or I come to you. Write and tell me *exactly* how you feel alone—with fondest love, ever your affectionate husband, Dickie." Marion did not mind being on her own for a short time, and she always enjoyed the chance of striking up interesting new aquaintances at the hotel. In the absence of her family she could also devote herself to reading: "Finished Mrs Gaskell's *Wives and Daughters*, v.true to life but so long and wordy glad to get through it" was one diary entry, and another, "Sat out after tea, actually felt dull, no book to read. Have finished Morley's Miscellanies, Robespierre, Byron, Macaulay, Emerson and Carlyle." French writers were still favourites, with Voltaire, Rousseau, Maupassant and Balzac appearing amongst other lesser known names. Some English authors whom she enjoyed were Matthew Arnold, Wilkie Collins, Olive Schreiner and Anthony Hope, but most of the comments on these books are unfortunately extremely brief, ranging from "most interesting" to "tiresome" or even "waste of time".

Marion's health remained poor. In November 1899 she went on her own to

Thanet for a week to convalesce after a bout of illness, but she chose Broadstairs rather than Ramsgate. The usual prescription was meted out by the local doctor: "Mr Treves came to see me, weakness and cold due entirely to nervous prostration, to rest in bed as much as possible." Although she was able to enjoy a Christmas visit to the Messels at Nymans that year, she was too ill to go with the rest of the family to Tabby's in January. By the end of February she was still "very seedy indeed" so Maud and Lennie asked her to go with them to a hotel in Ramsgate for a month. It was pleasant to see so many of her old friends after such a long absence, but Marion could not help noticing how age and infirmity were taking their toll. "Saw Mr Warre, looks v.shaky" she wrote, and "Think Mr Burnand looking much older & v.depressed, his old genial ways gone." On her return to London there were other friends who had not worn well: "To see Fildes' Stone's & Colin Hunter's pictures— met usual dowdy crowd!" was the diary entry on Picture Sunday 1900. But somebody who did please her very much in these turn of the century years was the ex-patriate American writer, Bret Harte, who would often call at Stafford Terrace for a morning gossip, or come to dinner *en famille*. He and Marion got on together very well and she found him a stimulating and amusing companion. They discussed literature and lent each other books, and he would write her little thank-you notes in his miniscule handwriting. Nearly all correspondence from people outside the immediate family was thrown away, but Bret Harte's letters were carefully preserved. Besides having been quite a celebrity in his youth (he was now in his sixties) it is possible that he was the only person Marion knew who genuinely appreciated her intellect and wished to hear her views on modern authors. Unlike her husband, he did not scold her for being "self-opinionated".

Linley posing in army uniform. In the years leading up to the Boer War England developed a very jingoistic attitude, which was reflected in the cartoons of the time.

The Boer War broke out in the autumn of 1899. Trouble had been brewing in South Africa since 1877 when the British had annexed the land south of the Vaal river where the Dutch colonists, known as Boers, had established a republic. After a decade of sporadic violence here it became clear that war was inevitable. The first engagements took place in October, but though the British were victorious they suffered unexpectedly heavy losses. On 30 October Marion wrote in her diary, "Terrible disaster to our troops near Ladysmith, had to surrender 2 battalions." The fighting was fully reported in the press and was very shocking to a people who had not known full-scale war since the Crimean campaign of 1854-6. Maud, safe at Nymans with her baby, wrote a letter which presages the feelings of those who were to be exposed to a greater conflict only fifteen years later:

> My darling Mother. It is such a heavenly morning. I am writing this in bed with my window wide open and I can hear the birds singing away in the trees. It seems terrible that while everything is so peaceful and beautiful here there is so much sorrow all round us. Two men that were in the same house at Eton with Lennie are killed and he feels it very much. We wait with sinking hearts for the paper each day. . . . Oh think darling how awful it would be for us if our dear ones were fighting. . . .

By the end of the year the Sambournes were taking a close interest in events, as Marion's brother, Edgar, was a Captain in the Lincolnshire Regiment and it seemed likely that he would be sent out to South Africa. Many people were predicting that the war would be over by Christmas, so that Edgar was much concerned that he might miss this opportunity to go on active service. Great was his elation when the call came in December. As soon as Marion heard his news she sent him a present of chocolate to supplement the expected hard rations, and on 4 January 1900 wrote, "Edgar sails with the 7th division for S.Africa today." She was to receive several letters from him during the next few months, giving fascinating insights into the progress of the war.

British troops suffered more reverses in the early weeks of 1900. "January 29th. Bad news from war. Spion Kop abandoned after loss", but those at home only became more determined than ever to press for victory. Roy wrote from Oxford, "Lots of men are going from here to the war—I wish I were too. Edgar will I hope get through the campaign all right, I study the papers daily on the chance of seeing his name mentioned. . . ." By the end of February things had taken a turn for the better and Marion recorded on the 27th, "Good news from S.Africa, Cronje surrendered." This was the British capture of Paardeburg, where Cronje, the Boer General, surrendered with 4,000 men to Lord Roberts. Unknown to the Sambournes, Edgar's regiment had taken part in the battle, and a month later a long letter about the campaign arrived at Stafford Terrace.

Edgar's letter was headed "Paardeburg Drift, Modder River, about 34 miles east of Jacobsdaal", and was written in pencil on very poor quality paper:

My dearest Marion. I received two letters from you last evening. It is very good of you to write & send me the handkerchief. Any little thing of that description, a piece of soap, a towel, anything of daily use is acceptable. Also a sheet of paper & an envelope ready addressed facilitates my answer. I am very hard up for writing paper, this is some I got in Cronje's laager (camp) after his surrender. We got here a fortnight ago having marched 34 miles the longest march I have ever done. . . . On the day previous to our arrival there had been an unsuccessful assault on the laager by our troops. They got up to 80 yards of the laager by night with bayonets & were driven back, casualties 700. If you could see the Boer defences after the surrender as I have you would term it simply murder to assault them. The following day or rather night we marched back to the river Modder and blundered into the outposts of the Boers. At about 3.30 am shots were heard and shortly after the retire given. I managed to keep my company together and formed it up and faced about but I found some of our own people and our wagons in front of me. The shot & shell was falling thick about us and eventually the whole regiment got in with two officers wounded slightly, one sergeant killed and 13 men wounded. The mercy is that we didn't have half the regiment slaughtered. I wonder whether this has appeared in the papers. I strongly suspect not but be careful in not making what I write public property. . . . My best love to you dear, ever your very affectionate bro, Edgar.

At the end of March Edgar had a few days rest behind the lines at Bloemfontein which gave him time to write again:

This is a very pretty place indeed and the country all around is beautiful grass for miles and miles. It is a lovely climate but when it rains it does rain. The whole place in about 10 minutes is simply a pond. Another officer & myself came here yesterday for a change and to get out of the camp. The place is crammed with officers, there are something like 6,000 troops in & around Bloemfontein. Every-thing is at war prices; last night at the hotel we could get nothing to drink except St Julien claret at 9/- a bottle, no whisky to be had. The great comfort is that there is plenty of food. A good dinner is rather a treat after bully beef and biscuit for a month. . . ."

Later letters reveal that Edgar was engaged in more fighting, but in spite of heavy losses, difficulties with transport, sickness among the troops and some bungling from the leaders, morale in the army seems to have remained high and victory was always only just around the corner. At home Linley pasted into his diary the brief and poignant death notices of those young men of his acquaintance who lost their lives in the campaign. Several returned maimed, but the dreaded enteric fever was a more common cause of death than battle wounds. The relief of Mafeking, besieged

by the Boers for two hundred and fifteen days, was cause for great national rejoicing, "Kept awake half the night with noise & shouting" wrote Marion on 19 May. On 13 July the family at Stafford Terrace received bad news: "Edgar severely wounded in left ankle. Five companies of Lincolns & Scots Greys surprised by Boers. Wire from Sophy." Sophy at once sailed to South Africa to succour her husband, leaving her sister-in-law feeling "Most anxious & unhappy". There was disturbing news too from the other side of the world, where in China a fanatical sect called the Boxers had risen in rebellion: "Terrible accounts of massacre of all Europeans in Peking — tragedies of the middle ages returned" wrote Marion on 15 July. Fortunately Edgar's wound proved not too serious and by October 1900 he was back in London. "Lovely day. To see Edgar, looks wonderfully well & 10 years younger" was Marion's comment. Edgar was forty seven: the campaign had been the crown of his career and he had thoroughly enjoyed the experience.

Apart from the progress of the Boer War, the most important event of 1900 was the *Exposition Universelle* held in Paris. Linley was asked to represent Great Britain as a juror for Class 7 of the Fine Arts section; a great honour which must have pleased him very much. On 3 June Marion went with him to Paris for a busy and enjoyable fortnight, although the French capital was not quite the wonderful place it had been in former years. Not only had the war in South Africa put the English out of favour, but the overcharging and poor service in shops and restaurants was very marked: "Nothing worth buying, dearer & not half so pretty as in our own shops" was Marion's verdict. But she had come on purpose to see the Exhibition and was determined to do the whole thing thoroughly. Linley was busy most days so she had to fend for herself, which she managed perfectly well even though it was all very tiring. "Fearful crowd, great heat & dust" she wrote, "Magnificent buildings, walked through pictures & statuary, endless." Each country had its own pavilion and Marion looked at three or four of these each day: she liked the Belgian and Japanese the best but found the English pavilion disappointing. As usual the diary contains hardly any comments on the exhibits themselves; one would have liked to have had her opinion on the Gallerie Rodin with its much discussed studies for *L'Enfer*, while the significance of the entry "Saw Pasteur bottles!" is lost on the modern reader. Marion and Linley usually met for a quick lunch, and in the evenings they joined various English friends who had also come over for the exhibition — Mr Spielman, Mr Ernest George, Admiral Keppel, Mr Davis, Mr Yeames — for a convivial dinner.

Linley took over the position of "First Cartoon" from Sir John Tenniel on 1 January 1901, three days before his fifty-seventh birthday. Tenniel was a remarkable and much loved personality, still hale and hearty at eighty years of age. He had worked

for *Punch* for fifty years, so Linley's step up when it came at last was a real challenge. The Queen died on 23 January, so he soon had to demonstrate that he could rise to a great occasion. The whole country was plunged into mourning. "All silent & hushed, gloom prevailing, festivities postponed, Lin greatly worried with work" wrote Marion. She went into Hyde Park on 2 February to watch the Queen's funeral procession pass by. Although she was not able to see much, the atmosphere was unforgettable: "Intense crowd, never saw anything like it, all silent & in mourning." No one can have doubted that they were witnessing a historic moment; the Queen had reigned sixty-four years and only the very old could remember any other monarch. A great and glorious age was over, the nineteenth century had truly ended.

The gay nineties now gave way to a slightly less hectic epoch. King Edward VII's influence had been felt in Society during the previous decade when he had made no secret of the fact that he enjoyed good living, the company of rich bankers and the attentions of pretty women. He was sixty when he came to the throne, so his wildest days were over. To the surprise of his subjects he soon made a reputation for himself as a wise statesman, exercising a beneficent influence over an increasingly restless and troubled Europe. In England all was apparently calm, with the *nouveaux riches* and the professional classes establishing themselves ever more firmly in the hierarchy of power and influence. The Sambournes' middle age, settled, happy and comfortable, mirrored the glow of the Edwardian afternoon. Linley had achieved his goal, Maud's marriage was everything that her parents could have hoped for and Marion worried far less about money, though she still meticulously noted all the buying and selling of her shares and cast up her accounts on the end-papers of her diary. It was a matter for great satisfaction that nearly every year brought in a few more pounds than its predecessor. Lennie sometimes made a little speculation for her and the profit from these deals was very welcome, but expenses were very much less than they had been during the Ramsgate years when the children were growing up.

Maud and Lennie had bought a country house of their own early in 1900. This was very close to Nymans, in beautiful unspoilt countryside. When Marion visited it for the first time she wrote: "To 'Glovers' Charlwood. Found darling Maud, Baby & Lennie well. House & grounds charming both outside and in. My room sweet." Maud as usual pressed her parents to stay for as long as they liked, so that Marion was able to dandle the baby and get used to being a grandmother, while Maud busied herself organising curtains and sofa covers for her new home. At weekends Lennie was an enthusiastic gardener, planting quantities of primroses and other simple county flowers around the house. Both he and Maud were admirers of the new informality in gardening (as preached by William Robinson and Gertrude Jekyll) and later they too became well known in the horticultural world.

Marion always remarked every time she saw her daughter whether she was pale and tired or looked seedy, and now that Maud was no longer directly under her care she worried about her more than ever. Maud had inherited her mother's constitution and probably some measure of her hypochondria as well: both she and Lennie were constantly plagued by various colds, pains, aches and fevers. Lennie suffered from eczema and headaches, and Marion often described him as "very depressed". For a

Roy posing as a supercilious young man
about town.

young couple in their twenties with every good thing in life at their command the catalogue of ills seems extensive. The pattern of behaviour established long ago between Marion and Mrs Herapath was to be repeated with uncanny similarity in the next generation: "Maudie not so well, most anxious & feel such a wreck myself" and similar entries became a regular feature of Marion's diary, while Maud's letters in their turn constantly urged her mother, "Be sure to *rest* and take great care of your precious self."

Roy had left Oxford at the end of the summer term 1900, after having been there less than three years. Once again his parents thought that the only way to get him through his exams was to send him to a crammer, but this, predictably, was not a success. "Roy getting very tiresome again, debts, bills & general indiscretions spoiling his better nature" wrote Marion that autumn. A little later she was sighing, "Wish boys were as little worry as girls or Roy as manageable as darling Maud was." By the end of the year the family had at last concluded that it was no good pushing Roy any longer. He never returned to Oxford to take his degree, but was sent to work — in an unspecified capacity — for a Mr Devitt in the City.

Roy had no idea what he wanted to do with his life, except to become very rich and have plenty of leisure. It was probably the Messels who encouraged him to take up stockbroking; certainly their example must have made it look an easy way to make money. Lennie kindly offered to help by putting up the money necessary for the young man to become a member of the Stock Exchange, but temperamentally Roy was neither a plodder nor a gambler and the nervous stress of trying to cope with high finance merely exacerbated the strain of manic-depression in his nature.

185

After the day's dealing he would come home to Stafford Terrace either wildly elated, noisy and "tiresome", or else deeply depressed and morose, casting a blight over the whole household. Good manners, hard work, and a cheerful spirit in the face of difficulties were part and parcel of Marion's code of living; Roy's behaviour had often distressed her, and she was baffled by his failure to get to grips with adult life. "Roy depressed, wish he had more pluck & energy, seems to hopelessly rely on others instead of on himself" she wrote, and "Roy v.odd evening, must have had too much, nearly maddened me & felt v.unhappy & worried." Over and over again she returned to this problem, the one area in her life which was manifestly a failure. Roy, too, must have suffered from a sense of inadequacy and a feeling that he could never be the son his mother wanted. Although Marion wrote, "Roy *most* trying at dinner, worries Lin so after his tiring work", it seems from Linley's diary that he and Roy did not really have much trouble in their relationship, being bonded by their masculinity, love of good living, and a passion for all kinds of sport.

A handsome charming bachelor, even if impecunious, is always an asset at parties and Roy was much in demand. Marion took his repeated absence from the family dining table as another slight, though in view of their difficulties it is hardly surprising that he preferred to go out. At weekends and holidays he often went to stay with his bosom crony, Mr Stern, whose lavish spending habits made him even more discontented with his lot. Marion never mentioned the possibility of finding her son a suitable girlfriend, though she must have often wished that he could be distracted from the charms of Edna May. Roy's aunts were always very kind, pressing him to stay with them in the country, so that he was thrown much into the company of his three pretty young cousins. Photographs of Dora Langley and of Gwen and Eveleen Fletcher hang on his bedroom walls at Stafford Terrace: marriage to one of them would have been a wonderful solution to his problems. Both Midge and Tabby set their sights high and neither would have considered their nephew adequate as a son-in-law, but it is intriguing to note that as each daughter in turn became engaged it was Roy who received the news before it was announced to anyone else.

PART FOUR
1902-1914

Marion. A studio portrait taken in 1910.

CHAPTER FOURTEEN

GRANDCHILDREN

AUD'S SECOND PREGNANCY did not go as smoothly as her first, and during the latter part of it she spent several weeks laid up at her London home warding off the threat of premature birth. Thus Marion was greatly relieved when she was able to write on 8 February 1902: "My darling Maud's little baby girl born 5.20 pm, Lin & I there. Brought on on account of flooding last night & all over in under 2 hours. Baby weighs 6½ lbs, miracle it lived." However an anxious time followed as Maud was very weak after her haemorrhage, and four days after the birth developed pleurisy. Baby Anne was also ill with severe convulsions and for a time both lives hung in the balance. To crown all, Roy contracted mumps and Marion was forbidden to see her daughter for fear of carrying the infection. She was frantic with worry, but fortunately the crisis only lasted a few days. On 14 March she was allowed to visit Maud for the first time: "Went to my darling, lunched & had tea there, better than I dared expect. Baby still very delicate-looking. Lovely being with Maud again."

With two children and a new partnership agreement which doubled his income, Lennie decided to move to a larger country house. His choice fell on an estate near the village of Balcombe in Sussex, a few miles to the south east of Nymans. Marion was taken to see it while Maud was convalescent. "With Lennie to Haywards Heath, took fly to Balcombe House. Charming house, not picturesque like Glovers, but roomy airy & convenient. No pretty flower garden, parkland round, good kitchen garden." This early Georgian building, with its elegant wrought iron verandah, had the sort of old-fashioned prettiness that was just beginning to be admired, rather than despised as too plain. In fact Balcombe was very much the kind of house that Nymans had once been, before Ludwig Messel carried out his extensive rebuilding in the 1890s. Maud and Lennie did not want to modernise: they were much more

Left: Maud with little Linley and baby Anne, 1903.

Balcombe House, Sussex, the country estate that Lennie bought in 1905. He and Maud lived there for over twenty years.

interested in the genuinely antique. Marion went to stay with them in August 1902. "Balcombe House charming, furniture shows up much better & all painted white is so fresh & clean, a great sense of space & room," she wrote. After her experiment with country life at Glovers Maud now knew what she wanted; Balcombe was very much her own creation, and it made the ideal background for her beauty and good taste. Her children grew up here and were devoted to the place: everything about the house and garden was perfect and they resented the move to Nymans, which took place twenty years later when Ludwig Messel died and their father came into his inheritance.

Lennie had another new acquisition early in 1902—a motor car. He was not the first in the field; Marion had seen an electric carriage in the Park in September 1897, and Linley had had an exciting outing in April 1898: "Lin to Guildford with Mr Roger Wallace on motor. Wire from him during dinner, arrived safely, enjoyed it immensely." Her own first experience of this mode of transport had been at Glovers in 1901 when a friend of Lennie's had come visiting and had offered a ride: "Maud & self in motor, rather nervous, wizzing down hill and round corner, near shave of accident". Lennie's first motor was a Panhard, and he proudly took his in-laws out for drives—to Hampstead to demonstrate how well it dealt with the steep gradient, and to Windsor to show its turn of speed. Linley timed their trip from Kensington to Windsor and back (about 40 miles) at 1 hour and 40 minutes. It was this speed, and the fact that there was no need to rest the horses, which was the key to the eventual

triumph of the motor car over the carriage, though it took much longer than the bicycle had done to become established as transport for the masses. A chauffeur was essential in these early days, and a trained mechanic too, as the engines were most unreliable and the tyres extremely weak. Marion recorded several breakdowns when she had to get out and walk, or wait to be picked up by a passing farmer's cart. Comfort was a low priority and Marion preferred to ride in a carriage because it had better springs and fewer draughts. Despite these draw-backs, motoring was a delightful new way of spending money, and very soon all the Sambournes' rich friends and relations owned a motor. They themselves never bought one, and as they grew older used their own carriage less and less. With Maud ever ready to lend either her open victoria or carriage-and-pair (both so much nicer than their own one-horse brougham) they had little need to keep up the stables in Phillimore Place. Linley no longer rode, and even the bicycle was beginning to lose its charm, but he refused to consider selling the horses or making economies in this department and nothing Marion said would change his mind.

After Edgar's safe return from South Africa Marion lost interest in the Boer War and did not mention it in her diary until peace negotiations were set in hand two years later. These were very protracted, but by the end of May 1902 it seemed as if agreement might be reached at last. "Lin finished Peace drawing but no peace certain yet" was her entry on 25 May, and on 1 June she wrote, "To Lady Hickman's, tennis for Lin & we dine there after." That evening it was "Peace news real this time, heard at Sir Arthur's" and the next day, "Streets & every place gone mad with peace news, great crowds."

The coronation of King Edward VII had been arranged to take place on 26 June 1902, a fitting celebration, it was hoped, to usher in a new era of peace and prosperity. All the preparations were made, streets decorated, stands erected, the special issue of *Punch* already published, when it was suddenly announced that the King was gravely ill and would have to be operated upon at once for appendicitis. On 24 June it was "General alarm and anxiety about the King's operation", and on the 26th, "Coronation postponed—all gloom and anxiety for the King." It was not only a dreadful anti-climax for the nation, but a matter for great perturbation also, as any operation on the internal organs was a life-threatening matter. "Appendicitis" was a new word which the public grasped with avidity, even though the condition itself had long masqueraded under various other names. It is quite surprising how many of the Sambournes' acqaintances were to suffer from this affliction during the next few years, and some of them died of it. Amongst those who could afford it the operation for removal of the appendix became very popular and was usually successful, though it still carried a very high risk factor until the introduction of the sulpha drugs two generations later.

All the decorations for the coronation were hurriedly taken down, but the week did contain some bright spots as the list of Coronation Honours was not cancelled and Frank Burnand received his longed-for Knighthood. Marion hastened round to The Boltons to offer congratulations to her old friend, now Lady Burnand. Another of Linley's friends, Mr Henderson of Buscot Park, became Baron Farringdon, and Arthur Conan Doyle (the creator of the Sherlock Holmes stories) was knighted. Linley's cartoon, which he did at great speed to replace the one already prepared for the next issue of *Punch*, received many compliments. "Everyone delighted with dear Lin's drawing 'The Vigil'" wrote Marion on 2 July.

Soon after the Sambournes first became grandparents their participation in the gyrations of the London Season had begun to wane. Marion continued to make a point of calling on all the right people as the Season opened (twenty-four calls in two days made sure that everybody knew that the Sambournes were in town), but there seemed fewer party invitations worth accepting and no more dinners for twelve were held at Stafford Terrace. She still went each year to the Academy private view, but usually in Maud's company rather than in Linley's: "To Academy. Maudie fetched me 2.30 looking sweet in red dress, everyone admires her greatly. Saw Lockyers, Burnands, Fildes, Stones, etc etc etc. Stayed till past 5.30, had tea with Maud." Entertainment at home was gradually reduced to what it had been in the early eighties—family gatherings with the occasional addition of one or two couples of congenial friends. Marion spent more time reading to Linley while he worked, and diary entries like "Lin & self quiet little evening alone, very cosy", which had been non-existent in the nineties became commonplace by the time the new decade had passed its halfway mark. Weekend house-parties were now the favourite form of social gathering, as they gave Linley the sport and Marion the company they each so much enjoyed. The Galbraiths were now renting Terregles, Dumfries, where they entertained the Sambournes for several years running. Newer friends like the Howldens, the Johnson-Fergusons and the Beales also took big country houses, so that Marion and Linley were regular visitors to Renishaw, Springkell and Drumlanford. The Bakers at Pangbourne were pressing in their hospitality, while Midge and Tabby were as free with their invitations as ever. Things had settled down in South America after the worries of the early nineties and Hamilton Langley's estates there were thriving. He and Midge were now permanently based in England, renting Gatley Park in Shropshire in 1902 and Stoke Edith Park in 1903 before settling at Bedstone Court in 1904. The Fletchers divided their time between The Anchorage on the Hampshire coast and Pyt House in Wiltshire, and Marion spent several weeks of each year at one or other of her sisters' houses. Hamilton Fletcher was still passionate about yachting and had the 340 ton steam yacht *Joyeuse* built to his own specification in 1898, while in 1902 he made a lucky shipping speculation which brought him in £72,000, a sum he hardly needed.

Maud in 1903, at the height of her beauty.

Maud's third and last child came into the world with little trouble. On 13 January 1904 Marion wrote, "Maudie's dear little second son born. Only awakened at 6 o'clock in morning & all over by 10! I arrived at 10.15 & found my darling looking so well. Such a clean strong happy baby. Remained at Gloucester Terrace all day." The child throve, and was christened Oliver.

Soon after Oliver's birth Marion wrote a letter to her brother Edgar. Edgar had retired from the army with the rank of Major and a DSO after the Boer War, and decided to take a journey round the world before settling down to the life of a country gentleman. He and Sophy had left England in November 1903 and at regular intervals long interesting letters arrived at Stafford Terrace, full of their experiences. Like the good sister she was, Marion wrote to each far-flung port of call on Edgar's itinerary, to make sure that he had news of all the family at home. Her letter dated 28 February 1904 (addressed to Honolulu) arrived too late to catch him and was returned to sender. This is the only one of Marion's many letters to her dear ones which has survived, and it is delightful to find that it reinforces all the impressions already formed by reading the diary. She had just been to the wedding of her niece, Dora Langley, to Paul Foley:

Hamilton & Midge are at the Coburg Hotel. They left home a week after the wedding which was a great success, altho' a pouring wet day. Dora looked lovely & they made a very handsome couple—they have so much in common & I trust they will be very happy, they have all that this world can give to make them so. It was very nice being together at Stoke Edith, we all wished you & Mervyn could have been there too. Con was most funny & Ham F in splendid form, it was very jolly indeed. If only Maudie could have been there too dear little thing. . . . Ham & Midge met us at our box yesterday at the Criterion—such an amusing piece by Capt Marshall, we roared. H misses Dora v.much & he seems to feel the parting far more than Midge, & all their friends seem to pity him most. They are both dining here tonight, & were here last Sunday also, when Midge & I talked! as we of the family can do!!! when we get together. . . . Tabby & H go to Paris on 7th March where H takes possession of his beautiful motor, 24 horse power, & they go by motor to Biarritz! isn't that delightful? They expect to be away 3 weeks. Lin Roy & I go to Pyt for Easter. Lin is so anxious for me to go & Tabs is v. dear & says I am not to wriggle out of it this time—I love going but my whole heart is with Maud she is so dreadfully delicate. She was getting on so nicely & baby 5 weeks old when she was taken with fearful pain & is now in bed & not able to move with threatening of appendicitis & is allowed to see me only for a little while each day— however they hope with care to avoid an operation as she is not strong enough for it. Baby will be 7 weeks old on Wed, such a dear boy & so good. . . . Poor Aunt Barbara wrote me yesterday saying she has been v.ill—there is no chance of my getting to see her—every moment of the day is rushed in domestic duties & fitting in time to be with Maud & my 1½ hours with Lin who is injured if I don't sit with him parts of the day—his meals take him about 5 minutes each! & that long after I have had mine. . . ."

Edgar and Sophy settled at Ravendale Hall, Lincolnshire, when they got back from their trip round the world and this made yet another pleasant place for Marion to spend a fortnight or two each year. She became very attached to Edgar as the years passed: he was always so kind and considerate, nothing he could do for her comfort was ever too much trouble. Most of the men in her life were rather self-centred, and Edgar's sympathy went a long way towards compensating for the fact that he never was, and never could be, "amusing". This word was reserved for Spencer, who retained the knack of making her laugh, but Marion's closest ties of affection had always been with her sisters. It is hard to say which of them she loved best: she saw Tabby more often perhaps, but Midge had always been more fun, and as she grew older was increasingly described as "witty", an epithet earned by no one else in the family. Conrad and Effie were seldom encountered after 1900. Their marriage had been showing signs of strain for a few years and it seems as if the couple had elected to live apart. Although both were still occasionally entertained at

Stafford Terrace, they no longer appeared together and there were no more holidays with them in the country.

After 1905 another relation was often to be found at Stafford Terrace— Annie's daughter, Edith. Mrs Herapath had kept up an affectionate correspondence with Edith during her childhood, but it does not seem as if any other member of the family ever acknowledged her existence. Marion must have had this neglect on her conscience, so when she had recovered from the shock of Annie's death she wrote to this long-forgotten niece asking her to spend Christmas 1899 at Stafford Terrace. Edith was a year older than Maud and earned her living by teaching music in Hamburg; though Marion said little about the visit in her diary uncomfortable feelings prickle on the page. Maud promised to help: she attended to Edith's hair and fitted her out with some clothes, but no welcome or hospitality was extended by Spencer, Edgar, Midge, Tabby or Mervyn, and when Edith returned to Hamburg in January everyone was rather relieved.

As the years passed Marion became reconciled to the existence of Annie's children. Edith's brothers had spent all their lives in Australia, first in the orphanage and then in menial jobs. When they discovered (after their mother's death) that they had a long-lost sister living in Hamburg, they came over to Europe to join her. The elder boy, Herbert, visited England with Edith early in 1905. Once again the

Edith Furrell, Annie's daughter. Taken in Hamburg, where she studied music.

195

Sambournes were the only ones to receive them, and Lennie—urged by Maud to extend a helping hand—offered to find the young man some employment. Herbert was a harder pill for Marion to swallow than Edith had been: she gave him a tip of five shillings when he first came to see them, and later sent him an old suit of Linley's. Edith and Herbert decided to try life in England, so they set up in a little flat together: he worked in a bank earning £150 a year while she gave lessons in music and German at a school on one day a week and to Maud's children another day. When she was not working Edith often came round to Stafford Terrace, where she played the part proper for an impecunious spinster niece—running errands, mending underwear and tidying drawers. In return Marion took her calling, gave her theatre tickets, and had her to dinner when they entertained friends. (Herbert was only asked when no one else was present.) Although Marion felt uncomfortable about Edith's clothes and rebuked her for wearing rouge ("Such bad form") she became quite fond of her and appreciated her usefulness and good sense. One hopes that Edith too found pleasure in helping her aunt and was grateful for the kindness—even though belated—shown by one branch of her mother's family.

When Oliver was a year old Maud and Lennie decided to have a larger London house. Gloucester Terrace was too small for three children and their nursery staff, nor was it any longer a sufficiently imposing setting for Maud's entertaining or Lennie's art collection. Early in 1905 Marion wrote, "Drove morning to Maudie, went over 104 Lancaster Gate, charming house, so bright & sunny." The move took place in the autumn and set the seal on the young Messels' worldly success. The ranges of tall ornate stucco buildings along the Bayswater Road (of which Lancaster Gate is only a part) face due south across the great open spaces of Hyde Park and Kensington Gardens. They show the typical London house in its grandest manifestation: only Nash's terraces overlooking Regent's Park are more noble. Here Maud and Lennie could enjoy fine rooms and have space for numerous servants, whilst the children in their nursery were level with the tops of the trees. Hyde Park was still the special playground of the upper classes, a place to ride and drive, meet and talk, see and be seen. The nursemaids with their perambulators congregated in Kensington Gardens, where they could stroll along the shady paths, or sit by the bandstand listening to music on summer afternoons. Here too was the Round Pond, where the children fed the ducks and sailed their model boats. It was in Kensington Gardens that the writer J.M.Barrie met the Llewellyn-Davies children, who became the inspiration for his play *Peter Pan*, first produced in 1904. Their mother was Sylvia Llewellyn-Davies, daughter of George du Maurier. Mrs du Maurier had moved into London from Hampstead, so now it was easier for Marion to call on her and the two ladies became quite friendly: sometimes Sylvia was with her mother and it was a special pleasure for Marion when she met the famous Mr Barrie in their company.

Like everyone else in that circle she was saddened when she heard of Sylvia's tragically early death in 1910: "What a sorrow for her poor mother & her 5 boys — so young & so beautiful."

Marion had always enjoyed walking through Kensington Gardens. From Stafford Terrace to Lancaster Gate would have taken her about half an hour, and if this walk was followed by lunch with Maud, an outing in her carriage to go to the dressmaker or pay calls, and then tea with the grandchildren, she considered the day quite perfect. There were many such days, and one can imagine all her feelings of pleasure and satisfaction each time she settled into Maud's comfortable victoria and went bowling across the park in the sunshine, with all the world turning to look at the young and beautiful Mrs Messel in her lace and pearls and lovely hats — and perhaps sparing a thought too for the lady at her side, the wife of the well-known *Punch* cartoonist. Even then the cup of pleasure was not full, as there was the happy prospect of long restful holidays at Balcombe, where Maud and Lennie insisted on a very private life and to which only relatives and very close friends were ever invited. Maud was always asking her parents to come down to stay, so that Marion and Linley spent many weeks of every year enjoying the tranquillity, the country walks and drives, and the garden full of flowers.

In 1905 the Sambournes decided to treat themselves to an extravagant spring holiday. They had not been abroad since their trip to Paris in 1900, and a Mediterranean cruise (organised by the travel agents Thomas Cook & Son, who made their fortune by inventing the package tour) was the newest way to escape the winter. Accordingly they crossed the channel and took a train to Marseilles, where they boarded a P&O steamship on 18 March. Unfortunately the SS *Orient* was overcrowded, the organisation muddled and the cabins dreadfully cramped. There was little of the luxury to which Marion and Linley had become accustomed on their holidays with the wealthy, and not very many congenial souls on board either. But what really contrived to spoil the trip was Linley's new camera, which was found to have been damaged in the packing. It was typical of Marion's lifelong antipathy to photography that she was quite unable to appreciate what a disaster this was for her husband. He spent the whole of the first week of the cruise trying to mend it, getting increasingly overwrought and despairing each day, while Marion became more and more impatient with him. "Dined at table with Lord Mount Edgcumbe, had interesting talk. Peaceful happy day except for camera" she wrote, and next day, "Have hateful headache, dear Lin so worried over trifles worries me, gets so upset about nothing instead of keeping calm and quiet."

While Linley stayed in his cabin struggling with the camera, Marion sat on deck chatting to the other passengers and watching the lovely scenery. The SS *Orient* steamed through the Straits of Messina, within sight of Stromboli and Etna, and on to Corfu. They both spent a whole day ashore at Corfu, ("a picture of beauty" according to Marion) and another at Olympia, where the red and purple anemones grew wild amongst the broken columns, but the accident to the camera blighted everything. "Lin livery & absolutely absorbed in his injured camera — hoped to have got away from this hateful photography it seems so much more trouble to him than

to anyone else & is always being lost or broken" wrote Marion crossly, but she was determined to carry on and enjoy herself in spite of everything.

The ship arrived at Athens on 24 March. "Excellent night's rest, up at 8.30. Beautiful view of Acropolis as we approached Piraeus. Huge natural harbour full of ships, counted 18 on one side alone." Everyone went ashore and had a strenuous day's sightseeing: though it was cold and wet the Sambournes tramped round all the sights and Marion pronounced everything delightful. The next day Linley got his camera temporarily fixed by a man in Athens, and was able to take a few pictures. "Walked to Dionysius Theatre where Lin took photos, Temple of Theseus & Acropolis most beautiful even in the rain which made distant hills deep grey blue."

From Athens the ship sailed along the coast of Smyrna. "The Asiatic coast reminds us of some of the milder parts of Norway, wooded hills & snow capped mountains", wrote Marion, thinking of their cruise on the *Palatine* fifteen years earlier. The weather continued wretched, just as bad as at home, "Dull raining & bitterly cold as we steamed thro' the Dardanelles, saw the Hellespont. Walked on deck but miserably cold & finally sat in our cabin the only restful place as every other is crammed." However Constantinople was enjoyable: Linley cheered up ("very glad Lin at last realises his camera hopeless in its present condition") and they were both much impressed by Santa Sophia. They watched the Sultan go by in procession to the mosque, viewed the Treasury, and bought attar of roses. They also met the British Ambassador and his wife, Sir Nicholas and Lady O'Connor, who were "very gracious" and invited them to luncheon at the Embassy next day.

From Constantinople the SS *Orient* headed south. The weather became warm and pleasant at last, but all too soon the passengers began to complain of the heat. Everyone disembarked at Alexandria and took the train for Cairo, where the Sambournes went to Shepheards Hotel. On 6 April Marion wrote, "Left at 9 o'clock for Pyramids in carriage. V.hot. Arrived at Mena House Hotel where our horses refused to move so had to walk up hill in hot sand! Too nervous to take camel & donkeys bad. Wonderful sight Sphinx & its temple underground. Excellent lunch at hotel, left at 2.30 for museum, saw Rameses II & many others! & the newly found treasures from Thebes." Next day, "Left at 9 o'clock in motor for steam launch for Memphis & Sakkara. Good lunch on board at 11.30. At 12.30 to Memphis on donkeys, v.hot. Saw colossus of Rameses II, wonderful granite statues." Linley was never comfortable in hot weather and was dreadfully bitten by mosquitoes, so it was a relief to return to Alexandria and the SS *Orient*, "Quite cool on board after infernal heat of Cairo, like another planet", wrote Marion. Four days later the ship was back at Marseilles. After a muddle with the luggage and an unpleasant channel crossing the Sambournes were thankful to reach home safely on 16 April.

CHAPTER FIFTEEN
LAST YEARS

T THE END of 1906, when she was fifty-five, Marion fell seriously ill. At first the doctor thought it was influenza: Maud came every day with flowers and presents to make the stay in bed more comfortable, but by the tenth day the fever had still not abated. The family were all worried about her condition, and Maud urged a second opinion, recommending her own physician, Dr Pollock. He thought very seriously of the case, diagnosed kidney trouble, and arranged for a nurse to come to the house. Another week passed—during which Marion was too ill to write in her diary—before it was decided that an operation (the exact nature of which was never disclosed) would be the only way of saving her life. Linley wrote on 23 December: "Terrible news that dear M must have an operation tomorrow. The greatest blow I have had in my married life. Miserable & wretched." The next day was Christmas Eve: "Dear M resigned. Sat with her 1½ hours until turned out at 12.30. Terribly anxious. At 1.0 Dr Hayford, Dr Pollock & the anaesthetic man came. Spencer Mite & Lennie here. Over at 2p.m with good news."

Later Marion filled in the gap in her diary with the words, "Awful time. Would much prefer to have died." Her daily entries were not resumed for six weeks, and another nine months were to pass before they regained their usual brisk tone. She spent almost the whole of 1907 away from home, staying in the country with her sisters and depending on the constant services of a trained nurse. All that time she regarded herself as an invalid, staying much of the day in bed, or taking little outings in a bath chair. There was a great scare too about the drains at Stafford Terrace. The Sanitary Inspector came round and condemned them in March and Marion, in her weakened condition, was afraid to set foot in the house until they had been completely overhauled.

Just after Marion's operation Linley had a nasty bout of influenza. To aid his recovery Maud and Lennie proposed that he accompanied them on the European tour which they took every spring, so in March 1907 the three of them set off for Spain. They sent back a shower of affectionate letters to Marion (who was staying

with Tabby in the country), full of how much they were enjoying themselves in Biarritz, Madrid, Seville and Granada, and how often they wished she could be there with them. Marion did not need much cheering up, as the Fletchers were kindness itself, providing every comfort and pressing her to stay on with them for as long as she liked. But just before the travellers were due to return she and Tabby heard sad news—Conrad had died suddenly of heart failure, aged fifty-one. Apart from Annie, who had not been "family" for thirty years, Conrad's was the first death to break the Herapath circle. Marion was especially distressed that both Edgar and Linley were abroad and unable to attend the funeral, that most important focus of family sympathy and solidarity.

Linley returned from Spain on 25 April, writing, "Saw dear M first time since 11th March." They had never been separated for so long before, and for the rest of Marion's time away from home he made sure to come and visit her every weekend. She was always so pleased to see him: Conrad's death, her own feebleness and the thought of more separation made her weepy and nervous. She fussed about Linley being so much alone at Stafford Terrace; he was not really well, his cough was bad, his pallor distressing. In fact his condition, along with the worry about the drains, occupied her thoughts obsessively during the months of her convalescence. Sometimes she was sufficiently depressed to think that her operation, and the long struggle back to health after it, had simply not been worth the pain, effort and expense.

Tabby moved to Leweston Manor in May, so Marion came back to London to stay for a month with Maud at Lancaster Gate. July was spent at Buxton in Derbyshire (where the waters were said to be especially good for kidney trouble) and for the next two months she stayed with Midge in Shropshire. At the end of September she went back to Maud at Balcombe, and finally returned to Stafford Terrace on 12 November. The drains had all been done by Nash, the builder, during the summer, and the fearsome bill (the thought of which had caused her many sleepless nights) was paid by Maud and Lennie. They also paid the surgeon's fees for the operation and for the nurse, so it was no wonder that Marion felt infinite gratitude. On 31 December 1907 she gave thanks in her diary for "Maud's loving thought & goodness to me all through a most trying time—a lifetime of devotion on my part could never repay the dearest best & most unselfish little daughter in the world, a sunbeam of joy to us all."

By the beginning of 1908 Marion seemed almost herself again, though she remained invalidish for the rest of her life. A dragging pain in her side recurred whenever she got tired, and the various doctors she consulted had only the usual panacea to offer: more rest. However it was pleasant to be able to be at home again, to make rounds of calls on her old friends and to visit the dressmaker. On 30 November Linley took her to a matinée. This was a real treat after twelve months' abstinence, but it was still some time before she felt able to go out to any parties. Family affairs, always of paramount importance in Marion's life, were now quite enough to keep her busy. Maud's health, and that of her children, was of course a fruitful topic for the diary: fortunately the children only had minor ailments, and their good looks and charming manners were the source of much pleasure and

satisfaction. Their earliest infant scribbles, and then their letters (addressed to "Darling Ganna") were as carefully and lovingly hoarded as those from her own children had been. Though "the darlings" were usually "sweet & good", like most grandmothers Marion was critical of the way they were brought up. Too much chocolate cake, lax discipline in the nursery and fidgetting in church all brought adverse comments, while their noise and high spirits could be very tiring to someone frail and (by the standards of the time) old. Although she saw the children quite a lot when she was at Balcombe, they were always hedged about with nannies, whose presence Marion sometimes resented. She much enjoyed inviting them one at a time to Stafford Terrace, and this was often combined with a little treat—a matinée, a visit to the toyshop, or a drive to the zoo. On 18 December 1907 she wrote, "Little Anne to tea, as good as gold & so sweet." Anne was six years old and it was more than a year since she had last been to Stafford Terrace. The dark house full of exciting treasures, the rather formal tea with grandmother, of whom she was somewhat in awe (no doubt Maud had impressed upon her the fact that grand-mother was still an invalid to be treated with care) and the relief and delight when grandfather came down from his studio to join them, making everyone laugh with his jokes and tricks, made this a day she remembered for the rest of her life.

Marion always looked forward to seeing her sisters on their frequent visits to London. Tabby and Midge were both grandmothers now, so there was even more to talk about whenever they met. The Fletchers and the Langleys took suites in the best hotels; Claridges, Browns, the Carlton, and the Coburg in Bayswater Road, were all sampled in turn. The Sambournes would dine with them there, or Marion would ask Maud and Lennie to a meal and everyone then came round to Stafford Terrace for a real family evening. Dora was the favourite niece for whom Marion always had a special welcome, while Spencer's son, Douglas, and Conrad's sons, Geoff and Fitzroy ("such a dear boy"), dropped in whenever they were in town.

One thing which gave Marion especial pleasure was the discovery that her youngest brother, Mervyn, had talent as a sculptor, something which had been quite unsuspected in his youth. Mervyn was now forty-three, and had continued to travel all over the world, even after his marriage, which (like Edgar's) remained childless. He had always seemed a happy-go-lucky rolling stone, so it comes as quite a surprise to find him and Ethel settled in a studio flat in Wimbledon. Maud and Marion went to call on them there in the autumn of 1907: "Mervyn looking so handsome & distinguished in his working holland blouse. Very pleased with his 2 statues of guards mounted & Don Quixote, v.clever." To the family's delight, not only did Mervyn exhibit the Don Quixote at the Royal Academy in 1908 but Hylda, Spencer's daughter, had a picture hung too. As Linley was a regular exhibitor that made a triple triumph.

From 1905 onwards Linley's health gradually deteriorated. The winters were always bad for him, and a lifetime spent smoking—admittedly cigars rather than cigarettes— had not helped his lungs. Bouts of coughing made him breathless and giddy, as well as keeping his wife awake at night in the double bed which they continued to share. Marion wished he would not rush about going to a shoot nearly every weekend instead of resting quietly at home, but he brushed aside all her suggestions, refused to see a doctor, and continued to work and play as hard as ever. Although Linley did his best to ignore it, the ageing process was manifested in many little ways. Not only did he write in his diary "very tired" or "seedy and bilious" increasingly often, but also the more ominous "short of breath". His brisk and competent attitude to life began to change too; he became anxious and pernicketty, while little trials like unpunctuality and things mislaid flustered and upset him. By the autumn of 1908 his general condition was worrying everyone, so Maud arranged for her own doctor to see him. "Dr Parker came to see Lin, says exactly what I have known & felt for months" wrote Marion. "The muscles of his heart are weak & his blood vessels too full. Must diet & drink v.little & not over-charge system. Feel v.anxious & dare not think much." Next day she was still worrying: "Lin ought to rest week-ends—this almanack work too much for him. Afraid he is v.depressed about himself but he seemed bright at dinner & talked after."

After this scare Linley seemed better, and Christmas was spent happily at Balcombe. Marion had been at death's door in 1906 and in 1907 had been staying with Tabby, so that in 1908 Maud—whose greatest pleasure was in cossetting her loved ones and loading them with gifts—welcomed them with more affection than ever. Marion was able to set her cares aside for a while: "December 25th. Slept well & woke to find 2 lovely Xmas trees fastened to either post at end of bed with many presents!!! Never saw anything so pretty before. Lin a dressing-gown & various things, 3 pretty baskets fitted for each room for work, a lovely brown silk tie-box. From darling Anne a handkerchief made by *her*, beautifully worked, endless pretty things. All went to church except Lin & self, he worked all day. To Nymans in car, 7.30. House party, Dr M, de la Penhas, Gibbs, Lorings. V.amusing evening, charades after." The next day was delightful too: "December 26th. Not in bed till 1 o'clock, rested late morning. Lin hard at work all day until 3.30, light failing so went for our walk. Maud gave away oceans of presents at 4.30 to all household. Lennie splendid as old Father Xmas in red silk dressing-gown & hood. 22 to dinner here, whole party from Nymans, 3 tables all most charmingly arranged. Charades after, excellent." On New Year's Eve there was another happy party, "V.jolly evening, saw old year out, sang auld lang syne."

The early part of 1909 was very foggy and cold in London, not good for anyone's health. Linley's chest was bad again, so the Sambournes went to Bournemouth for a change of air. This was not, in the circumstances, a very happy choice. "To Highcliffe Hotel, same as my dear parents were at in 1883 & I with them", wrote Marion, adding next day, "V.bad night, Lin's cough most trying & exhausting." As she penned these words her mind surely went back to the time when she was young and strong and had to watch over her dying father. He too had

202

coughed all night, and had lived for exactly one year after his visit to Bournemouth. One wonders how much dread and foreboding Marion felt when she came to that page of her diary which marked the sacred anniversary: "My beloved father died, 13th March, 1884."

These worries faded during the summer. Linley cut down on his smoking, coughed less, and was bright and cheerful, almost his old self. With the encouragement of the new *Punch* Editor, Owen Seaman (Burnand had retired in 1906), his drawings were better than ever and Marion repeatedly remarked on them. During the Season the Sambournes did a little entertaining again, and attended several afternoon parties, though Marion usually refused invitations to go out in the evening: "Greatly fear I cannot go, I get so dreadfully tired." Linley still enjoyed company and was sometimes able to persuade her to accept if it promised to be a particularly interesting party. "May 10th. Lin & I dine at Sir Norman Lockyer's. V.pleasant evening, saw wonderful photos of London taken from a balloon" was Marion's comment after one such evening. Lockyer was a well-known astronomer and keenly interested in new inventions: conversation that evening must surely have turned on the latest exciting topic—man's conquest of the air. Even though H.G. Wells had written *The War of the Worlds* more than ten years earlier, his story of battles in the sky was still being dismissed by most people as pure fantasy. But something was very soon to happen which would bring that vision of the future a little nearer. With heavy underlining Marion filled in her diary: "July 26th 1909. *The channel crossed yesterday at 4.am from Baragne by a frenchman Bleriot to St Margaret's Bay in 23 minutes.*"

The pace of innovation and invention was quickening in other ways too. In 1904 Marion had seen her first coloured photographs, and also her first X-rays: "Midge Eveleen & self to Wigmore Street to see Eve's arm under Rontgens rays. Had it photoed." In 1905 a gas stove was installed in the kitchen at Stafford Terrace, much to the satisfaction of the cook. In 1907 the first taxi-meter cabs appeared in London, and by the following year this form of transport had almost replaced the horse-drawn cab, "Lin & self to Victoria, took under 10 minutes, man drove v.fast" wrote Marion in 1908. Another labour-saving device was added to Stafford Terrace in 1909: "Telephone put up, used it at once to Maud." (Telephone jokes first appeared in *Punch* as early as 1878, and "Spoke through the telephone" was a phrase used in Marion's diary several times during the previous five years, so the Sambournes were rather slow with this new idea.) An ever-increasing number of "cars" for the middle classes were now on the roads, competing with the chauffeur-driven "motors" of the rich. Marion was at Balcombe in 1907 when she wrote: "Mr Stuart & his wife came to tea from Worthing in their small Rover car which he told me cost him £150 second-hand. He has had it a year & had no mishap, he drives it himself & it costs him ½d a mile!!!"

In the summer of 1909 Marion and Linley decided to go abroad for three weeks for a cure. Spa waters had been all the rage during the early years of the 19th century, and many attractive little towns had grown up round mineral springs. A change in fashion had led to their decline, but by the beginning of Edward VII's reign the spas had entered another boom period. Like the modern health farm, these places were much frequented by rich ladies with little to occupy their minds, or by gentlemen who had spent a lifetime over-indulging at table. For both categories the strict regime insisted upon by the local doctors made an interesting change. To be obliged to take 4 glasses of foul-tasting water every day, have carbonic acid baths and the latest kind of electric therapy, (or any other of the expensive treatments recommended) often convinced the hypochondriac that a genuine cure had been effected. Over the last few years Marion had taken short breaks at various English spas, Harrogate being her favourite. In spite of the fact that she always complained that she never felt any better afterwards and that the expense had been terrible, she thought something similar might do Linley good. European spas were considered the best: Edgar urged the Sambournes to try Vittel but they chose Homburg, a resort much liked by King Edward before he discovered the charms of Marienbad.

The trip to Homburg was a failure. The food at the hotel was horrid, the medical regime debilitating. Both the Sambournes felt decidedly poorly and Marion was very worried to see her husband losing strength daily. The only interesting event was the Dirigible Balloon Exhibition held at Frankfurt, which they made a special effort to see, "To Frankfurt by 11.58. Saw Zeppelin starting & great crowd but missed seeing it rise from ground. Another large white dirigible near it, wonderful sight" wrote Marion. Later she had a better view, "Saw Zeppelin III distinctly & people moving in her."

After three weeks Marion and Linley returned home, far less healthy and more depressed than they had been when they left. "V.v.bad night & felt so sick. Lin not still one moment. Fear shall be ill again if bad nights continue, feel an utter wreck in nerves" wrote Marion on 20 October—their thirty-third wedding anniversary. Even the inattentive Roy became worried, "Lin so breathless, tired & white at dinner. Roy & self anxious—feel so sorry for him poor boy, it is so sad for him one of us always seedy." The doctor came and told Linley that his heart was weak and that he must go to bed at once, but he insisted on getting up the next day to work as usual. On 27 October he finished the almanack drawing for that year; on the 28th he began the week's cartoon. He had a great struggle to finish it, but it was done by 8 pm on 29 October. "Beautiful drawing" wrote Marion, "Lin v.seedy indeed, wretched night, got no sleep till 5 o'clock, head feels so bad." It was the last time she was able to admire her husband's work: Linley never drew for *Punch* again.

Linley was put to bed in Roy's room, nursing help was organised, and a strict diet imposed by Dr Kingscote, another of Maud's physicians. Massage and electric vibrator treatment were also recommended, as well as oxygen to ease the patient's difficult breathing. The absence of a Sambourne cartoon in *Punch* two weeks later made headlines: "Account in all papers of dear Lin's illness. Telephone going all day long & doorbell enquiries & paper reporters." Amidst all the worry and strain

Marion, taken in March in 1910. "Will look a fine wreck after months of anxiety" she wrote. But she was quite pleased with the result: "My photos came! Quite nice, wonder if they are really like me."

Maud was a tower of strength. "Maudie with Lin, she is marvellous & soothes him more than anyone & reads him to sleep," was one of Marion's diary entries, and another, "Maudie as usual doing all, bless her, paying, writing, arranging and supplying our every want, so brave & good, a perfect marvel." Roy's behaviour gave no cause for gratitude. Linley's illness frightened and depressed him and he absented himself from the house as much as possible, not helping his mother or supporting her in any way. His attitude grieved her deeply: "I pray that Roy may never suffer for his unkindness to me, he makes me v.unhappy often & I would do anything to make him happy if I could" she wrote despairingly when everything looked very black.

Marion's account of Linley's long last illness has great poignancy. Her diary faithfully recorded each change—for better or worse—in the patient's condition, but the downward slide, so heartbreaking to watch, was seldom halted for long. Saddest of all for Marion was the change in her husband's character. Gone was the bustling merry spirit, the lively intelligence, the steady affection on which she had depended for so long. Instead he became irritable and morose, rejecting all her tenderness and solicitude in his effort to concentrate his failing energies on the one thing left which really mattered—to live, not die.

Linley seemed a little better by Christmas, though still nothing like his old cheery self. With a nurse in attendance he was able to get up, be dressed, and be taken out for drives. On 21 January there was a brief announcement in *The Times*, "Mr Linley Sambourne is now convalescent and will leave London tomorrow for Ramsgate to recuperate." But the sea air did him no good and the doctor advised returning to London for different treatment. Marion found his depression at this set-back hard to bear, "Lin v. silent, all interests gone, makes me feel so sad", but it was the long weeks of broken nights listening to him coughing and tossing which exhausted her. "My head so bad from nervous strain, utterly broke down, nurse v.kind, lay down until 4.30." she wrote on 15 March. The family urged her to have a rest, so she went to stay with Tabby for a week. This made her feel better and when she returned Linley was much stronger too: in her absence he had got up and insisted on being taken to the *Punch* dinner. The improvement lasted a few weeks. Marion took him for little walks in the park and they even went to the theatre together ("To see *Trelawney of the Wells*, enjoyed play immensely") and to the zoo, where they admired the polar bears in their new quarters, but it was impossible for anyone to feel really hopeful.

Linley. He had always enjoyed having his picture taken; this was the last of many.

At the end of April Marion was again persuaded to have a rest. This time she went to Ramsgate, where the sunshine and fresh air were, as always, a tonic for her jaded spirits. The Burnands had her to dinner in their new little house—"Fear finances tightening, but all happy & cheerful"—there were other old friends to see, and she could draw comfort from a visit to St Peter's: "Took arum lilies to our beloved parents' grave, looking so beautiful with purple & white hyacinths, yellow tulips & forget-me-nots." It was a wrench to return to the gloom of London. "Do not feel any improvement in Lin, depression very contagious, poor darling seems to care for no one or any thing" she wrote sadly.

King Edward VII died on 6 May. Linley and Marion went for a drive: they passed the Palace, "All flags half mast, great crowds outside", and went on through the parks where all the trees and shrubs were bursting into bloom. A fortnight later Linley took a sudden turn for the worse. He became dropsical, was sometimes comatose or wandering, and had to have both day and night nurses. Oxygen administered at frequent intervals was the only thing which gave any relief to his breathing problems and it seemed as if the end could not be far off. But May gave way to June, June to July, and still he would not give in. Marion was very near the end of her endurance, with all kinds of worries piling onto her. In his lucid moments Linley sometimes tried to write letters or sign cheques, and would not give his wife power of attorney. As far as she could gather (from spending a day turning out the desk drawers with Roy) their affairs were in a terrible muddle, with several hundred pounds worth of outstanding bills to be accounted for, as well as the huge medical expenses which mounted daily. The worry about how she was to manage everything, added to the misery of watching her husband suffer, seemed at times really more than she could bear. One great blessing, for which she was continually thankful, was the love and support given by the whole family. Maud did most of all, but Lennie too was ever kind and generous. Spencer and Mervyn rallied round, Edgar, Midge and Tabby came up to town to be at hand. At least one of them called at Stafford Terrace every day, taking it in turns to sit with their sister for an hour or two and going up to speak a few words of comfort to the dying man.

By the end of July there was still not much alteration in the patient's condition, so Dr Kingscote and Maud made Marion go away again. "July 27th. Maudie came early, to stay during my absense. Dear Lin about the same, would have his drawing board, compass etc, seemed wandery. Had not the heart to tell him I was going to Ramsgate." She had only been there for two days when a telegram from Maud called her back. "Returned, found dear Lin greatly altered, Dr K says most critical v.little hope. My dear one scarcely recognised me." Two terrible days followed, with Maud and Marion taking it in turns to watch by the bedside all night, until the change they were longing for came at last. "My darling looked so happy all afternoon, smiled at us & kissed us & seemed to see friends, his whole face lighted up." Linley then lapsed into unconsciousness and died peacefully in the early hours of the following morning, 3 August 1910.

Relief that the struggle was over at last must have been the thought uppermost in everyone's mind. Marion could only find conventional phrases to express her

feelings: "The saddest & most desolate morning of my life now my dear husband's spirit gone. God has given him rest & peace after his long illness. Our dear children a great comfort in their love & all my dear brothers & sisters. God is indeed good & merciful to me, may I have strength & courage to do what is right," is the first part of the entry for 4 August. But it had never been her habit to invoke God for long, and the familiar individual tone of the diary was quickly resumed: "Dear Edgar arrived morning. He & Maud to St Peter's by 3.30 about grave, remain night. Lennie Mervyn & Spencer here, Edgar & Lennie to lunch. Tabby arrived after luncheon, all so dear & kind & what a comfort their love is in my sorrow. *Great* many beautiful wreaths and flowers arriving all day & endless telegrams & letters all so appreciative of my darling's talent & character. Tabby Spencer dear Roy Lennie to tea. Tabby took me for a walk, felt so much better after. She left 9.30. I spent half an hour in my darling's room. The lovely expression of perfect peace on his face beautiful, cannot remember anything else. . . ."

The funeral service was held at St Mary Abbots, Kensington, followed by cremation at Golders Green. Roy, Lennie, Spencer, Edgar, Mervyn, Hamilton Langley and Hamilton Fletcher were chief mourners at the church, which was full of the Sambournes' many friends, while Marion and Maud stayed quietly at Stafford Terrace to read through the burial service together. Linley's ashes were brought home in a bronze urn, and two days later were taken down to Thanet. "My darling Lin laid to rest in our own ground at St Peter's. Edgar Spencer Lennie & Roy left here 10 o'clock. Service in church & all struck with beauty of church & grounds, so happy my dear one lies close to our beloved parents who loved & were so proud of him."

Linley had not left any instructions about his funeral, so that Marion had been able to make whatever arrangements she liked. She had never made any attempt to bring a priest to his bedside during his long last illness, but it was important to her that the conventions of mourning should be observed. Her own attitude towards religion had always been equivocal; over the last twenty years her interest had waned and she had attended church less and less. It was not obligatory to follow the customs adopted by the majority of respectable Victorians. During the latter half of the Sambournes' marriage, whenever they stayed away with friends or relations, Marion would write, "All to church except Lin & self." Even when alone with Maud (who was a keen churchgoer) Marion could nearly always think of an excuse to stay at home. Curiously, remembering her earlier interest in alternative religion, she was as shocked as the rest of the family when Tabby became a Roman Catholic in 1909. But where Marion remained constant was in her attitude to death and mourning. Her parents' grave had always been the focus of strong emotions, and now that Linley's ashes were buried in the adjoining plot—where she too planned to rest—St Peter's Thanet became more than ever a place of pilgrimage.

The week after the funeral was spent sorting and tidying everything away. There was so much to be done that Marion hardly had time to think. It was not until she went to stay with Tabby, where there was nothing to do except answer all the letters of sympathy which had come pouring in, that she could give way to sorrow. "Found all well here at Anchorage, all most kind. How terribly I miss my dear one" she wrote. Every day the pain felt worse. "Miss my darling Linley more than ever, life seems so empty without him. . . . Wrote 7 letters, felt v.bad writing. . . . Wrote letters, felt wretched, wept my eyes out. . . . Miss my dear one at every turn & his bright happy face. . . . Dreamt of my dear Linley that he was so well & happy. . . ." From Tabby's she went to Balcombe, where there was even more to remind her of past happy times: "Felt terribly the blank of my dear one here—miss him more than I can express."

At the beginning of October Marion returned to London. "Feel v.lonely without darling Lin. . . . *begin* only to realise what life means without him." Her old friend from her girlhood in Brussels, Toula Frick, came to stay with her for a time and was a great comfort and support. Over the years Toula (Tilda) had often been a visitor at Stafford Terrace and in her widowhood Marion came to depend very much on her company. Together they embarked on a great turnout of Linley's studio, which no one had dared touch during his long illness. Getting rid of dust and dirt always gave Marion a glow of satisfaction, though she was a little startled to find how many packets of nude photographs were lurking in the drawers. The drawings were all parcelled up; some were given to Bernard Partridge, Linley's successor at *Punch*, but many had to be sold to pay bills. A few the family could not part with: "Roy & I put up dear Lin's lovely Hans Andersen drawings which Roy has had framed in his room—they look beautiful." Then there were all the legal and financial problems for Marion to cope with, debts, death dues and legacy duties, endless muddles to be

Marion (centre) with Edgar and her old schoolfriend, Toula Frick.

resolved, papers to sign, and decisions to make. She managed it all in spite of some bad days, "Feel v.shaky & seedy, had a tiresome weep." It was a relief to have all money matters under her own control at last, Linley in his will having left her everything for her lifetime, except for an annuity of £200 to Roy. When all the paperwork was completed it was estimated that Linley's and her own investments would bring in an income of about £1,000 a year, enough, Marion hoped, to manage on without difficulty.

Christmas was spent quietly with Tabby. "As pleasant and happy as possible without my dearest who I miss more than ever" wrote Marion. From there she went to Balcombe before returning to London to pick up the threads of her old life. Her neice, Edith, and Toula often came to stay or spend the day at Stafford Terrace, and they warded off loneliness with many kind attentions. There were calls to make on many old friends—Mrs Bosanquet, Lady Bergne and Lady Hickman (all three newly widowed like herself), Mrs Joachim, Lady Margaret Watney, Mrs Spofforth, even Laura Stone: "Sat for an hour with Mrs Marcus Stone. Felt v.sad, reminded me of dear old times." There was still a lot of sorting and tidying to do, but Marion planned to spend as little time as possible at Stafford Terrace. Roy was poor company for her, though he did make the effort to write to her regularly when she was away. His letters always began and ended with an endearment; it was only when they were at home together that she felt the lack of empathy so acutely.

Shortly after Linley's death Roy wished to enter into partnership with his colleague Mr Pohl, and Marion arranged to sell some investments to provide the £5,000 he needed. Luckily she quite liked Mr Pohl, a steadier influence than some of Roy's other friends. ("Wish Roy did not hanker so after great wealth & would be satisfied with what we have" was one of her regular complaints after he had been out with Mr Stern.) But even with Mr Pohl's assistance Roy was never able to make money in the way that Lennie found so easy, and each letter to his mother had the same doleful theme: "Times have been very bad and I have found myself as you know very hard up" he wrote, and "Still absolutely hopeless in the City—no business and no money to be made at all—it is really worse than ever I have known it even in my short and rather unlucky experience."

Roy was no use as a prop for Marion to lean upon but there were many other people in her life happy to provide support. Tabby, Edgar and Midge always welcomed her with open arms and the years after Linley's death were spent moving from one sheltered haven to another, with only short spells in London. Maud especially was full of plans for her mother's entertainment. In the spring of 1911 she invited Marion to go to the south of France with herself, Mr and Mrs Messel and their youngest daughter, Muriel. They all stayed at the California Hotel, Cannes, and revelled in the warmth and sunshine. "The scenery along the coastline too beautiful for words. Mimosa trees in full bloom, pines & palms, the sea a glorious blue & sky the same, felt like being in a heavenly dream after the grey skies of home." The party went on several expeditions to Antibes, Grasse, and Monte Carlo (Marion felt dreadfully nervous in the Messels' motor on the coastal road with its notorious hairpin bends) and watched the Battle of Flowers. Although she found the

Messels rather trying—she would so much rather have had Maud all to herself—the holiday did her a lot of good. It was followed almost at once by a month in Ireland with Maud, Lennie and the children. This was a wonderfully happy time, and the beauty of the Irish scenery struck Marion even more keenly than the south of France had done.

The first anniversary of Linley's death was spent at Ramsgate. The dear familiar place with all its happy associations meant much to Marion. The sea air, the view, the walks, the old friends who had known Linley in his prime and who spoke to her of him with such affection and respect—all made her sad, yet happy too and grateful for a life much blessed. Nearly every day of this visit she took the tram to Broadstairs and went to St Peter's, where she placed wreaths on the graves, watered the flowers and snipped off dead blooms, "Stayed for an hour, so happy there" she wrote, "All looked so beautiful, loved being near my dearest." Once, in nostalgic mood, she went a little further afield: "Took fly & drove to dear Westwood & got out to look up drive. Many fine old trees cut down, some patchy flower-beds about, nut walks immensely overgrown."

In the autumn of 1911 Roy was taken up again by his old flame Edna May, who was now married to Oscar Lewisohn, a rich American. The Lewisohns lived at Cranbourne Court, near Windsor, and here luxurious living could be combined with blissful worship at Edna's shrine. This was probably one of the happiest periods of Roy's life. "Yesterday we had a grand day at the races everything wonderfully done and the most charming people," he wrote to his mother. "Edna had a glorious dress from Paris and to my mind looked far the most beautiful lady I saw. We have a private luncheon room at the back of our box and I feel I am a very lucky person to have such good friends who always seem pleased to see me. Edna says she never saw me looking so well in my life and I feel it too . . ." Even though Edna had become respectable, Marion still could not consider her a good influence: "Roy returned from Mrs Lewisohn's, always seems discontented after these visits, & depressed."

Of course it was Maud, more beloved than anyone else, who did most for Marion in her widowhood. Her daily letters were longer and more affectionate than ever, urging her mother to take holidays abroad or at the seaside, offering unlimited use of Balcombe, cheering and comforting as only she knew how. She was as keen as Marion to preserve every relic of Linley's career—keener perhaps, as it was she who gathered all her father's papers together and was most insistent not only that nothing in his drawers be touched but that as little as possible be altered in the house itself. Early in 1912 it was decided that things had got a little shabby at Stafford Terrace and that some re-decoration was necessary. Paint and paper were applied to the hall and staircase, and possibly the dining-room and morning-room also, though not the drawing-room. "I have been to Morris's about the papers & they have all our dear old patterns. They sent me a large packet to see, & some chintzes too", wrote Maud, who then supervised everything (and almost certainly paid for it) while Marion was away staying with Midge.

In April 1912 Marion went to bed with a gastric chill. The doctor came; he thought nothing of the chill but took a grave view of something else: "Dr Croft Hill

came morning, seems to think seriously of lump under arm and in right breast, wishes me to see surgeon tomorrow. V.annoyed, wish I had never mentioned lumps!" Speedy arrangements were made for an operation, to be performed at home as usual. (The surgeon's fee was £100, which Marion thought outrageous.) Edith came to help, Maud was summoned to return from holidaying in Ireland, and even Roy behaved well: "Dear Roy v.kind & sympathetic, sat long time morning and afternoon in my room before leaving for Mrs Lewisohn's." Marion was remarkably stoical about the whole affair, but there is no knowing whether she, or anyone except her doctor, realised that the lumps were a death sentence. So much secrecy surrounded such things and very few diseases appeared to have names; "cancer" as a blanket term for malignant tumours was not part of common parlance. Bronchitis and heart-disease were rife among men, and were openly acknowledged as serious threats, but more and more women were falling victim to a plague which could not be discussed in public, and only with the greatest reluctance mentioned in private. In death as in life, both Marion and Linley proved typical of their generation.

The operation was not such an ordeal for Marion as her previous one had been and she was only out of action for a short time. Her brothers and sisters rallied round as usual ("All *most* kind,") and a fortnight later she was able to go to stay with Tabby. After a happy peaceful time there ("Enjoyed it immensely, all so dear and kind to me") she went on to Balcombe and Maud's loving care. She had not long left to live, but in many ways these last two years were happier than some which had gone before. Her grief over Linley's long illness and death became less acute, while the beauty of nature, the blossoming of the grandchildren, the love and kindness of family and friends, were remarked on more often than ever. "Happy day," she wrote over and over again, "*Very* happy day."

Marion was well and busy throughout 1913. She travelled around from one set of friends and relations to another during the spring and summer, then settled at Stafford Terrace for a winter which was almost as full of activity as the old days had been. A stream of people came to stay, there were calls to make, little dinner parties to hold, and clothes to buy, "To Marshall and Snelgrove, new dress, £9 ready made!" shows that the era of the dressmaker was nearly over. Some other newfangled ideas were not much liked: "Wish Roy would give up Ragtime, so senseless and frivolous, not worthy of him," and "To lunch with Mr Llewellyn, cocktails served, just tasted mine only & even that gave me indigestion for rest of day! Pernicious habit!!!" were two of Marion's disapproving comments. However a "Tango Tea" at a Kensington hotel was much enjoyed, and a visit to the theatre was still one of life's great pleasures. "By Om to Adelphi with Florrie, *Girl from Utah*. Enjoyed it immensely, v.good indeed & no trouble going or returning. Good front row seats 5/6 each, tea on return. Darling Maud sent me lovely flowers & fruits & Midge also. How more than thankful I feel for all the blessings I have" was Marion's entry on 28 February 1914. On 3 Marsh she noted the first symptoms of what proved to be her final illness—fever, a pain in her side, and a lump close to the scar of her first operation.

The doctor was sympathetic and cheerful. The lump was flatulence, nothing

more, and after a fortnight in bed Marion felt well enough to get up and go for little drives with Maud. "To Ranelagh, perfectly lovely there, felt v.tired but so happy being with my darling." Sea air was, as usual, recommended, and the shortest possible journey advised, so Marion chose Westgate for her convalescence. This was two stations nearer to London than Ramsgate, but still within the borders of her beloved Thanet. Comfortable lodgings were found by Maud, and Marion, with a nurse in attendance, travelled down on 28 May.

The summer of 1914 was wonderfully sunny and hot. The papers were full of troubles abroad and the possibility of war with Germany, but this was nothing new: as long ago as January 1910 Maud had undertaken to set up a Red Cross station at Balcombe to receive wounded soldiers from European battlefields. She and Lennie had had a most enjoyable holiday in Germany in 1911, when Maud had written: "There is something so lovable in the kindly faces who greet one on every hand. Can these be the people we want to fight—oh surely not!" Public feeling gradually hardened against the Kaiser; he had built up his armed forces to such an extent that it now only needed one excuse, one spark, to set all Europe on fire. But it was a long time since Marion had made any mention of international affairs in her diary and she had no desire to do so now; the cancer, dormant since 1912, was spreading rapidly. For six weeks she sat out in her long chair, facing the sea—"so beautiful, like opal"—with the blessed sunshine warming her bones. Sometimes, supported by a strong arm, she walked a little way along the front. Although her discomfort and nausea increased daily, she still took pleasure in the air, the view, and the precious company of loved ones. They must all have known that she was dying: one by one they made their pilgrimage to Westgate to see her. "Tabby came, looking so pretty and smart . . . Dear Mervyn came for day, delighted to see him . . . Midge came, looking so well . . . Spencer and Ada to tea . . . Roy dined here, think him pale and thin, wish he looked stronger . . . Dear Edgar here, took me for lovely drive along coast . . ." and, most welcome of all, "My darling came by early train, a great joy." Her writing begins to straggle on the page, but it retains its characteristic outline until the very last entry: "July 9th. Glorious day. Mrs Hawtry sent me charming bunch of flowers."

Maud must have gathered her mother up and taken her back to London, as Marion died at home, aged sixty-two, on 25 July 1914. Maud and twelve-year-old Anne were with her at the end, holding her hand; Roy signed the death certificate. She was buried, as she had wished, beside her husband in St Peter's churchyard. A few days after the funeral, on 4 August 1914, war with Germany was declared: not just one woman's life but a whole way of living was gone for ever.

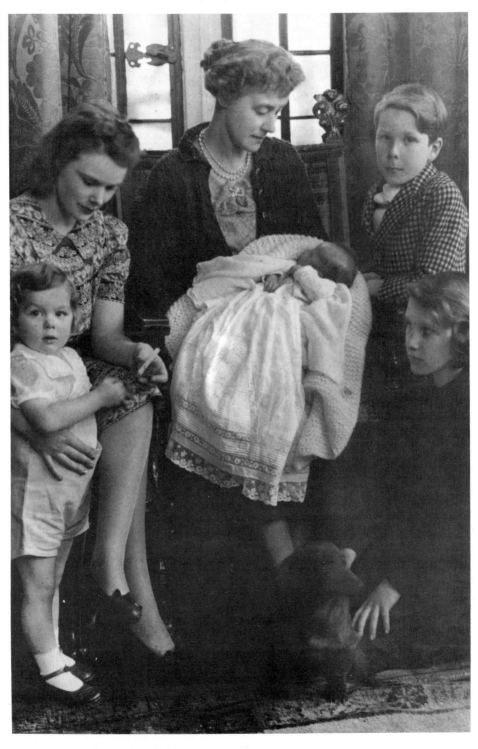

EPILOGUE.

ARION WAS LUCKY to be spared the horrors of the next four years. All the young men of the family went into the army; Roy came through the war unscathed, as did Spencer's son, Douglas, and Conrad's sons, Geoffrey and Claude, but the youngest boy in that family, Fitzroy, was killed in action. Tabby had a double sorrow: her elder son, Gareth—the apple of her eye—and her son-in-law, Lawrence Fisher Rowe (Eveleen's husband), were both killed in 1915. These dreadful gaps torn in the family circle would have grieved Marion greatly, but there were other indignities to be borne by those she loved which would have given her much pain. On the outbreak of war a wave of violent anti-German feeling swept over the country. All the Sambourne's many friends with German-sounding names were slighted and ostracised; some, like Toula Frick, obliged to languish in prisoner-of-war camps. The Messels still had relatives in Germany and forty years spent as an Englishman could not stifle old Ludwig Messel's affection and concern for those who were now technically his enemies. He died in 1915, allegedly of a broken heart. Lennie's service with the Territorial Army before the war (he had held the rank of Major since 1908) stood him in good stead, but even this could not save his wife and children from the embarrassment of having a German name. They must all have greeted the end of the war, when it came at last, with a special kind of thankfulness.

Lennie inherited the Nymans estate and a large part of his father's fortune. The garden at Nymans was especially fine, though Maud did not care for the house at all; the improvements made in the 1890s were now considered hideous. After the war it seemed sensible to build a new house on the site, and the Messels were soon absorbed in planning what they hoped would be a worthy successor to their beloved Balcombe. Although still in the tradition of Victorian and Edwardian stately homes, this was not to be a battlemented castle or a red brick Queen Anne mansion, but a

---

Left: Maud, with Anne and her four children. Tony and Susan Armstrong-Jones (right) with William and Martin Parsons, sons of the Earl of Rosse. Taken in 1939.

faithful rendering of a rambling Elizabethan manor. Maud and Lennie loved this period and had already collected much fine furniture, as well as tapestries, wood-carving and metalwork, for their other homes. Now all these treasures could have a larger and more suitable setting, in long stone gallery, great hall, and noble library. Part of the garden was re-modelled too: Maud planted old-fashioned roses while Lennie introduced new camellias and euchryphias to the horticultural world.

Young Linley Messel followed his father into the family firm, but Oliver had no taste for city life. He went to the Slade School of Art and developed a passion for the stage which was to mature into a highly successful career as a theatre designer. Anne inherited her mother's charm and good looks, making all heads turn at parties and dances during the sparkling twenties. In 1925 she married a rising young barrister, Ronald Armstrong Jones. Two children were born, Susan and Anthony, but the marriage was dissolved in 1934 and both parties married again. Anne's new husband was Michael Parsons, the handsome and dashing young Earl of Rosse, whose home was Birr Castle in Ireland, a much older and even more romantic and beautiful building than Balcombe or Nymans. It too was filled with all kinds of fascinating treasure trove to delight the heart of one who had inherited her parents' love of the past.

Roy came into a substantial sum of money when his uncle Edgar died in 1933, satisfying at last his ambition to be well-off. He continued to lead the same pleasure-filled bachelor existence that he had enjoyed before the war, but his moody and depressive temperament precluded real happiness. He never married, and would probably have been more comfortable in a service flat, but Maud continued to regard her childhood home as a sacred place and forbade her brother to think of selling it. She would not hear of him emptying drawers or throwing things away, and herself dealt with any small alterations and improvements which were absolutely necessary. Roy had always been "idle" and even in middle-age could not summon up enough forcefulness to over-ride his successful elder sister. He was thus condemned to spend his life in surroundings which became ever darker and more depressing as the years rolled by. Gloom settled heavily upon him as he aged, and it is sad to think of this lonely old man and his two ancient retainers below stairs struggling to come to terms with food rationing and fuel shortages, bombs and black-out, during the anxious weary years of the Second World War.

Roy died in July 1946, aged sixty-seven, leaving his house and all that was in it to Maud. Few people were keen to buy an unmodernised terrace house in Kensington at that time, and as for the furniture and effects, their antique value was almost nil. Everything Victorian was at the very nadir of popularity. All over the country people were clearing out similar houses in an ecstatic burst of welcome to a brave new world—clear-glazing windows, painting everything white, banishing heavy drapes, fringes and stuffed birds, and consigning all the dust-collecting clutter of a period now mocked and despised to jumble sale or bonfire. Only Maud's sentimental attachment and the fact that she had no pressing necessity to sell prevented the same thing happening to 18 Stafford Terrace.

Just a few months after Roy's death Nymans and everything in it was destroyed

by fire, a tragedy which made Maud even more reluctant to part with any relics of the happy past. The Messels moved to Holmsted Manor; they still kept up the magnificent garden round the burnt-out shell of Nymans, but they were never able to rebuild their dream. Lennie died in 1953; Maud lived just long enough to hear the news that her grandson, Tony, had become engaged to Princess Margaret. She died in March 1960, aged eighty-five.

Maud had been determined that her parents' old home should be preserved intact, so a few years before her death she had given 18 Stafford Terrace into the care of her daughter, Anne, Countess of Rosse. In spite of the low esteem accorded to everything Victorian in the 1950s, Lady Rosse could see that a revival of interest in the arts and manners of the nineteenth century was bound to come. With the support and encouragement of her husband, she decided to restore the house to the condition that she remembered so clearly from childhood visits to her grandparents. Some war damage had to be repaired, modern plumbing installed and a few articles replaced, but fortunately it was possible to preserve intact the decorative schemes in the main rooms. Over the next twenty-five years Lord and Lady Rosse cherished their unique London home, entertaining here many famous names from the worlds of literature, painting, ballet and the theatre.

In February 1958 Lady Rosse invited several friends who shared her enthusiasm for the past to a party, at which she proposed the founding of a "Victorian Society" to encourage the preservation and appreciation of hitherto neglected works of art and architecture. This grew and flourished, and it is largely due to its efforts that much of our magnificent heritage of Victorian building has been saved from demolition. After Lord Rosse's death in 1978 it was felt that the time had come to open 18 Stafford Terrace to the public. Arrangements were made for it to be run as a museum by the Victorian Society, and in the autumn of 1980 the first paying visitors crossed the threshold.

Fate works in strange ways: one thinks of all the famous friends the Sambournes had; those morning-rooms in which Marion gossiped and had tea, the dining-tables round which she and Linley sat talking and laughing into the small hours, the drawing-rooms where the cream of Society gathered; all gone, vanished without trace. Many people in their circle were charming and witty, great and good; their legacies of art, literature and science have enriched the world—yet not one of them has left behind so vivid and tangible a record of daily existence as can be found at Linley Sambourne House. The light filtering through the stained glass windows, the glint of polished brass, the ticking of the clocks, the tinkle of the fountain in the water-garden; these are the unchanged sights and sounds that Marion knew and loved so well. If she could step through the front door today she would surely smile and say, as she used to long ago, "So glad to be home."

Acknowledgements

My grateful thanks to Anne, Countess of Rosse, firstly for having preserved everything at 18 Stafford Terrace, and secondly for allowing me to quote extensively from her grandmother's diaries. I also owe a special debt to Spencer Douglas Herapeth, Marion Sambourne's great-nephew, as without his help I should never have unravelled the intricacies of the family tree. I have not been successful in contacting every descendant of the first Spencer Herapeth, but three of them, Lord Snowdon, Victoria Allison and Alexander Hamilton-Fletcher, have been most kind and helpful. My many friends in the Victorian Society have all given invaluable advice and encouragement; in particular I should like to thank Ian Grant, Hermione Hobhouse, Stephen Jones, Leonee Ormond, Alistair Service, Teresa Sladen, Robert Thorne, Alyson Wilson and Christopher Wood. Most of all, I thank my husband and children for being unfailingly supportive and critical (in the best sense of the word) during the periods when my thoughts were centered not on them, but on another family.

All the black and white photographs are from the collection at Linley Sambourne House, with the exception of those on the following pages: Royal Borough of Kensington and Chelsea 54, 59, 69, 79, 86; BBC Hulton Picture Library 111, 127; Ramsgate County Library 94, 114; Country Life 140; courtesy of Punch 14, 61, 81, 84, 115, 168; courtesy of Thomas Messel 165; National Monuments Record 2.